CW00554159

The Inner Circle

Editor's Note

The meaning of certain words and the hyphenated style of some military titles have changed over the past 60 years. For the sake of authenticity, these have all been kept in the text as they would have been at the time of the Second World War. Thanks are due to the Publications Department of the Imperial War Museum for their assistance in this matter.

The Inner Circle
A View Of War At The Top

by

JOAN BRIGHT ASTLEY OBE

The Memoir Club

© Joan Bright Astley 2007

First published in 1971 by
Hutchinson & Co. (Publishers) Ltd

Published in paperback in 2007 by
The Memoir Club
Stanhope Old Hall
Stanhope
Weardale
County Durham

All rights reserved.
Unauthorised duplication
contravenes existing laws.

British Library Cataloguing in
Publication Data.
A catalogue record for this book
is available from the
British Library

ISBN: 978-1-84104-166-7

Typeset by TW Typesetting, Plymouth, Devon
Printed by the MPG Books Group

For Philip and Richard

Contents

List of illustrations

Between pages 100 and 101

Acknowledgement

A special one to Edward Weeks of Boston, Massachusetts, who as Editor of *The Atlantic Monthly* waited twenty-four years with patience and encouragement for this book.

. . . and now, thirty-five years later, to Valerie Collins and Malcolm Harradine for their support of this edition.

CHAPTER 1

Shorthand and typing essential (1910–1936)

IT WAS 1945 – THE WAR in Europe had ended – and I had just come back from Potsdam where Churchill, Attlee, Truman and Stalin had met and where, for the last time, I had been 'administration housekeeper' to the British delegation. I was at a party when a lady bore down upon me smiling sweetly.

'You've had such a marvellous war,' she said. 'I wonder if you can tell me how my daughter can get a job like yours. She can type.'

'If she'll learn shorthand, spend two or three years slogging away in some office until she becomes of some use . . .'

'Oh, she doesn't want to do *shorthand*, be a stenographer . . . so dull.' The lady turned away.

I was irritated out of proportion to the occasion. It was not the first time I had heard of girls who regarded shorthand as a menial qualification and typing by itself as enough of an asset to lead quickly to executive rank. Shorthand was rather boring – so many fearful outlines on so many pages to be translated back into words – but without it I would not have had much to offer. With a shorthand pad and a typewriter I could be a valuable and mobile interpreter of others' thoughts, a human machine with the power to give and receive confidence. Without them I could not have done any of the jobs I had had, and I certainly would not have had 'such a marvellous war'.

Since 1941 I had been responsible for a Special Information Centre in the War Cabinet Offices in London. It had contained a complete filing section covering all matters which came before the British Chiefs of Staff Committee and it had supplied top secret information for the British commanders-in-chief at home and abroad. As well, I had been to many overseas meetings between the American President and British Prime Minister, including the three at Teheran, Yalta and Potsdam when Marshal Stalin had been present, where I had been an administrative officer for the British delegation. Luck had had something to do with it – it always does – but only in so far as being in the right place at the right moment. For the rest, it had depended on my having had a good secretarial training and some years of experience as a shorthand-writer and a typist.

As a profession it had been for me an obvious choice, not only because, after a six-month course, I would be self-supporting, but also because, in my private thoughts, the typing part of it came nearest to my own dream of being a professional pianist. In the performance of my dream I never got beyond mediocrity but at least I would still interpret, if not music, words.

We were an average family with a less than average income, and we were particularly lucky in our parents. My father was modest, elegant and charming, of a humour and kindliness which formed for each of us the pattern of how a man should be. He was very happy with my mother, a sturdy Lowland Scot whose shrewd insight, firm convictions and tolerant understanding of human nature were held together by a true, if somewhat austere, Christian faith. They had five daughters – Betty, Nancy, me, Pamela, Felicity.

My father's parents, George and Tempe Bright, reared their children comfortably and liberally, ignoring the fact that there would be very little money for their five daughters and none at all for their two sons whose education at Winchester College, with its school motto of 'Manners Makyth Man', did not entirely fit them for competitive wage-earning in an industrial world. Uncle Ashley became a regular soldier and died fighting the Boers in South Africa in 1900. His elder brother Trevor, my father, passionate in his love for the English countryside and its pursuits, joined the banking and shipping firm of Antony Gibbs, went to Chile and Argentina and thereafter spent most of his life in hot climates. His tidy mind and mathematical ability helped him to tolerate office work; he became a first-class accountant but never lost the tastes, which he could not afford, of a cultivated English squire.

My mother's kin, Harpers and Lindsays, were hard-working, straight-thinking Scots. Mary, my mother, went to the United States in 1894 to be a governess-companion with the Bancroft Davis family in Boston and then came home to train as a nurse at the London Hospital. Fate led her on to keep house for a bachelor brother in Buenos Aires, where she met and became engaged to my father, who by then was working for the Argentine North-Eastern Railway. In a letter home she found no fault in him except 'a hasty temper and he smokes too much'.

Betty, Nancy and I were born in the Argentine, and I was nearly three when, in 1913, we came back to England for a holiday. The outbreak of war prevented our return, and, though he volunteered for military service, my father was forty-four, not robust and was turned down.

The sinking of the liner *Lusitania* in May 1915 decided the whereabouts of our next home. My father was on his way to try for a job on the borders of Canada and the United States when his ship was delayed picking up survivors and by the time he arrived the vacancy was filled. This, combined with the difficulty of finding fitting work in England to keep his wife and, by then, five daughters, led us to southern Spain where he had been offered an accountancy post with the Zafra-Huelva Railway in Andalucia. Like the Rio Tinto Mining Company in the same area, this railway was an English concern, and here, he was told, we could 'live for a song'.

But neutral Spain did not turn out to be such a paradise for the poor. Rising prices and the limited scope of my father's job gave a tinge of failure to the five years we spent there. Not to us children, however. My mother had a genius for giving any rooms in which we lived an atmosphere of solid security and comfort. The very small house on the outskirts of Huelva, to which we moved because the apartment in town was too expensive, had features which were unique for us but which must have been hell for our parents. There was one staircase and it was outside and uncovered – lovely in the rain when we rushed it under umbrellas; a wooden ladder led out of the nursery window into the garden – to stop us trooping through the only sitting-room; vineyards lay around us where, just before harvest, we could hide, the great grapes at nose-tip giving off rich sweet smells from their shining white and purple clusters; and there were gypsies encamped in caves nearby. Their wailing flamenco songs and rhythmic clapping as they passed along the high road by our house made me shiver with fear of incomprehensible things; when the moon was full and their dogs bayed from the other side of the vineyards I lay cold in my bed, prey to the horror stories which our Spanish nurse told us to keep us good – of mad dogs running straight, of knives in the darkness, and of black-haired men who carried little girls away if they were naughty.

In the bright sunshine it was different. We bowled our hoops along the road, shared lessons with other English children, played English games, went to the English church, and spent golden summers at a golden place called Punta Umbria where there were miles of beaches and dunes and to which the only access was by steamer up the River Odiel and then along boardwalks laid over the hot sand.

Here we were all happy as we took temporary ownership of one or other wooden house standing high on stilts, lent to us by one or other kind friend. My father, loving the good things in life, was always gay on holiday, whether it was a half-day, whole day, weekend or, as in Punta, two weeks or more. Anything we did with him that was out of the ordinary was an excitement, a treat, something to be looked forward to and remembered always. It was harder for my mother: she was naturally gay but she had to conquer the Spartan side of her character before she could enjoy enjoyment for enjoyment's sake. She must first be quite sure that it was deserved and that it would not tempt any of us to lose our sense of duty. Even at Punta we had, after breakfast, to fulfil some task or do some service before we could kick our heels and race to the beach to play with our friends. Once her conscience was satisfactorily dealt with, then she too was fun. My parents enjoyed their daughters and we enjoyed them.

Betty wore spectacles, was bookish, dreamy and shy, but her apparent gentleness hid an iron will which she used to some effect to awe her three youngest sisters. Nancy should have been a boy, thin and wiry, finely tempered, a leader in any 'dare'. She was what our schoolgirl story-books called 'a madcap'. I was separated by two years from above and from below and because I had been sickly for the first six years of my life, I was rather spoilt, brash, self-confident and wheedling. I had dark brown hair and hazel eyes, and when, in our games, we pretended to be characters in Louisa May Alcott's *Little Women*, Betty was the obvious Meg, long-legged Nancy perfect for Jo, and, contrary to my private conviction that I was entirely right for the saintly Beth, they cast me as selfish Amy. But from below I was sure of admiration and acceptance from calm, humble Pamela and fat, giggling Felicity, who were always ready to fall in with any of my plans.

Our parents were strict but they believed in self-development and gave us a lot of freedom to mix with the local Spaniards, so that we all spoke their language with ungrammatical fluency. The English school dispersed when the teacher got married, and Nancy and I had a few terms at a Spanish–French school where we learned to speak French with a Spanish accent and to master the finer points of hopscotch. Sometimes we went to stay with other children at the mining settlement of the Rio Tinto Company where there were rocky hills and streams which ran blood red because of the rich deposits of iron-ore.

In 1920 Betty went to England to boarding-school, with my father in a cargo ship which sailed direct from Huelva and up the Avon Gorge to Bristol where his mother was living. Their trunks were packed with clothes for Betty and presents for Christmas, results of months of sacrifice and make-do on the part of my mother because she did not want our relatives to be confirmed in their belief that we were being barbarically raised. The captain of the *Marnetown* had his own plans for Christmas, took his ship a short cut in a fog off Vigo and struck a rock. All was lost, all but the crew and the two passengers who, when dawn came, were picked up from lifeboats and later re-embarked in a Royal Mail liner on its way from South America. My father and sister were dressed in bits and pieces lent them by the British Vice-Consul in Vigo and his wife, but, though on board there were one or two acquaintances who had received hospitality from my parents at our house in the Argentine, neither they nor any other first-class passenger thought it necessary to offer anything to them.

I remember two things: my mother's hopeless tears and my father's letter with a drawing of a fish nosing a collapsible opera hat at the bottom of the sea.

Shortly after, and presumably because of, my father's visit home, we were packing and saying goodbye to Huelva, to San Rafael – our vineyard home – and returning to a series of lodgings, first in Derbyshire, then Bedford. We children attended this or that local school until my father went to West Africa to another job with a railway and we settled in the city of Bath. Missing him dreadfully, we stood round my mother at the piano on Sunday evenings and sang Hymn 595 – *For Absent Friends*.

Because I was what my mother called 'nervy' and difficult to manage, it was decided that instead of school I should go to Norfolk and share lessons in a country house with the only daughter of friends of my father's. Just before my twelfth birthday my mother took me to Liverpool Street Station and handed me over to a dumpy figure in a black suit. She meant to be kind, old Nana, but her ignorant and limited outlook on life, alien to all I had known, dominated the four years I spent in the bosom of the Birch family.

'Oh . . . I do think of God', I wrote home, 'and I know He must have sent me here for some reason . . . but what I wonder is why God has sent me here and what His reason is.'

Whatever His reason, however homesick I felt in the isolated tranquillity of an old-fashioned English country house, there is no doubt but that the strong clean air, the regular routine of early nights and generous meals, built up for me a foundation of good health which has been of far more lasting benefit than the four years' fun I would have had in the stimulating atmosphere of my own home.

Major and Mrs Birch were very kind, and their daughter Ruby and I got on well together. We built up a mutual centre of experience and enjoyment, ignoring with the ingrown wisdom of the young the part of our lives which could never mingle. Miss Thorne, the governess, came daily from a nearby market town; due at ten, she never arrived before eleven: we practised the art of keeping her talking about the reasons why she was late, until half past twelve when the first lunch bell rang for us to go and wash our hands.

Ruby sang, rode her pony, I played the piano, struggled with the violin, and our academic education ran its leisurely course. When I was sixteen Major and Mrs Birch were ready to have their daughter to themselves, so I went home to Bristol, where my family had settled on my father's return from Africa in 1925.

In a final attempt to get me educated I was sent for a year to Clifton High School which meant bicycling across the Downs each morning with Pamela and Felicity. Having, during the past four years, become accustomed to climbing into a pony-trap at the side door of Crimplesham Hall, I was a poor and grumbling addition to their daily ride. But they were glad to have me at home again and their anxiety over my obvious dislike of the whole operation was tempered by their devotion to their Alma Mater. Never, they said, would they put powder on their noses nor relinquish the black stockings and navy bloomers which emerged below the straight line of their gym tunics. I was now the eldest because Betty was away in Mexico City working at the British Legation and Nancy was in London training to be a fashion model. I could not wait to be grown up myself and was joyful when it was decided that I should go to London and take a course at Mrs Hoster's Secretarial Training College.

I joined Nancy in a girls' hostel – prunes and rice pudding on Sundays – envying her her elegant figure and slim legs and doing my best to grow away from the fat calves and broad hips of my Norfolk life. We soon escaped from the prunes and found a flat, which we shared with another girl, in a tall building near the River Thames. We lived an economically restricted but happy life, seeing plays and musicals from high up in theatre galleries, tasting the romance of winter evenings in a big city when it seemed as though all lighted windows and quiet-moving limousines held the answer to unformed dreams of love and luxury. Our clothes were hand-me-downs and cast-offs, my best overcoat having been made by my mother from a plum-red tablecloth. If only she had kept quiet about it and not said 'Do look at Joan's coat: don't you think . . .?'

My first job was as a receptionist-secretary earning a pittance in the pine-panelled showrooms of Robersons, antique dealers, leading London sellers of expensive treasures from crumbling manor houses. There were more secretaries than jobs in those days and we who worked depended a great deal on the approval of our employers. I sat in the front of the shop, behind a screen, the servant of six salesmen; when the main doors opened to admit buyers of linenfold panelling or pieces of Hepplewhite, Chippendale or Queen Anne walnut, I sprang forward in welcome – and back to the rear where, in cubicles like horse-boxes, my salesmen waited for custom. The rota was strict, from Mr Wrigley at the top of the list down to young Mr Edwards. The prancing when Mr William Randolph Hearst came in was frenzied; all of them had at one time or another dealt with him or his representatives and there was violent competition as to who should earn the percentage on the thousands he might spend. Sometimes it was a caller for me – an aunt, cousin or girl friend; suspicious that I might be dealing myself with a customer, a salesman popped round the screen with a 'Who was that, Miss Bright?'

My most usual lunch was a length of French bread and some butter, and I was lucky to have any money left by pay day at the end of the week. I was content and I learned a lot, not only how to send out neat work and keep a card index but a bit else besides from reading a brown-paper-covered copy of *Lady Chatterley's Lover* lent me by a friend, which I hid under *A Specification for Decorating and Furnishing a Suite of Rooms at the Dorchester Hotel, Park Lane.*

For Robersons and all other dealers in luxury the Depression of 1929 brought retrenchment. I was sorry to leave.

Betty had just become engaged to a visiting legal adviser on the Anglo-Mexican Claims Commission and would soon be Mrs Godfrey Phillips. A suggestion from the aunt and uncle in Mexico City, with whom she had lived during her three years there, that I should apply for her job, brought a 'Send Miss Bright's sister' from His Britannic Majesty's Minister.

It was a rule that clerical staff in faraway places like Mexico must be 'locally employed'; in other words the British tax-payer should be relieved of the burden of paying passage money; none the less the Foreign Office felt it was their duty to test the would-be applicant if the would-be applicant happened to be in England. Having only taken one examination in my life, and that on the theory of music, I was scared and wrapped my right hand in bandage and sling. I felt dreadful because they were so nice about it, and when I got the job and went to Mexico I felt dreadful all over again when I read my personal file and saw that 'unfortunately Miss Bright was unable to take the test owing to an injury to her right hand'.

The Bancroft Davises in Boston invited my mother and Betty to accompany me to the States, so it was quite a family party on board the *Berengaria* when she sailed from Southampton in the autumn of 1931. The price of her fare from Uncle William Holmes in Mexico City brought Betty with me in the steamship *Orizaba* of the Linea Ward when she sailed from New York.

Only too well aware that her younger sister was apt to be rashly affable, she said to me quickly and firmly when we were unpacking in our cabin: 'We will *not* dance with anyone – however often we are asked.'

All very well for you, I thought, you're engaged to be married; but the long years of respect overcame the wish to parade myself in a pair of four-dollar black satin sandals I had just bought in New York. We sat with frozen English faces and no one spoke to us at all. Since then I have skimmed those shoes over hundreds of miles of parquet flooring, and if my age could match their youth they would carry me over a good many more.

The Mexico towards which we were sailing was a country emerging from long years of revolution. Sudden eruptions from its many volcanoes matched the sudden eruptions in its political life, while round and about and below flowed the tide which was to expropriate foreign commercial interests. President Plutarco Elías Calles, strong man, dictator, was in control; under him had begun the familiar pattern of totalitarian planning – the distribution of land from the white hands of the few to the brown hands of the many, the formation of farmers' co-operatives and of a one-party political system. It was a formidable task to etch these lines of black and white on to the violent and complex colouring of a land where in a few hours it was possible to move from the cold atmosphere of 10,000-foot heights to the tropical jungles of banana, mango, parrot and alligator. In this great subcontinent aboriginal civilisations had been violently conceived, their monuments standing witness from Chichen-Itza to Teotihuacan; the Spaniard, touching with long finger the ruffle of his shirt, brought Western civilisation and left behind him embellished churches on the ancient land; and now the twentieth century is making its mark with soaring architecture of unequalled style. Mashed in between are the villages where the soft-spoken, long-suffering Mexican peasant pursues his calling, unchanged by his various lovers but beginning none the less to absorb their ways.

William Holmes – short, ginger-haired, unbribing and unbribable and therefore respected – my uncle by marriage to my mother's younger sister, managed the Mexican Railway, as yet British and unexpropriated. He met us and it was in his private managerial coach that we ground slowly up from the port of Veracruz to Mexico City. The coach was Victorian and solidly comfortable, with bedrooms, dining-room and sitting-room. It was at the tail end of the train, and we could sit on the observation platform and watch the narrow gauge railway line curl away and down behind us. When night came, the curtains were drawn across the windows because the temptation to aim stones was too great for the quick-armed Mexican. We passed through Fortín, a centre of gardenia culture, the sweet smell meeting us long before we saw the women in the lamplight of the station with baskets of white flowers lying on green leaves. From then on I knew that I had fallen in love with a strange and beautiful country, a love which was confirmed during the five years which were to follow.

How right my parents were to push us out into the world. In England I would still have been in hostel or shared apartment – poor Nancy still was – my pleasures bound by lack of means and opportunity, consisting most often of cocoa, oranges and chat by a gas fire with girl friends, or the occasional date with the oh-so-occasional boy friend. In Mexico it was different: I was 'William Holmes's niece', I 'worked at the British Legation', I was automatically accepted into the ranks of society.

'Society' in Mexico City was led by the upper-class Mexican families, descendants of Spain's aristocracy, absentee landlords who had spent much of their life revelling in the cultural and social climate of Europe. The tide had now turned against them and they had to live in Mexico because it was Mexico that gave them their bread and butter. Then came the 'colonies' – British, French, Belgian, German, Italian; the American, increasing fast; the Latin American. Their embassies and legations formed a relaxed and friendly group of people, far enough removed from their capitals to be indifferent to the more stylised forms of diplomatic etiquette. The United States, of course, had an embassy – a large one – where the understanding influence of Ambassador Dwight Morrow had just given place to that of Mr Josephus Daniels, the Navy Secretary responsible for making the US Fleet dry, who continued to pursue with vigour and tact his government's policy of friendship and non-interference in Mexico's struggle for economic independence. It was very dry, the Ambassador's residence, but the niceties were observed when, at the correct moment, soda water was served in place of champagne. In their homes, members of the Embassy staff were free from the laws of prohibition and most generous in their hospitality. They were an able and attractive mission, worldly, mature and very easy for all nationalities to get along with. Arthur Bliss Lane, the Minister, was later to become Ambassador to Poland, and his death in 1956 deprived the State Department of an original and experienced mind. His wife Cornelia, like her sister Peggy who was married to the First Secretary Stanley Hawkes, was cultured and delightful, the four of them being just the right type of people who were needed to represent the great neighbour sitting so large and firm on Mexico's northern frontier. With them were other naturally friendly people: Jack Simmons, tall, curly-haired, a former Princeton athlete and a future Chief of Protocol, his wife Nancy, Robert and Katherine

Newbegin, who made me godmother to their eldest son, bachelor Jo Satterthwaite, Military Attaché Bob Cummings – in 1942 he landed in North Africa as Chief of Staff to General Patton; they worked hard to apply their government's policy of being the 'Good Neighbour'.

Mexicans liked to play 'gringos' – Americans – off against '*extranjeros*' – Europeans – usually to the detriment of the former, but they knew, and we knew, where lay the balance of power. For most of us the battle was lost. All we could do was to stem the revolutionary overflow as it seeped through the built-up dykes of foreign capital during the years preceding the outbreak of the Second World War.

In the British Legation we de-coded and typed the telegrams and despatches which spelt the decline of our commercial influence. One after the other, the banking, insurance, transport, oil and mining companies, which we had planted in Mexican soil in the good old days of our overseas expansion, became nationalised.

Our work was steady but not overpowering, our office hours being those most convenient to the climate: from ten to one in the morning and from four to seven in the evening. There was plenty of opportunity to play golf and tennis, to swim, ride and generally to enjoy ourselves. The fact that we lived at a height of some 7,500 feet exaggerated all our doings; the rarified atmosphere was a stimulant that not only sent our golf and tennis balls further and faster through the air but also shortened our sleeping hours, lengthened our drinks and made many of us pack twenty-eight hours into each twenty-four. Most weekends were spent in Cuernavaca, a small town perfectly situated at a temperate 4,000 feet, where my uncle and other families had villas with swimming-pools. The three-hour car journey, after a climb to nearly 10,000 feet past a sombre treeless village called Las Tres Marías, descended gradually to the valley below, bringing to the whole nervous system a sensation of warmth and relaxation. Sometimes we went further – to Taxco, a silver-mining centre where William Spratling had just set up his workshop and was designing and making silver objects of merit and distinction; or, all too rarely, to Acapulco on the Pacific coast, in those days a small fishing port, where our hotel on Los Hornos beach consisted of wooden buildings raised on stilts with nothing but sand between them and the sea. At night the water shone with phosphorescence and was so magical that we could sit indefinitely under the bowl of stars, quaffing mouthfuls of Mexican cognac. A walk along the coast, past a fine beach where mighty rollers crashed translucently green on to the shore and sharks could be seen swimming along the shining silken curtain of water before it fell, took us to a torpid lagoon at Pie de la Cuesta. Here there lived a white beachcomber wearing a squashed and greasy felt hat.

Once we went there at dawn, hired a boat and spent abortive hours trying to shoot alligator between the eyes while tropical birds and pale flamingoes screeched and flew about us. Other times we got up at three or four in the morning (if indeed we had ever gone to bed) to go deep-sea fishing with the local boats; for twelve hours on the rolling circling sea we set our lines and harpoons for barracuda, shark, sting-ray, marlin, returning at sunset in a glow of pink fire. Always in the evenings there were the singers, the guitars and the marimbas, the whispering sounds of the night and the slap of sandals on the cobblestones.

Thirty-four years ago Mexico was a wonderful country to be young in; serenades, sometimes under your own window, to wake us from sleep, bullfights on Sundays, long nights of dancing, singing, listening, arguing; long days of picnics, sport and gossip. There were tourists, the 'visiting firemen' – George Gershwin, Noguchi, Foujita, Aldous Huxley; the bullfighters – Solorzano, Cagancho, Armillita, and weekends at bull-breeding ranches; favourite *guitarristas* like Maciste and the lamented dead Guty Cárdenas; painters – Diego Rivera, Siquieros, Orozco, Covarrubias; and always for me a job of work to be done. I had the best of both worlds, even if I did sometimes find it difficult to stay awake while I shorthanded the Annual Report for the Foreign Office. I had a reason for being there and a purpose to the fun I was having.

The affection for America and things American that my mother had kept alive by her stories of old New England was now part of my own equipment. I had many friends in the American colony – in fact more than in the British – and I found it easy to feel at home with them and react at once to their warmth and kindness. I made three trips to their country during the first three years: to New York to see Betty and my new brother-in-law Godfrey Phillips on their way through to his post with the Shanghai Municipal Council, and the second to San Antonio in Texas. From these scratches at the surface I regarded myself as an expert on all the States of the Union.

The third was not so happy. I had fallen unsuitably in love and His Britannic Majesty's chargé d'affaires, wishing to keep clean the record of his staff, suggested it was time I took home leave. This I did, but, except for the pleasure of seeing my family, I was lovesick and fretful, a worry and a disappointment, not giving them the full attention which so long an absence had deserved. I had left Mexico City under a cloud of gossip and criticism, good friends advising me to give up the whole thing and remain in England. My father put it in proportion. In his sensitive and reserved way he told me that it was up to me, that whichever way my decision lay he and my mother would back me up. The reason for my unhappiness would still be there on my return: which should I do? Admit defeat and leave the clouds behind me, lying low in the Mexican sky, or go back to them and face it out? If I chose the first, I felt I could never look on my years there as anything but a period of failure, so I knew that I would return. When I told my father he said nothing, but he understood.

Because on the whole human beings have dignity and forbearance I found that it was not so bad after all. The people who loved me welcomed me, and the malicious ones from then on mattered not at all. My last two years justified my decision, and I had a very happy, full and rewarding finish to my shorthand-typist career in the Diplomatic Service – its benefits so rewarding to those who qualify for them, so irritating to those who do not. Having learned some salutary lessons in human behaviour, not least of them a less emotional and more critical attitude towards men, I clung to my work in the Legation as to a beacon in a shifting world – with the result, of course, that I began to be of some use. By this time I was enough of a resident to be able to communicate directly with various *excelentíssimos y distinguidos señores* in the Mexican Ministry of Foreign Affairs and be called by them 'Juanita'. Whether or not this did much for Anglo-Mexican relations, it certainly did good to my ego and taught me a fundamental truth that a good secretary should be discreet in mixing sex and service.

During this time my uncle, for two years divorced from my aunt, re-married. I began to suspect a courtship when one morning at breakfast I noticed that he had not asked me what time I had got home the night before. In the past my answer had been an invariable 'Oh, about one o'clock', but as nowadays it really was one o'clock and not, as used to be usual, any hour up to dawn, I had failed to realise that for some mornings past he had not questioned me at all. Suddenly I knew why; he was coming in later than I.

Our relationship which, though good, had before been tempered by the fact that he knew I was lying but was too kindly to do more than purse his lips, now became excellent. When he did get married I felt more like a mother than a niece, moved into my own flat, had my first taste of real independence – and continued revolving like a squirrel in a cage.

In 1936 three newcomers gave fresh breath to our buffet suppers and cocktail parties. Known as 'the Insurance Men', they had come to Mexico to negotiate as favourable a settlement as possible for insurance companies in England. It was chance which led me to cross the room at a lunch party to speak to Mr H. G. Shaw, the quietest and most elderly of the three, because I thought he looked out of his element in his dark suit and stiff collar. That moment of impulse was to change my life for me.

Some of us decided to take them to Acapulco, sharing the expense of a small aircraft run as a taxi service by Fritz Bieler, an experienced German pilot with the face and keen blue eyes of an unusual and attractive bird. I had often flown with him when the First Secretary in our Legation, Harold Farquhar, a forceful and original personality, had bought himself a blue and yellow Beechcraft four-seater, largely from the proceeds of his phenomenal luck playing baccarat in the local casino. Harold had frequently taken me on short trips into the remote parts of the country. When he finally left Mexico, with Bieler he flew back to England by way of the Bering Straits and Siberia.

The easy and intimate familiarity into which our small society had settled might well have seemed odd to a newcomer, and none of us realised that Mr Shaw, who represented an older generation, might be shocked by the flinging round of well-worn jokes and doubtful stories; nor did we think of his reactions when we took our midnight swims and sips of cognac. The knowledge came to us all too plainly on the Monday morning when he refused to return with us by air because, he said, it was against his principles to fly with a pilot who had been drinking most of the night before. In chastened mood we returned to the capital, leaving him to cover the dusty seven-hour journey in a hired car. I felt particularly responsible because he and his two younger colleagues were under the wing of my office and I was doing their typing for them. I rang him up at his hotel to apologise for our seeming discourtesy and agreed to meet him for tea that afternoon at Sanborns in the Avenida Madero.

Without preamble, he said: 'Joan, it is clear to me that you have been in Mexico for long enough. I don't think you are as happy here as you think you are, and I feel, for your own sake, that you should go and re-settle yourself into a more prosaic life in England. If you cannot afford the fare, I would be very glad to pay it for you, and help you until you get on your feet there. We can charge this off as a loan to friendship, but I want you to accept it.'

As he spoke I knew most certainly that he was right, that I should accept his offer and thank God for it. I was well paid, but I was extravagant, loved clothes, and was always living so near to the constant repayment of back debts that I had given up hope of an early return home, except by a miracle. I was too ashamed of my financial inefficiency to ask my uncle for help, and my family, I knew, could not.

Here, then, was the miracle. I said 'Yes' without further hesitation, and next morning when I awoke I felt a great wave of relief and gratitude.

At dawn on the day I left in July 1936, Fritz Bieler fulfilled a promise he had made that he would fly me round the crater of Popocatépetl, the 'Smoky Mountain', snow-covered sentinel of Mexico's history. As the small aircraft climbed into the clear sky, the country extended below us and the peaks of the 'White Woman' Ixtaccíhuatl, Mount Orizaba and the Nevada of Toluca, stabbed clear. The heaviness of my altitude-conscious limbs, the lightness of my heart, the warmth of the sun through the windows, and the purity of the light around, came together in one unforgettable moment of conviction that what is past is in the present and in the future, and that none of it is lost.

CHAPTER 2

Irregular warfare (1936–1940)

MY DEPARTURE FROM MEXICO CITY'S railway station was the same as many another's, a send-off peculiar to a colonial community where farewells are made much of. But this time it was I who was going, for whom the marimba band played the songs which meant 'Mexico' to most of us: the people on the platform were my friends, their gifts in the coach mine; even the last minute thrust-through-the-window gift from Miguel Covarrubias of one of his own drawings was inscribed 'for Juanita'.

I plumped down on the seat and wept – not because I was leaving but because I had never expected it would be like that.

New York was a surprise because here, too, friends I had met in Mexico speeded me aboard the *Europa* and filled my cabin with their goodbyes and their 'See you again soon'.

The crossing could not go fast enough for me. At Southampton I had just enough time and enough money to eat two crumpets soaked in butter before my train left for Bristol. Then I was home.

Had it ever been different? I felt so changed and yet, after the first hour of exclamation and talk, there I was, right back in the family circle, trying hard to push my new self at them and finding that, after all, I was the same 'Joan' they knew so well. Nancy was visiting Betty in Shanghai, but Pamela was there, dear, calm, responsible Pamela, down from Edinburgh where she was doing what she had always wanted to do – train to be a hospital nurse. And Felicity, much grown up, her hair springing in curls, her snub nose still ready to button up with laughter; she was doing a domestic science training course in London. Themselves changed, they let me think I had; they gave me all I needed when they said that it made life more exciting to have me home again.

In September I went job-hunting to London. My ideas as to my own value made me feel that nothing was interesting enough, important enough or well paid enough to warrant settling down. An introduction to Mr Duff Cooper might have led me to part-time working on his book *Talleyrand*, but when I learned I would also be his wife's secretary I refused. I have never wanted to work for a woman, a prejudice which has made me modest towards those who have had to work for me. I could have gone – no longer 'locally employed' – to our embassies in Rome, Vienna or Paris, or I could have accepted an offer which came from the British Consul-General in Munich whom I had known in Mexico; Mr and Mrs Rudolf Hess wished for a girl to live in their house and teach English to their family. In view of what was to come, it was a pity I refused; at that period it would have been interesting to see Nazi Germany from the inside. I could have stayed on in the Royal Institute of International Affairs at Chatham House, where I worked for a while. I could have done any of a dozen different things, each of which would have led me up a different path.

Instead, I flitted from one temporary post to another, had fun, saw old friends and made new ones.

I had a large, furnished room in a house in Queen's Gate, next to a friend called Clodagh Alleyn, who worked in Elizabeth Arden's Beauty Salon and had a ribald sense of humour. We shared friends and jokes, and felt the same relief as we kicked off our shoes and fell into our armchairs when we came back from work in the evening. Once a week I went to dinner with Mr Shaw. The visit to Mexico had been his last foreign assignment; shortly afterwards he retired as foreign manager of a large insurance company and went to live a quiet, bachelor life in a flat off Victoria Street. I hoped I was in some measure repaying through my regular visits the kindness and friendship he had extended to me in Mexico. He had three nieces of whom he was fond, and the addition of another young person to his steady life gave him pleasure. He was not himself a talker, but he enjoyed listening to chat. He would never change, would always be loyal and true, hold on to his own strong principles, his religious belief, and his practical common sense.

In September 1938, when the Munich crisis made war seem immediate, I mobilised myself into typing action in the head-quarters of an anti-aircraft unit of the Territorial Army. In a drill hall in the suburbs of London I typed reams of Standing Orders and learned the difference between an ancient 2.5 and our most modern 3.7 gun, the latter a long-necked graceful weapon which was trundled to its site when Hitler roared and brought back again when Neville Chamberlain waved his umbrella.

The job was as temporary as the period of peace which ended it. War was striding inexorably across those months; a chance meeting made me a part of it in April 1939. John Walter, a childhood friend from the summer days at Punta Umbria, was mysterious when he said he could get me work if I went to St James's Park Underground Station at 11 a.m. on a certain day, wearing a pink carnation. There, he said, a lady would accost me. I did – and so did she, and led me to an office so anonymous that we had to change direction frequently in order to reach it unobserved.

A dapper colonel interviewed me, warned me of the tortures which would be mine if I were caught by the Germans, and then got me to sign the Official Secrets Act. Leading me to the window, he pointed to a citizen quietly minding his own business at the street corner.

'He has been there all morning – watching,' said the colonel. 'When you leave here, don't let him see you; turn left and keep going.'

It all seemed good clean fun and I was pleased to be joining an organisation in which fact and fiction played so smoothly together. I was assigned to section 'D/MIR(R)' and told that my bosses were four: Colonel J. C. F. Holland, Colonel Colin McVeagh Gubbins, Major Millis Jefferis and, from the Royal Navy, Commander Dymock Watson.

Colonel Jo Holland, a Regular Army Royal Engineer, had the ribbon of the Distinguished Flying Cross stitched to his tunic. In the Royal Flying Corps during the 1914–18 war he had leaned from the open cockpit of his aircraft and dropped by hand small bombs on the enemy. He was a chain-smoker, his ashtray filled with flattened butts, a habit, he explained, from those days when cigarettes were scarce, sorties frequent, and the precious end waited to be re-lit on return to base. He drew heavily on his loves, holding in the smoke until the last wisp of nicotine had reached his boots, when it was expelled with full force as he seized on some point of discussion. He had an independent mind, an acute brain, a loving and poetic heart; he was quick, imaginative, and of a fiery temper.

Holland had for the past year or two been the only member of a research section in the War Office, G.S.(R), set up by General Sir

Ronald Adam, Deputy Chief of the Imperial General Staff. Unhampered by departmental responsibility, his terms of reference were to consider how the coming war with Germany should be fought and with what weapons. A series of terse reports concluded that our means were three-fold:

(a) by Royal Naval blockade;
(b) by Royal Air Force bombing;
(c) initially, until the Army could be brought to its necessary strength, by well-planned irregular, or guerilla, warfare designed to fight the enemy at all possible points.

The last had grown from Holland's studies of Boer tactics in South Africa, of the Civil War in Spain, of the Sino-Japanese conflict and of his own experiences of the use made by the Irish of irregular troops during the 'Troubles'.

The conclusions were filed but not forgotten. The fears of Munich subsided, but those who had eyes to see prepared for war and among other things recognised the importance of denying oil to Germany. Under Colonel Holland a top secret section was formed in the Military Intelligence Directorate of the War Office. Called 'MI(R)' its purpose was to study how the enemy could be prevented, or at any rate hampered, from using the great wells of Romania; it should also look into any other scheme that might, in war, show a profit as, for instance, aid to the Poles behind the enemy lines if their country should be overrun.

Because of the irregularity of this form of warfare from a politico-military point of view and because, financially, it needed to be free from too close Treasury scrutiny, it was decided that the new section should start its work under the administrative cover of the Secret Service. It was this decision which brought Colonel Holland and his three staff officers to set up their office near St James's Park and provide a place for me.

We became part of Section D which, under Colonel Lawrence Grand, had also been pursuing means of disruption against the Germans. Holland and Grand were both Regular Army Royal Engineers, but here the resemblance ended: Grand was a volatile dreamer, Holland an unsmiling visionary. The line of demarcation between their future operational plans was clear however: Grand's Section D deeds would be done by undercover men, spies and saboteurs, who, if caught, would be neither acknowledged nor defended by their government; Holland's MI(R) plans would be subject to proper strategic and tactical requirements and carried out by men in the uniform of the established Armed Services for whom the normal conventions of war would operate.

Housed and administered by Section D, MI(R) was supposed to conform to its habits. So secret were these that some members of Section D's staff never emerged from the office in daylight for fear of exposure to an all-seeing compiler of the German Black List. Others, mindful of their instructions to pass in the street without salutation those with whom they daily worked, were sometimes taken aback when Colonel Holland, on impulse, shouted 'Boo!' at them and continued on his way. My sponsor, John Walter, grandson of the founder of *The Times* newspaper, lost some of Section D's trust in him when the Head of the Secret Service, on a tour of inspection, came into his room. He did not look up but remained bent on his work. Why, he was asked afterwards, had he shown such lack of respect? 'I'm sorry,' said John, 'but I thought we were not supposed to know who he was.' He lost all its trust and was shown the door when a letter he wrote to *The Times* correspondent in Paris, asking about a certain German, was regarded as a major breach of security. Colonel Holland, loather of pretence, happened to be coming in as Walter went out; he offered him a job with MI(R).

It was the mixture between true and false which irritated Holland and made him dislike the set-up and its elaborate web of concealment. There was no direct reason for his distaste; the Section did its best for the cuckoos in the nest; he and Grand got on well together; but from the moment we started work in our hidden rooms he began plotting for our return to the dusty and respectable confines of the War Office and the more formal umbrella of Military Intelligence.

Of all this, however, I was ignorant as I sat at my new desk and took stock of my surroundings. Besides my frightening Colonel Holland, there was Colonel Colin Gubbins, Royal Artillery, quiet-mannered, quiet-spoken, energetic, efficient and charming. A 'still waters running deep' sort of man, he had just enough of the buccaneer in him to make lesser men underrate his gifts of leadership, courage and integrity. He was a man-at-arms, a campaigner, the fires banked up inside him as glowing as those round which his Celtic ancestors had gathered between forays for glen and brae. He was dark and short, his fingers square, his clothes immaculate and in peacetime he wore a carnation in his buttonhole. A pair of smooth suède gloves lay across the corner of his table. He was Holland's best-picked and most devoted staff officer and destined for a distinguished career in the war.

'D/3', for such was his code name, was Major Millis Jefferis, who could never have belonged to any other branch of the Army but the Royal Engineers. Red of face, kind of heart, he was an inventive genius, his dreams and thoughts linked with all forms of infernal machine – and the bigger the bang, the louder his ready laugh. In a private house in Portland Place he set up his factory of destruction. From handy jam tins packed with explosive for throwing under the tracks of tanks, he developed such devices as the Sticky Bomb (anti-tank) and the W Mine (a floating underwater mine).

The W mine was developed for use in what was known as 'The Royal Marine Operation', a scheme which had been the follow-up of an idea of Professor J. B. S. Haldane, the biologist. During the First World War, when he was a young officer in the Black Watch Regiment, he had thought it would be possible for a man with a Davis escape apparatus to float down the River Meuse with, strapped to his chest, an explosive mine with a time fuse which he would then fix to the pier of a strategically vital bridge. He now put forward the idea that men, swimming and pushing explosive charges for attachment to bridges and barges on the River Rhine, could cause disruption of German supplies. A section to pursue this scheme was accordingly set up in the Admiralty. Small submersibles were considered, or such a floating mine as Jefferis's which could be dropped into the river, its striker set for release when the water had softened a retaining strip of material; on contact with bridge or barge it would explode. Prototypes were tested in the River Thames, Boy Scouts at strategic spots to catch them as they floated by. The result was sufficiently successful to lead to a quantity being made for the Royal Navy and concealed near Strasbourg with men trained and ready to use them. French agreement to their use came too late. The successful aerial mine destruction of the Mohne and Eder dams in 1943 showed what such mines dropped from the air could do.

Major Jefferis's Sticky Bomb caught the interest of Mr Winston Churchill, who was then First Lord of the Admiralty. He wished to see how it worked. Such a weapon might awaken interest when he next visited the French General Staff. With a bucket and a sample pack, his face alight, Jefferis hurried into the Admiralty and up to the First Lord's room. Except for a prolonged pause between adhesion and explosion, the demonstration was a success. Major Jefferis was told to be prepared to accompany Mr Churchill to France. In the interim each had thoughts about the pause: Jefferis succeeded in shortening it and at the same time producing a bigger and better bang; Mr Churchill decided that he would divert the attention of the French generals by leading them to one side and engaging them in a short discourse. The result was unfortunate; a deafening detonation to their rear pleased no one.

The fourth staff officer on Colonel Holland's establishment was Commander Dymock Watson, Royal Navy. He was a green-grass-and-white-flannels type of man, with brilliant blue eyes and a wide smile. His gentle ways belied an iron determination and a specialised knowledge of the flow of the River Danube and its importance to the oil wells of Romania. He stayed with us long enough to plan their destruction and then left us in order to carry it out.

Very soon another girl came to join me. Lesley Wauchope was proud, with the face of an untroubled Madonna, but she had a wicked wit, was a shrewd observer and no respecter of others' pretensions. We giggled at the same things as we typed our way through the hectic months of reality and idiocy which preceded the outbreak of war in September 1939.

Colonel Gubbins was compiling and producing three pamphlets: *The Art of Guerilla Warfare*, *Partisan Leader's Handbook* and, with Jefferis, *How to use High Explosives* – this last illustrated with line drawings showing how to fit a stick of gelignite under a railway sleeper or where to pack a lethal brown paper parcel under a bridge. Printed pocket-size on edible paper and translated into several languages, they were ideal textbooks for the use of spies and saboteurs, and for the men in the uniform of the established Armed Services.

Where were these men who would wear uniform and take part in an Order of Battle? Colonel Holland crossed Whitehall and called on the Director of Military Intelligence.

Major-General F. G. Beaumont-Nesbitt was tall and polite, an erect, good-looking man, his crisp moustache brushed up. In his bearing he was a typical Guards officer, in his actions perspicacious and far-seeing. Since the Munich crisis he had been convinced that, on the outbreak of war, his Intelligence Directorate would be shorn of its trained officers. He was determined to be ready with the right replacements. He had ordered one of his sections to comb the commercial and professional world for executives, writers, explorers, linguists, with specialised knowledge of foreign countries, who were on the Army Reserve list; and then to call some of them in for after office hours' indoctrination into the functions and operations of military intelligence. When mobilisation came they would be taken on the strength of a new branch of the Army, the Intelligence Corps. A badge was especially designed for this Corps; horticultural in its concept, it was soon described by its wearers as 'a pansy resting on its laurels'.

It is of passing interest to mention here that when the British Expeditionary Force was in embryo, no French-speaking British officers had been earmarked for attachment to it. From Beaumont-Nesbitt's list twelve were chosen – 'the Twelve Apostles' – who were, of course, more than valuable to the two corps and five divisions when they moved across to France.

From this same list Colonel Holland could choose his men. I was sent over to the War Office to make a preliminary sorting and then to pick out those whose qualifications seemed most suited to training in irregular warfare. To those selected – men like Peter Fleming, Geoffrey Household, Peter Wilkinson, Tommy Davies, Malcolm Munthe, Douglas Dodds-Parker – we sent invitations for interview in the War Office. Major Gerald Templer of the Military Intelligence Directorate did the interviewing, I made notes, and soon we had a core. These we sent to attend a course of lectures which informed them about the organisation of the General Staff; the part played by the Intelligence branches within it; the probable strategic picture of the coming war; the tactical opportunities for guerilla action and subversion; the use of clandestine wireless communications; and the co-ordination of local resistance and sabotage.

Also included was the use in military operations of the parachute and helicopter. The parachute, later in the war, billowed and swelled, but the military potential of the helicopter lay stillborn in those years, a fact which caused grief to Colonel Holland who had a passionate belief in it. He would have been glad to see its present-day role.

Lesley Wauchope and I organised the venue of the lectures. Because it was near and was a public building much used for weddings, conferences and borough meetings, we chose the Caxton Hall. The constant comings and goings gave good cover to the small and highly secret groups of young men in plain clothes. We kept the classes small for security reasons and must have been quite successful because Geoffrey Household said later that when he joined the Romanian Military Mission in Holland's office two days before it entrained he had never before seen any of the other members.

As the summer months flew towards the darkness of European war, our offices near St James's Park Underground became crammed with men and ideas. Colonel Grand was delighted with us, his imagination flaring ahead of our schemes, each one of which seemed to him a war-stopper. If, as often happened, one of his schemes or one of ours came to nothing, he showed no disappointment, called for more and never let his enthusiasm descend to the level of a cautious 'Wait and see'.

Two sensible business men had joined MI(R) and were studying two sensible ideas of Colonel Holland's. He had handed to Colonel Norman Crockatt a pile of books which had been written about escaping prisoners and which he had borrowed from libraries and friends. From these, the tall, dark Reserve officer was to think of means by which prisoners of war could be kept in secret communication with their home base and how the radios could be smuggled to them; and to work out practical methods of helping them to escape.

Into Colonel Eddie Combe's shrewd and sophisticated keeping he gave the other: a full study of all means by which the enemy could be deceived as to the size, scope and venue of any military operation; and the compilation of a list of operational code names for future use.

The pressure was on. As it became obvious that Poland would be the first target for overt German aggression, Gubbins was completely absorbed in plans for aiding their resistance. He flew to Warsaw in the early summer and made successful contact with their Intelligence Directorate. He had first dealt with the Poles when on service in Russia in 1919 and again when he had worked in the Polish Section of the War Office in 1932: they trusted and liked him. An MI(R) mission to move in advance of the outbreak of war into Poland was chosen from the 'Caxton Hall class', at the same time that Commander Dymock Watson was collecting his men together to go secretly to Romania. Peter Wilkinson was brought in to organise the Polish mission, and his intelligence and sense of humour, added to John Walter's ready wit, did much to help Lesley and me lengthen the shortness of our temper and shorten the length of our working day.

On 22 August, now carrying the respectable title of Chief of Staff to the British Military Mission to Poland, Colonel Gubbins returned from a second visit to Warsaw. It was obvious that his and Dymock Watson's missions must go – and quickly. They were given three days to collect and commission their men and report with them to a room reserved for the purpose on the first floor of the War Office.

On the 25th we saw them off from Victoria Station – twenty men in civilian clothes, their passports identifying them as insurance agents, commercial travellers, entertainers, agricultural experts – a deadly secret cell in a big body of naval ratings, soldiers and airmen hurrying back to the Middle East before the freedom to do so was denied them. It was a sign of our immaturity in such matters that the numbers on the brand-new passports were consecutive. (Colonel Gubbins managed to get them changed on arrival in Alexandria.)

I came away from Victoria with a heavy heart. Childhood impressions of wartime railway stations, with bands playing, women weeping and flags flying, had superimposed themselves on the prosaic send-off I had just been a part of. It was no comfort to look up to the sky and see the first barrage balloons, mute white forerunners of London's ordeal by raid. I was changing my bedsitting room from one end of Queen's Gate to the other, and I hated the fresh pink walls of my new home. I was also packing up the contents of the flat of a young man I had hoped would marry me. He had gone to Turkey, and I felt low, washed-up and afraid.

A crescendo of hysterical planning in Section D did much to restore my spirits. Colonel Grand had decided that we were all too essential to risk our lives under bombardment in London. He acquired a country house called The Frythe – (of course it was known as 'The Fright') – where, he said, we must sleep, where, he said, we must be preserved for our vital role. So insidious is romance that on 3 September 1939, pleased to escape annihilation from above by the Germans, I accepted with alacrity the offer of a lift in a white Rolls-Royce with an Irish brigadier (a balloon expert), Major Harris (key man in the organisation), and Miss Beecham (private secretary to the Director). Whispering (because 'the enemy has ears'), we made our way through an as yet incomplete blackout and swept into the Tottenham Court Road. Handling the car with confidence the brigadier shot down the centre of the road fair and square into a pedestrian island. In the ensuing silence, Major Harris groaned, blood falling from a cut in his forehead. We pulled him out and carried him to a nearby hotel. Clutching his chest, he cried:

'The papers . . . the papers. Take them, take them.' We looked, but he had none.

Next morning, sheepishly, we returned to a raid-free London to find much excitement over our accident. It took me some minutes to convince Colonel Grand that I did not need to go to Mr Macindoe, the great plastic surgeon, to have a minute cut in my cheek operated on and smoothed over.

With the declaration of war Colonel Holland took action. Within days we were swept through the streets into a room on the third floor of the War Office. As Lesley and I, our unburdened officers following discreetly behind, staggered up Whitehall carrying files and typewriters, we were not to know that we were the vanguard of a revolution. Up to then few civilian women had held any sort of 'personal assistant' or private-secretary type of job in a military stronghold like the War Office.

Our branch lost the 'D' and became once more MI(R). We continued to be supported by secret funds, from which we bought two Royal typewriters and were much envied by the other typists who had to press heavily on the keys of government-issued Imperials.

I became devoted to the War Office; to its ancient ways, its unwashed walls, the uneven watermarks revealing the length of the office-cleaner's arm, the ceilings thick with dust and the dim evenings in blacked-out rooms which held the stale smell of scores of smokes and dozens of thick-cupped, thick-made teas. The walk to the ladies' washroom was immodestly long, but it gave us a chance to stare and stop and exchange subversive remarks with junior staff officers – 'G.3s' – who breathed fiery revolt within and sweet acceptance without. In daily circulation were the jokes peculiar to the times and the building – the one, for instance, which claimed that the morning and afternoon tea trolley as it clanked its way round the third floor was, in fact, the only serviceable tank in the British Army. I liked the officers who were polite to women and the sturdy, loyal, flat-footed messengers who untiringly provided us with tea, cigarettes, drawing-pins and booty in the shape of pieces of carpet scrounged to cover the bare boards of our rooms. When the air raids came I liked Brigadier Humphrey Wyndham because he allowed us girls to hide behind his door when the wardens flew sharply about demanding that everyone should immediately descend to the shelters in the basement.

Early in 1940 each warning sent the General Staff speeding to these fortified rooms, where, rebellious, we sat murmuring that 'After all, this *is* the War Office and there is a war on'. More enterprising officers would step outside the building just before the punctual Germans came over; once outside, they were not allowed back inside until the 'All Clear' had sounded – a better way of spending a couple of hours than fuming on hard benches in idle rows down below.

The forced descent stopped abruptly one day when the emergency telephone system failed to link the new and more vigilant Prime Minister, Mr Winston Churchill, with his Chief of the Imperial General Staff. Thereafter we were allowed to remain in our offices.

A bomb did fall close by one morning just before nine o'clock; it killed a girl typing up on the top floor, where the general typing pool remained, air raids or no air raids, and flung large lumps of masonry on to our desks through the windows of the third floor.

Women were expendable in the War Office in those early days as they sat at their typing-tables, guarded by lady supervisors, with eagle eye and scratching pen, who noted their movements and checked as to whether 'Colonel B has had Miss K recently', or whether some other girl should have the dubious privilege. None of us, no female, was allowed to carry the red-lettered 'Top Secret Officers Only' files; it was a daunting experience to me at the time of Dunkirk – when even the tea-trolley stood silent and the jokes had ended – to be asked by a furious brigadier:

'Can't you *read?*' as he pointed at the 'Top Secret Officers Only' file in my hand.

But the rot had set in. By the time the bombs were really falling on England there was scarcely a senior officer without his female 'Personal Assistant' – a Temporary Civil Servant for the duration – her high heels beating an efficient and provocative tattoo up and down the murky corridors, in and out of the shabby rooms.

The Gubbins Mission was in Poland, but briefly; the German blitzkrieg had halted all major resistance. 'This tragic fortnight', wrote Gubbins on 16 September, 'has been an unceasing rush, tearing round night and day in fast cars over primitive roads, trying to find out what is happening and why; rushing back to send wires to London and then dashing off to some new area of activity.' The odds were too great; the Poles were doing their best but they had no defence against the German Air Force, whose pilots could do what they liked where they liked, coming down low to bomb open towns and shoot along roads crowded with refugees. Ruin and devastation spread quickly across the country, while its people looked in vain for overt allied support. On 17 September it was all but over and the Gubbins Mission crossed the border into Romania with the Polish Government and General Headquarters.

In Bucharest Commander Dymock Watson's group were observing Romania's neutrality from the office of the British Military Attaché, Brigadier Geoffrey Macnab. It was lucky that he not only had a ripe sense of the ridiculous but also an open and uncluttered mind which was prepared to accept the fact that the authorities at home had not gone mad but were really trying to forestall the enemy. But the Germans were on the right side of the frontier and the Romanian Government anxious to keep them there. All the MI(R) party could do was to wait. If the Germans had invaded, Plan 1 – destruction of the oil fields with the aid of the Romanian Army – would have come into effect; if the Romanians had been unwilling or unable to help, Plan 2 would have brought a trained company of demolition experts from Egypt where it stood ready. After the fall of France, Plan 3 – destruction of the high-pressure field at Tintea by the MI(R) party, helped by British employees of Unirea – was the final hope, but the secret leaked and thirty-six hours before the attack was due to go in, strong guards appeared at each well.

The mission left Bucharest as modestly as it had arrived, first sinking its virgin explosives, case by case, in a lake.

The winter waiting, or 'phoney', period of the war led those who were impatient for action to turn wild ideas into diverse, sometimes parallel, plans. MI(R) did not lag behind. We were part of the pattern, the hidden power of peace-prone Britain, moving, extending, retracting, seeking, till it could find the proper sphere from which best to strike the foe. By spring 1940, our establishment had swollen to a score of officers, and we were organising and sending missions to encourage resistance in many parts of the world. The men who formed them were various, the thread which bound them the taut thread of adventure and desire for individual action. We overdid it, of course, but those were serious, burdened, rushing days, and the holes in the dyke called for all the fingers in our hands. The engine which drove us was Colonel Holland. We admired him, feared him, loved him; we all felt that by bragging about him and supporting him we could add in some way to his already, to us, considerable stature. He was too outspoken to be liked by the majority of his colleagues, and to us he could be very rude indeed. I can feel now the quick downward movement by which I ducked the impact of a book flung at my head one day on opening the door of his office. He held fiercely to his motley army and to each person he gave the feeling that the job he had to do was paramount.

The opportunity to shake off the fluff of Secret Service which still clung to us and get his section under proper military control came in February 1940 when, in Paris, the Supreme War Council decided to seek permission from Norway and Sweden for an Anglo-French force to occupy Narvik (later Trondheim, Bergen and Stavanger were included), reinforce the Finns against the Russians, and seize the Gallivare ore field on the Gulf of Bothnia. Colonel Holland succeeded in getting agreement to the despatch of an MI(R) trained ski-team to Finland and for five officers to go ahead to the chosen Norwegian ports as observers and co-ordinators of local resistance. At last his individual trainees could fulfil the role he had intended for them.

The Germans, swift and secret, took the initiative and invaded Norway on 9 April. Hastily and untidily the British and French forces detailed for the landings crossed the North Sea. By then, one MI(R) officer had been captured, three were making their escape back to Britain, and the fifth – Peter Fleming – attached himself to General Adrian Carton de Wiart's regular force when it landed at Namsos.

There were other signs during the early months of the year that more serious attention was being given to the use of irregular forces. It was agreed that a training establishment for guerilla warfare should be set up at Inverailort in the West Highlands of Scotland, and that small units for raiding operations should be formed from men of the

Territorial Army. The size of these would be as set out in a report produced by Holland and Gubbins; an infantry company with signal and engineer sections, and a nucleus of officers and non-commissioned officers linguistically capable of encouraging local resistance groups and living with them off the country. They would be independent and self-sufficient, knowing where and how to use the explosives they brought with them. They would be called Independent Companies and, initially, ten would be raised. In the very short time available, five of them were ready to go to Norway where, under command of Colonel Gubbins, they made a very respectable showing.

What was more important was that, by their presence, they represented the kernel of Holland's belief that irregular warfare should be controlled by, and undertaken in conjunction with, the actions of regular forces.

Chapter 3

Twelve o'clock in London (1940)

There had been a heated session of criticism and recrimination in Parliament that aid to Norway had been badly planned and inefficiently carried out. In the branch of War Office Military Intelligence responsible for press and propaganda, Major Denzil Batchelor was at his desk summarising a report of the proceedings.

The tape machine sprang to life. 'Ticker-tacker, ticker-tacker'; it rolled out its sheaves of paper onto the floor. The Major heaved himself out of his chair, crossed the room, picked up a sheet, and read:

> Hotler's troops have overrun Luxembourg; Dutch and Belgian Cabinets appeal to France; Hotler proclaims fall of Belgium and Holland; Hotler says he will crush Britain; Hotler says . . .

The machine paused; there was silence. Then hiccup and out came a single sheet. Major Batchelor picked it up.

> Correction [he read] for Hotler read Hitler and the meaning will immediately become apparent.

Whether Hotler or Hitler it made little difference; his successes were there for all to see. On 15 May the Dutch had no recourse but to capitulate; on 27 May the Belgians did likewise; on 28 May the great evacuation from Dunkirk began. In the corridors of the War Office the jokes stopped. Now it was questions: 'How's it going?'; 'How many have got out now?' By the morning of 3 June it was all over and the answer came loud and clear: '224,585 British and 112,546 French and Belgian.'

The loss of equipment was enormous, but it was the men who mattered, who had been rescued from the exposed beaches by some eight hundred ships of the Royal Navy and a citizen fleet, which had gone back and forth over a period of three intensely felt days. Four-fifths of the British Expeditionary Force had been saved, and with this – one of the finest armies we had ever sent into battle – we would start again.

On 10 June Italy declared war on us, and on the 17th the French asked for an armistice. It was as if the past month had been four hours, four days or four centuries, as if the North Sea had been a stream and the English Channel a huge ocean. Reality lay in the knowledge that we were now alone: it brought with it an odd sense of relief and fatality. We knew that, for the duration of the war, our persons and property belonged to our country; we felt certain that we would be supported and sustained by our Commonwealth relatives, our captive friends and, through the only door, the Atlantic wall behind us, the peoples of the United States of America.

On 24 July I cut from the *London Times* the reprint of an article which had appeared in the *New York Times*. It summed up for many of us what we felt:

> It is twelve o'clock in London. Hitler has spoken and Lord Halifax has replied. There is no more to be said. Or is there? Is the tongue of Chaucer, of Shakespeare, of Milton, of the King James translation of the Scriptures, of Keats, of Shelley, to be hereafter, in the British Isles, the dialect of an enslaved race?
>
> Let us try to see clearly. We have to look back a good many centuries to find the beginnings of English liberty. We see it as a rough and obstinate growth, heaving the rich soil under the oaks of lordly estates, breaking out in Wat Tyler's time and in Cromwell's and in the day of the second James, forcing through the Reform Act, never perfected, never giving up. We see the spread of democracy and of empire, side by side, confused and turbulent. But we see democracy ever marching on.
>
> It is twelve o'clock in London. Not twelve o'clock for empire – there is no empire any more. Not twelve o'clock for the old 'dominion over palm and pine'. Twelve o'clock for the common people of England, out of whom England's greatest souls have always come. Twelve o'clock for all that they are and have been, for all those things which make life worth living for free men.
>
> Twelve o'clock – and the wisest prophet in Christendom cannot say what is to come. The old, old towns of Britain, the hills and cliffs and shores and meadows, rich with history, the homes and lives of forty-five million people, the great British traditions of human worth and dignity, the folk sayings, the deep wisdom and the long-suffering hopes of a race – these, not being pleasing to Hitler, are condemned.
>
> We know little, and for a time shall know little, of this unparalleled spectacle of the nation rising as by a single impulse to the defence of

> This blessèd plot, this earth, this realm, this England.

From our own shores we cannot see the shadow over ancient gardens, over houses hoary with age, over the graves of poets and philosophers, and the tombs of the martyrs. We know only that one of the green and lovely oases of civilisation in the wilderness of man's time on earth is foully threatened, and that the whole world for evermore will be the poorer if it falls.

Words falter. There are no phrases for the obscene ambition that attacks, for the magnificent mobilisation of a people that defends, unshaken and unafraid. We can only pray that soon the time will come when the vultures no longer defile British skies, and the cry goes out from John o' Groats to Land's End: 'Twelve o'clock and all's well!'

CHAPTER 4

Small cog on an oiled wheel (1940–1941)

'WINSTON IS IN!' On 10 May idealistic 'peace in our time' Neville Chamberlain resigned and Winston Churchill became Prime Minister, his government a coalition of the three major political parties, his cabinet a War Cabinet. Where sat those critics of the past who had called Mr Churchill 'a warmonger'? With head bent, we hoped, thanking God that the man and his destiny had met and that, now, they might have a chance of being alive when twelve o'clock struck.

In speeches of immortal phrase the new Prime Minister made it clear that, so far as the British were concerned, this was the aim. For the immediate present, all depended 'on winning this battle, here in Britain, now, this summer'.

The battle for Britain began on 10 July when the Germans launched the first of many large-scale daylight air attacks aimed at destroying docks, shipping, airfields and centres of communication. One after another, each wave as it came across the Channel was met and fought by young pilots in Spitfires and Hurricanes of the Royal Air Force. Repeatedly, day after day, with little rest, they beat off and crippled the enemy until the sky was clear. After that daylight raids were sporadic and could be dealt with in a normal order of battle.

On 7 September the Germans switched their main offensive to the night bombing of centres of population, mainly London, and this continued with varying intensity throughout the winter, killing and injuring some fifty thousand civilians by the end of 1940.

Vacillation and fear had by September stopped their plans for invasion by sea.

From Washington men of all shades of opinion watched closely the deportment of Britain during these vital months. Those who put America first, the isolationists, were doubtful of her ability to survive and therefore chary of giving aid. Others, among them the men who had formed and supported a Committee to Defend America by

Aiding the Allies, fought hard for the conviction that in Britain lay America's first line of defence. Roosevelt, a presidential election due in November, did his political best to hold the balance, to show support for Britain without prejudicing the chances of re-election for his own Democratic Party. Among the steps taken towards the former was the agreement of 3 September whereby the British leased to America, free, certain sea and air bases in Newfoundland, Bermuda and the Caribbean in return for fifty over-age destroyers badly needed to support the battle for her sea communications.

At a much lower level – at what might even be called a personal 'subversive' level – collaboration had begun between the two countries earlier in the year. Mr William Stephenson, a trusted and respected business man, had been sent to the United States by Military Intelligence to look discreetly into the possibilities of developing an organisation which, in co-operation with the Federal Bureau of Investigation, could seek means of countering enemy subversion in the Americas. He was advised by friends in London who knew Colonel William J. Donovan, not only as a valiant officer of the First World War but also as a man whose support could be relied on, to get in touch with him. Colonel Donovan's forceful, sensible and intelligent personality, his certainty that aid to Britain was of paramount importance if the Axis powers were to be contained, and the fact that he had the President's ear, were factors which helped Mr Stephenson and made Donovan a welcome visitor to England. In July the President sent him as his personal representative to London to get a view at first hand of Britain's will to fight. An introduction from Stephenson to the headquarters of the Secret Service resulted in Colonel Donovan being shown without reserve the work of British Intelligence in all its parts. He learned also of the importance being attached in Whitehall to the use of all forms of irregular warfare.

The contact with Mr Stephenson and this visit convinced him that, when the United States entered the war, it would be profitable to draw into one body the many Intelligence agencies which worked independently of each other in the departments of War, Navy and State, and to include in this body the study and implementation of unorthodox methods of war such as were now being pursued in England. When Colonel Donovan's Office of Strategic Services was set up in Washington in 1942, and came to be recognised as a proper arm of America's fighting services, he had an advantage over the

London equivalent, the Special Operations Executive. In spite of jealousy, criticism and obstruction, he did succeed in having a combined Intelligence Staff within his command.

But as yet MI(R) and Section D did not know what this equivalent would be. In early June of the fateful 1940, General Beaumont-Nesbitt, the Director of Military Intelligence, and Colonel Holland proposed a reorganisation of MI(R) and Section D into one War Office directorate for irregular activities. Mr Anthony Eden, who was Minister for War, showed their report to the Prime Minister, but it was too late. By now the Chiefs of Staff Committee were recommending 'the creation of widespread revolt in . . . conquered territories' as a means of getting at the enemy, and Mr Churchill was urging immediate aggression in the form of 'butcher and bolt' raids across the Channel. For these he had fired into orbit a Combined Operations Headquarters to take over the extant Independent Companies, their training centre at Inverailort, and to press on with the formation and training of self-contained units of men who henceforth would bear the name 'Commandos'.

An organisation was needed to co-ordinate and direct subversive warfare, and a decision needed as to which department should have charge of it. It had a powerful political potential if it was given a life of its own, and the Foreign Office was anxious that its growth should be controlled by civilians. The Director of Military Intelligence did his best to keep it in the War Office but he was submerged by the Minister of Economic Warfare, Dr Hugh Dalton, who claimed that his was the proper quarter to give it shelter and that he was the right man to watch over it.

'Do you really think, my dear General,' he said, 'that subversive activities can be directed by disciplined soldiers like yourself?' On 16 July his Ministry won custody of the clandestine child with all its goods and chattels: the Foreign Office had a seat on the board and the new organisation was named the Special Operations Executive (SOE).

In August Brigadier Humphrey Wyndham was appointed Deputy Director of MI(R), his terms of reference to review our structure and operations in relation to the new set-up. Because we knew this spelt our end, we did not feel warm towards him, but soon realised that, as Colonel Holland said, the man 'is a gentleman doing an unpleasant job in an extremely nice way' and that we should support him. This we did, and soon recognised that his cool judgment, his ability to cut the cackle and go straight to the root of a problem, and the example he gave of only speaking when there was something worth saying, were just the qualities needed to break up an association such as ours.

By October the operation was complete and the members of MI(R) dispersed. John Walter went as an attaché to the British Embassy in Madrid, and Colonel Eddie Combe to the War Cabinet offices as head of the Inter-Services Security Board and allotter-in-chief of code names. Colonel Norman Crockatt remained in the War Office in charge of his expanding and invaluable Prisoners-of-War Interrogation Centre.

Major Millis Jefferis's future was secure. In his history of *The Second World War* Mr Churchill wrote: '. . . I decided to keep under my own hand as Minister of Defence the experimental establishment formed by Major Jefferis . . .' and in a minute to General Ismay dated 24 August 1940, he asked: '. . . By whom is he employed? Who is he under? I regard this officer as a singularly capable and forceful man, who should be brought forward to a higher position. He ought certainly to be promoted Lieutenant-Colonel, as it will give him more authority.' So promoted, Jefferis with his small staff remained for the rest of the war under the hand of his Prime Minister, his ingenuity and inventiveness free from departmental surveillance.

Major-General Colin Gubbins, the Distinguished Service Order awarded to him during the Norwegian campaign sewn alongside the 1914–18 Military Cross, had spent the summer months organising, with Home Forces Headquarters, pockets of military resistance in the form of self-contained 'Auxiliary Units' against what looked like certain invasion. In October he reported back to the War Office confident that he would be assigned to a war front. It was not to be: the Special Operations Executive needed his know-how, and it was there that he took his wide experience, imaginative brain, power of quick decision and qualities of leadership. In 1943 he became its Director-General, his command embracing active cells of resistance in every country from Norway to the Far East, its own training establishments, laboratories, wireless communications and aircraft. Irregular operations had travelled far since Colonel Holland's idea had been given its start in the War Office Intelligence Directorate. Many parts of the enemy-occupied world were now being secretly and boldly exploited for the benefit of the Allied cause by missions sent out from Donovan's OSS and London's SOE The two organisations appreciated each other and pooled their resources whenever it was necessary to do so.

Peter Wilkinson went with Gubbins: so did Lesley Wauchope. She and I parted with sorrow, feeling like the last members of the crew of a sinking ship. We were, only I was still on board and would no longer have a colleague to laugh with.

Last of all, sadly, we said goodbye to Colonel Holland. He went back to straight military duty as Director of the Royal Engineers in Northern Command Headquarters at York. He was content. He had never sought personal aggrandisement in the work he had begun, and the fact that it had outgrown the conventional garb which he had hoped for it did not inspire him to continue in it. He could, if he had wished, have regarded himself as the man who began it all. Without his persistence in the early days, Romania, Poland and Norway would not have had the small advanced support which, if things had worked out, would have been there to encourage and sustain them; nor would the way have been eased for the expanding operations of SOE without the preliminary placing of the many MI(R) missions which have not been named in these short chapters.

He had established on solid ground his belief in the value of clandestine operations as a weapon of war; the essence of it he left to be carried in the heart and stomach of the men and women who took part in them during the years that lay ahead.

'There is one office to make for', said Colonel Holland as he cleared his desk and made ready to go, 'and a man at the top of it for whom you should work. The office is the Office of the War Cabinet and Minister of Defence, and the man General Ismay.'

His letter of introduction to Lieutenant-Colonel Ian Jacob, a fellow Royal Engineer, led me down Whitehall into a quiet and tidy room.

'I am sorry.' The Colonel's eyes stared unblinking through round spectacles. 'We don't employ women here as private secretaries: we draw officers from the Navy and Army, but I will send your name round.' With an austere smile he showed me the door.

In the October sunshine I took off the blue corduroy hat which matched so carefully my new suit, dusted myself off and crept back to the War Office.

Under the quiet and authoritative direction of Colonel Dudley Clarke, his equable temperament so different from the dynamic and uncertain humours of Colonel Holland, a section had been formed to liaise with Combined Operations Headquarters and raise, equip and administer ten Commandos. No longer Independent Companies under Intelligence, but Commandos under Military Operations, I said to myself and thought of Colonel Holland.

I was on its establishment and remained there for the next two months, part of my time spent in collating a War Diary for MI(R). Military formations in the field had to keep War Diaries, and the same rule applied to the military bureaucrats. Ours was complicated by the fact that our use of Special Funds outside the supervision of the Treasury had to be accounted for. The result was, I am sure, chaotic, and for any auditor a nightmare. Easier for me, because I have always loved records, files and documentation, was the collation and selection of memoranda, letters and reports, each of which as I sorted and filed them represented the ideas of individuals, their hopes for them, their burial or their implementation of them. Little by little, from these, I extracted what was needed for the chronicle of our actions and recommendations during the eighteen months of MI(R)'s existence.

My life outside the office was based in an attractive apartment on the top floor of an old house in Curzon Street, Mayfair, let to me furnished, for a modest rent, by a friend who was on service overseas. Here at night I spent the Blitz period, sharing the staircase, when the raid was particularly bad, with the only other occupant, the janitor Mr Hulford. Together we fire-watched and shared jokes with the 'ladies of the town' who resided by the gross in that area of London. They were a cheerful lot, on excellent terms with the local air-raid wardens, and their lack of fear was a real test of one's own nerve. A beautiful girl rushed in one night and asked to use the telephone. We heard her say:

'Hello? Oh, darling, remember you said you'd do anything for me?' Expressions of assurance, we presumed, ensued from the other end of the line. Then:

'Well, sweetie, hurry over, will you? There's an unexploded bomb right outside our house and I want you to come and take it away.'

Dinners with colleagues and friends were strictly 'for the duration'; when the eating, or the eating and the dancing, were over we parted – he to his home, me scurrying along to mine, sometimes dropping flat into the gutter if the swish-sh of a bomb sounded close – and not caring a damn if I misjudged it, overdid the act and had to arise in a silent street and face any passers-by.

There was one colleague in Dudley Clarke's section who was a source of joy and laughter to us all. Captain David Niven had a wit which was well up to John Walter's standard, and a supply of funny stories, told with perfect mimicry, which could be exceeded by no one. The War Office was his stooge and he had fun with it. Two hats, one in his room and the other, with a folder of typescript, in the porter's entrance lobby, meant, he said, that no one knew whether he was in or out. He lived a full personal life outside the building and kept his immediate superior, a serious and earnest officer, in constant uncertainty as to his whereabouts. John Walter had also had a ruse to disguise his, more often than not, late return from lunch. We had often watched him, with knees bent ready in the sitting position, skimming in and landing on his chair behind the door of the MI(R) officer's room, with a document in his hand and a beaming smile on his face.

For a time Captain Niven waged a relentless psychological war against a superior young aide to the Chief of the Imperial General Staff. Because the aide, on their first encounter, had not returned his 'good morning' salute, Niven made it his business to be there to greet him more loudly and more unctuously each day, until at last the aide cracked and the sortie ended.

In November my fortunes changed. My flat was hit by a bomb, one of a stick of three, the only ones to drop on London on that particular Sunday night; and Colonel Jacob's note with my name on it matured into an invitation to dinner from Lieutenant-Colonel Cornwall-Jones, Secretary of the Joint Planning Staff in the War Cabinet Offices and Ministry of Defence.

The destruction of 14 Curzon Street was sad, not only because I would no longer see the trees in the adjoining garden of Crewe House. I had that morning decided that the worst of the Blitz was past, and cleaned everything, unpacked my clothes from cases which had been kept ready for instant flight, and had laid the breakfast tray ready for next morning. I had also forsaken Hulford at a time when we often sat together in his basement room to listen to the late night news. I had gone round to Berkeley Square to have a drink with friends, had heard the bombs drop near and had returned to find the house bombed and empty. From the local air-raid warden I learned that Hulford was in St George's Hospital with minor injuries. I slept the night in a nearby hotel and next morning went to see him. He was all right, and when I said how sorry I was I had not been there with him he told me that the bomb had come in at an angle and that he had by luck been in the one spot in the room which had escaped heavy falls of debris. His cat, who had always warned us by his unhappy restlessness that there would be an air raid, had been killed. Later that day, I found that, by its angle, the bomb had left the top floor shaky but intact, and the owner's and my effects recoverable.

The interview with Colonel Cornwall-Jones took place in Hatchett's basement restaurant in Piccadilly. To the thump-thump of a dance band he offered me a job on his staff and talked about the overall design and importance of war planning at top levels, while I bleated on about the value of MI(R) and the work it had done. A truce was called, I accepted his offer and next day gave in my notice to Colonel Dudley Clarke. Colonel Holland was pleased; it was the office he had wanted me to join, but not yet the man.

In December 1940, with my three stalwarts – the Royal typewriter, a pair of scissors and a ruler – I moved over to Great George Street, into a deeply constructed citadel under the heart of Westminster. Here I found myself in a square box of a room attached to the Joint Planning Committee Secretariat at a salary of £185 a year plus overtime. My boss, Colonel Cornwall-Jones (or 'C.J.' as he was generally known), was a capable, dedicated man with a bellyfull of the sort of fire with which good priests are fed. He had no thought for himself and believed in the waging of the war with all the energy compact within him. He wanted me to start a card index showing, on specially designed cards, the dates, meetings, decisions, arguments, of each operation, real or planned, and of all problems, real or probable – in short, a day-to-day summary of the war. It was an idea to which my filing-clerk type of mind reacted well, and I set to it with a will. I ordered large white cards edged with different colours, gazed at them and decided to zone the war, alphabetically and by colour, in the following divisions:

A, with an orange edging: Major Strategy and Policy.
B, mauve (an indeterminate colour which seemed right for talkers): Departments, Conversations, Conferences.

C, green-edged, to suit the United Kingdom, Canada, USA, N. Ireland, Eire, Channel Islands, Greenland, Iceland.
D, blue: Europe which included the Free and Vichy French, Baltic States, Finland, Russia, Scandinavia.
E, pale pink: Iberian Peninsula, Atlantic Islands, West and North Africa, Latin America.
F, bright pink: Middle Eastern countries, the Balkans, Italy and her dependencies, East Africa, India, Russia in Asia.
G, white (no edge) Far East, Australia and New Zealand.

The world was easy to manage. I padded on, and soon presented my first progress report. 'I have,' I said, 'cards for:

A/STRATEGY/1: Major Strategy.
A/STRATEGY/2: Strategy in the Middle East.
A/POLICY/AIR/1: Bombing Policy.
A/POLICY/NAVY/1: Naval Programme.
A/POLICY/ARMY/2: Proposal for General Purposes Expeditionary Force.
A/SPEC. OPS/1: Planning for Irregular and Subversive Activities.
B/FOES/1: Formation of Future Operations (Enemy) Section.
B/SOE/1: Formation of Special Operations Executive.
C/COMB. OPS/1: Landing Craft and Assault Shipping.
D/FREE FRENCH/1: Operations by the Free French.
E/ATLANTIC ISLANDS/1: Atlantic Islands: proposals.
E/SPAIN/1: Suggested Preparatory Measures.
E/NORTH AFRICA/1: Assistance to the French in North Africa.
E/WEST AFRICA/1: Establishment of French Forces in West Africa.
F/GREECE/1: Assistance to Greece.
F/GREECE/2: Demolitions in Greece.
F/SARDINIA/1: Capture of Sardinia; of Cagliari.
F/LIBYA/1: Situation in Libya.
F/SOUTH AFRICA/1: Move of 2nd South African Division.
G/FAR EAST: (Not attempted yet).'

The file, or card, titles were usually similar to those heading the War Cabinet, Defence Committee and Chiefs of Staff Committee memoranda and the minutes which referred to them. It was interesting to see later, when I built up a filing section for the Chiefs of Staff Committee Secretariat, that the simple form I had chosen for the titles and the continued use of the colour system, only on files instead of cards, worked quite well; the rhythmic and descriptive wording of the titles made the subject easy to locate.

The card I got furthest with, because by April 1941 it was 'hot', was the pink-edged 'Assistance to Greece'. Onto it went the dates and document reference numbers, summaries of discussion, decisions, telegrams, appreciation; and the column for cross-reference showed, for instance, that anything to do with the 'Availability of Landing Craft' – crux of all military operations – was repeated on the green-edged 'Landing Craft' card.

As an idea, however, it was too ambitious. How could the immense and intense preoccupations with our decision to send forces to defend Greece be set out on cards measuring eight by five inches? History cannot be so confined; the urgent present lay with us and too much was happening for it to be possible for one person to click from typewriter to card all that was going on. What should one include, what leave out? I scratched my head and dithered, the minutes of high-level meetings and the telegrams which whizzed back and forth piling up on my desk while I tried to decide how to give the future historian the most accurate view. I thought then, as I think now, that a place for a war record-keeper should be as urgently available on any operational establishment as, say, for a logistics expert.

Quite apart from the amorphous quality of the work I had been given to do, I was unhappy. The MI(R) War Diary, which I had brought with me to finish, represented the life I knew and liked, and I missed my firm position on the third floor of the War Office with its chats and jokes and smiles of recognition. Here I was neither officer nor clerk, and it took quite a time for the juniors of the regular Civil Service to accept me as a colleague and not regard me as a usurper of their rights. I was never tempted to push myself into the underground Officers' Mess and was careful to keep to myself social outings with any of the officers with whom I worked.

I sat in my room, neither fish nor fowl nor good red herring, and tried to assimilate the intricate pattern of committee and personality whose job it was to work together and reduce to paper the strategy of World War II. The labyrinth of brightly lit and varnished rooms and passages, their air-conduit pipes gaily painted red, had been planned and constructed before the war to serve as headquarters for the Cabinet and Service Chiefs and their staffs, and was proof against air attack or, if the worst happened, equipped for siege. Mr Churchill's Blitz suite of rooms was here and the telephone on which he talked with President Roosevelt across the lively waves of the Atlantic.

In this warren were offices, conference rooms, canteens and bedrooms guarded and staffed by dark blue uniformed Royal Marines. The Joint Planning Staff, the Joint Intelligence Committee, the Strategical Planning Section, Future Operations Planning Section, the section devoted to thinking out the enemy's intentions, the section to produce ways of deceiving the enemy about projected operations, Colonel Combe and his code names – here they all were, dug down deep. They bloomed with sprays of officers and civilians – tall, short, fair, dark, frank, devious, dull, spirited. The culture and pruning of these brilliant, sometimes exotic, growths was in the capable hands of men like Colonel Cornwall-Jones. He and the other Secretaries of Committee were hand-picked civilians and service officers, some of whom had been brought in from high professional positions in the outside world. They formed the Cabinet Secretariat, which was headed by Sir Edward Bridges, Secretary to the War Cabinet and Head of the Civil Service, and Major-General Sir Hastings Ismay, Deputy Secretary (Military) to the War Cabinet and Chief Staff Officer to Mr Churchill in his capacity of Minister of Defence. Sir Edward Bridges, son of a poet, with a poet's unruly hair, a man of shy charm, held his high post with such modesty that he managed to merge his considerable intellect into a balanced whole of unobtrusive leadership and tactful co-operation with colleagues trimmed for war. His relationship with General Ismay was one of mutual respect and forbearance between two widely different temperaments, and there was no shadow of disloyalty or intrigue between them. They were immune to the measles of over-staffing and kept the War Cabinet Offices compact and flexible, as expeditious as a well-oiled machine.

On the military side, at the centre sat the Chiefs of Staff Committee, responsible for joint military opinion and the day-to-day direction of military effort, subject only to the overriding authority of Prime Minister and War Cabinet. Besides the First Sea Lord and Chief of Naval Staff, the Chief of the Imperial General Staff and the Chief of the Air Staff, General Ismay sat in as Chief Staff Officer to the Prime Minister and Minister of Defence. When Combined Operations became the fourth leg of offence, their chief, Admiral Lord Louis Mountbatten, attended the meetings as required. The

Secretaries to this committee were Colonel Leslie (known as 'Jo') Hollis, Royal Marines, and two others, of whom Lieutenant-Colonel C. R. (George) Price, Royal Engineers, was permanent and the other changing. The practice of moving secretaries periodically between Whitehall and the various theatres of war was a good one and avoided stagnation.

Colonel Ian Jacob was Secretary of the Defence Committee (Operations) and (Supply), a two-part committee which Mr Church-ill used a lot, because it was so constituted as to be able to deal at one and the same time with politico-military strategy and policy, its members being the Chiefs of Staff and those Cabinet Ministers most closely concerned.

From General Ismay down, the military side of the Secretariat, like the civilians under Bridges, were, so to speak, members of the same club; certainly where the Planning and Intelligence members were concerned, they worked, ate, argued, together under one roof from early morning, when they breakfasted in the Mess, until late into the night when wearily they pushed back their chairs and went to bed.

Most powerful, most flexible, most outstanding, was the Prime Minister and Minister of Defence, whose presence in the building could be felt by all. Under the dynamic direction of Mr Churchill the creaking machinery of a Great Britain awaking to its destiny became the mighty truth of a Great Britain unshakeably and unmistakably meeting and matching it. His noble use of the English language was not confined to his speeches; each minute that he wrote, each draft for telegram or letter, was worth reading, not only for what it said but for how it was said. His choice of words, the brevity with which he expressed his views, the wit, humour and deep feeling which came through them, were part of the character of an extraordinary man. They revealed his meticulous attention to detail, made clear his singleness of purpose and unrelenting sense of duty. It would have been impossible to be anywhere within reach of his genius and not react to his unique gift for communication and the power it gave him to reach into the heart.

Gradually I became a part of it. Nostalgia for the War Office, for sabotage and sneak raiding, began to give way to the realisation that here, at the centre, even if a paper was simply entitled 'Move of the Nth Division to Timbuctoo', it really did have a direct and vital bearing on the outcome of the war. With my ruler I drew a line at the end of the MI(R) War Diary and sent it across Whitehall for burial in the military archives and eventual resuscitation by the historians.

At the same time I took a personal step upwards. Colonel Cornwall-Jones's Assistant Secretary, Major Anthony Head, called me in one day to take dictation. Smarting from my position of being neither clerk nor stenographer, not seeing why I should be used for work which the other girls regarded as theirs, I struck.

'No', I said to the astonished officer. 'It is not my job. I am not a shorthand typist.'

In January 1941 Colonel Cornwall-Jones went to Washington as Secretary to a most secret mission. Called the Anglo-US Technical Conversations, these were the first of all the wartime Anglo-American conferences. By now the drums were beating in American ears and it was timely that men from war-encrusted Europe could talk across the table to their American counterparts, could sift facts at first hand and widen the view of those who were not yet in the struggle but – to the far-seeing – soon would be. Overall agreement was reached that if the United States and Japan became involved Germany would be dealt with first and then Japan. More practical because less hypothetical was the establishment in Washington of joint staff missions for present exchange and future partnership. By the time the talks had ended, the Lend-Lease Bill had become law, President Roosevelt was asking for a seven thousand million dollar appropriation and promising 'the end of compromise with tyranny . . . aid until victory . . . ships, planes, munitions'.

It was a strange life that we led in those days in our quiet dungeon galleries where the only mechanical sounds were the tap of typewriters and the hum of air-conditioning fans. A noticeboard showed us if it was 'fine', 'wet' or 'windy' outside, red or green lights if an air raid was 'on' or 'off'. If it was 'on' we heard nothing of it until we were outside the heavy steel doors of our cage. Then we would know by the frequency of crump, boom or crackle whether or not it was worth going on out into the normal Blitz life of London. Long hours of work did not give anyone much opportunity for this anyway, except for punctuation marks of reality like an outside date for lunch or dinner, for haircuts and shampoos. The Planning and Intelligence Staffs lived on assumption, based their appreciations on likelihood – facts behind them, assumptions with them, likelihoods ahead of them. Daily truth belonged to the Map Room. Well equipped, manned by retired officers from the three Services, it was our one centre of fact, a haven not because any news it gave was good but because it represented a peg in a shifting world and because its caretakers were informative, helpful and charming. Here we could know the whereabouts and condition of such-and-such convoy ploughing the Atlantic Ocean or squirming its way through to the encircled island of Malta; we could see where the bombs had fallen the previous night, how stood our shipping losses, our civil and military casualties. Coloured pins showed that the Eighth Army was withdrawing in the Western Desert, was being pushed back towards the Egyptian frontier. The flags had gone from Greece and Yugoslavia where the German invasion had been strong enough to end national resistance and had forced the withdrawal of the British Expeditionary Force which had been sent to their aid. The flags showing the dispositions of our forces in the island of Crete, in their fierce battle against a swift and deadly German airborne attack, were now lifted and pinned on their Egyptian base camps. The days of March, April, May, June were black, lit only by the Royal Navy's victorious assault on units of the Italian Fleet at Cape Matapán and the sinking of the German battleship *Bismarck*.

I seldom slept in the underground bedroom with my name on the door, preferring to nip across St James's Park to the St Ermin's Hotel where I had parked myself when my flat was destroyed. My room cost £3 a week including early-morning tea, and I bought my own bread and butter. I was able to afford this convenient living thanks to an allowance from Mr Shaw, whose kindness to me since Mexico had remained steadfast.

One night I awoke to a bedroom glowing red, fitfully red; the church across the road was alight, set on fire by incendiary bombs sizzling down from the sky. In April and May the air raids were particularly severe. On 16 April St Paul's Cathedral was hit; till then it had escaped damage and had stood supreme in wreaths of flame. One night in May the House of Commons, Westminster Hall and Westminster Abbey were hit; we saw it all from the roof of our office building and, by the light of the fires surrounding us, we could read the print on charred pieces of paper which fell around us in a cloud of dead bureaucracy.

Like every other quarter, street and public building, the War Cabinet Offices had its team of air-raid wardens and fire watchers. We were on a roster, those of us not needed for essential executive or clerical duties, and most of us had had a course of training in civil defence. Under the direction of the fully trained wardens we patrolled the building, checked that the blackout was complete and in incendiary raids carried bucket and spade ready to scoop up each small fire bomb and shove it into the sand-filled bucket. They spluttered and fizzed like squibs the size of hand grenades. I was not a brave fire-fighter, but I was there – and if there had not been others with me braver than I, I would probably have been brave. I cannot remember feeling afraid; by now most of us were conditioned to air raids and more conscious of gratitude for being alive than fear of being dead. Real fear came much later, with the V.1 and V.2 flying-bombs and rockets, when we were, so to speak, 'out of training'.

I can see why men become monks and women nuns; it is a satisfying condition when the trappings of material life are cut away and the mind and body become sufficient to themselves, a relief to feel responsibility within one's own limitations for one's own salvation. At this time I was not the only one who hugged London to my beating heart. London was ours from the hour the blacked-out night hid its beauty until the morning siren signalled the coming day, most triumphantly ours when the full moon rose and shone on its age-old face and we knew the Germans would not be coming.

During this period of sky-high death the night-time meetings of the War Cabinet took place in the underground Cabinet Room. It gave me a feeling of importance to be able to walk down the passage, peep through a small window in the door and know what it was they were discussing round the blue baize table. The sense of importance which this knowledge of great secrets gave me came with me into the outside world and made me feel superior to those who did not know what I knew.

The smug look was wiped off my face when the secrets of March became the public news of April: our military withdrawals from Greece; the air raids which destroyed Coventry; the cruel and mounting score of merchant ship losses; Mr Attlee's grim recital to a silent House of Commons that the total British casualties in the war to date were 39,856 civilians killed, 40,897 injured, 37,607 fighting forces dead, 25,895 wounded.

Rudolf Hess arrived in May, his parachute swinging him down mad and alone on his private peace mission. I imagined myself sent for by the Foreign Secretary. 'Miss Bright, you alone in England know this man. Go and see him. Here is your ticket for Scotland.' Yes, certainly I should have accepted to go to the Hess family in Munich in 1938.

More yielding of good, though not so spectacular, was an invitation to lunch one Saturday with General Ismay. Over a chilled bottle of Chablis he asked me if I would like to come upstairs and run an information room for commanders-in-chief. I was not immediately enthusiastic. For one thing I was well into, and fond of, my card-index history. I felt a sort of non-acquiescent reaction against General Ismay's charm and his assumption that I would jump at the chance of going up to the higher regions of war-planning. I knew that Colonel Cornwall-Jones, in order to establish me on his staff, had had to break down quite a bit of resistance to non-Civil Service women, and I had feelings of loyalty to him and to my fellow-workers below stairs. I was not being offered a rise in pay and my knowledge of commanders-in-chief was limited to a belief that they could get any news they wanted at any time anywhere. 'No, thank you very much,' I said, 'I think I'll stay where I am.'

Far more vivid at this period was my preoccupation with my own home. In May my father had felt ill, had had an X-ray and had fainted. In June he was in bed and the doctor told my mother he had a year to live. On the 28th I went to our cottage in Somerset and held his twisted arthritic hand for the last time. The sweet williams were blazing in our front garden. On 3 July he died, and it was the open black telephone – not the top-secret red nor the security-equipped green – which brought my mother's voice with its sad news to my ear. Betty and her two children were still in Shanghai where Godfrey was now Secretary-General of the Municipal Council; Pamela was with the 26th (Scottish) General Military Hospital in Palestine, had been there for the past six months. Only Nancy, married and living in Bristol, and Felicity, who had joined the Women's Royal Naval Service and was stationed at Bristol, were there with me and our mother when we buried him.

Because he had had no security of pension he had worked longer than he should, had never complained as he walked each morning the two miles from our house to Freshford railway station to take the train to Bristol and return the same way at night. With the cancer in his throat so far advanced, it must have cost him much effort. He and my mother had planned for his retirement by moving from Bristol to the cottage, and he was keenly looking forward to the day when he could live there entirely and have time for his sketching, his stamp collection, his reading and his pleasure in the countryside.

Germany's invasion of Russia on 22 June was to me personally, at that time, a matter of indifference.

CHAPTER 5

Information by degree (1941)

IT HAD BEEN MR CHURCHILL'S HABIT, when he had presided as First Lord of the Admiralty at meetings with his Home commanders-in-chief, to treat his listeners to a masterly summing-up of the war situation. When he became Prime Minister the comradeship in meeting with his admirals gave place to the formality and scope of a full War Cabinet or Defence Committee agenda. At one of these meetings a naval commander-in-chief had looked mystified during a discussion of certain naval operations. Mr Churchill lost no time in minuting an order to General Ismay. He was 'anxious', he wrote, 'that Commanders-in-Chief should be kept fully informed of the situation, but reluctant to increase the circulation list of highly secret papers'. General Ismay should 'organise a special secret information centre in the Office of the Minister of Defence which Commanders-in-Chief could visit whenever they came to London. No trouble should be spared in organising this centre which should start functioning by 1 July at latest.'

General Ismay was unwilling to increase his uniformed staff and decided that it was the kind of section which could be perfectly well handled by a civilian woman. He decided to approach 'the girl C.J. brought in'. Hence our lunch. My lukewarm reaction did not deter him. He returned to the attack, this time with success. I deserted the card index and came upstairs into a room, very near General Ismay's Private Office, on what is known in Whitehall jargon as 'the second, or principal, floor'. On the strength of what it was hoped would be a constant stream of distinguished visitors, I was given a carpet, a long polished table, wall maps, an easy chair and some official secrets.

Around me, compared to the busy burrows from which I had come, it all seemed very calm and dignified. Important-looking people passed up and down the passage outside my door, snatches of conversation floating on the air behind them; 'Number Ten . . .', 'The P.M. . ..', 'President Roosevelt . . .', 'an offensive . . .', 'decision must be taken . . .' Each morning, be-medalled, in khaki, dark and light blue uniforms, the three Chiefs of Staff disappeared into their Committee Room. General Ismay, from his office two doors away, with Colonel Hollis and one of his two Assistant Secretaries, joined them and the door was closed. After an hour or so, more footsteps and bursts of conversation signalled the end of the meeting for the day. Then, in Colonel Hollis's Private Office, the work began; by that afternoon the minutes had been written, discussed, typed, duplicated and sent out.

I had no idea what my visitors, when they came, would want to know about, so, as a start, I put the visitors' book I had been given on the table, and beside it Intelligence Reports and Situation of the War summaries which now were sent to me automatically.

'Nobody come yet?' asked General Ismay, popping his head round my door. 'Don't worry; they will.'

I did worry – not because my room was empty of commanders-in-chief but because I feared that when they came they would be critical of it looking like a doctor's waiting-room presided over by a girl who looked like a girl. I need not have: it turned out – as it so often did – that General Ismay was right. They liked to be greeted by someone who did not spring to attention and say '*Sir!*', to relax and read and express strong views which would be agreed with and then forgotten. For overseas commanders-in-chief, home for consultation, the Special Information Centre filled a real need. Separated from the power and security of their own headquarters they felt adrift in Whitehall, where their particular problems were regarded as being only part of the whole and where their ranking opposite numbers were usually too submerged in work to be able to give them more than just enough attention. The room on the second floor offered them a tranquil mooring and the freedom to chart for themselves the shifting tide of war.

'A nice set-up, but not quite what I expected', remarked the first visitor, Admiral Sir Percy Noble, Commander-in-Chief of the Western Approaches, a figure as maritime and handsome as his operational title.

It turned out to be not quite what I expected either. At first there was a rush of callers as air marshals, generals and admirals, feeling they should put in at least one appearance before the Prime Minister asked them whether they had signed their names against such commands as

The Nore, Eastern, Western, Scottish, Fighter, Bomber, Orkneys and Shetlands, Rosyth. Then there would be long gaps during which I collected and collated all I could in the way of restricted information. It was not easy. General Ismay's Private Office, of which my section was a part, consisted of a Paymaster-Commander Royal Navy, Maurice Knott, and three girl secretaries of whom Betty Green was the chief. They did their best for me, but it was not always possible to borrow their files, not only because they were jealously guarded but also because they were nearly always in use. The less vital papers, informative and valuable, came to me regularly, but the purpose of the Centre was to give my visitors background to the discussions and decisions being conducted and reached on all aspects of the war, and these were, by their very nature, 'hot'. A commander-in-chief seeking information on the likelihood of military action in a theatre other than his own, with its accompanying threat to his supply position, was not likely to be pleased to be handed a list of the number of aircraft or guns in hand and in process of manufacture in the armouries of the United Kingdom.

There was a kind of condescension towards commanders-in-chief implied in such remarks as: 'Is it necessary for them to know about this? It has nothing really to do with them.' This was infuriating: it made me feel as if I, on their behalf, was being nosy about secret things. But I had my job to do, so I tried, by keeping my eyes and ears open, to present to them the sort of knowledge for which the Centre had been formed, and I let them read themselves into any subject they fancied. Once I showed the commander of a subordinate theatre of war some papers which the Chairman of the Chiefs of Staff Committee, General Sir Alan Brooke, thought he should not have seen and told Ismay so in no uncertain terms. All General Ismay said to me was:

'How silly of old . . . to show off his knowledge to "Brookie" like that', and he laughed.

Together we began a series of regular telegrams to all commanders-in-chief at home and abroad. Called 'COS(D)' (Chiefs of Staff (Defence)), they were coded top secret and contained the sort of background information which commanders-in-chief would not otherwise get and, where possible, plans for the future. Here care had to be taken, not because of any doubt of the addressee's discretion but because future planning was subject to events outside its control and not, therefore, necessarily unalterable. Regular appreciations of the politico-military situation and future policy and strategy did, however, give the commander-in-chief the feeling that he was being kept informed from the inside.

Collecting the contents together and preparing summaries of the telegrams for General Ismay represented for me a first step into the inner circle of the War Cabinet Offices. I could now by right not only ask for news but also have a direct reason for becoming closely connected with his Private Office.

When I had lunched with him I had felt cheated in some way by General Ismay's easy charm and the lack of crusty power which had been in Colonel Holland's character. I mistrusted his good manners and smooth sophistication and wondered at Colonel Holland's high regard for him. When I began working upstairs, my superficial appraisal began to fall apart, and I saw that here indeed was the man at the centre of the web, a remarkable man. He held the balance between the Prime Minister and the Service Chiefs, presenting the views of each to the other with clear-headed verity and simplification of divergencies. He supported, and was on excellent terms with, Colonel Hollis and Colonel Jacob, keeping their trust and giving them freedom of action. Right down the scale of his integrated Defence Staff and its many military subcommittees, he was respected and liked. This was the man, then, for whom Colonel Holland hoped I would work.

Some qualities they shared: an inability to compromise on any problem involving their own moral standards; a quiet and direct faith in the unseen power of Almighty God; an inability to lobby for themselves or to seek personal advantage out of any mixture of circumstance; an ability to cut out pretensions and concentrate on fact; an inability to wait and see how the cat might jump. Both had kind hearts, loyalty to those above and below them, and a delight in laughter.

There the resemblance ended. I had changed my awkward, antisocial, shy, ailing and aesthetic colonel for a man, urbane and approachable, of superb physical appearance, with a pronounced taste for the good things of life. The nervous energy which had kept Colonel Holland smoking innumerable cigarettes, and the powerful physique which he had used to its limit, had spilled themselves into round shoulders and chronic stomach ulcers with constant pain which he impatiently disregarded. General Ismay was tall, calm and broad-shouldered, light on his feet; he carried his weight with an ease which betrayed his cavalry and polo-playing past. Characteristic of straightforward and practical commonsense were his round head and square, capable hands, the other side of his nature being compound in his large brilliant eyes. These mirrored a clairvoyant foresight, a psychic perception of men's foibles and, more often than not, a sure discernment of their true motives. They also made him a formidable cardplayer who knew the whereabouts of any card in the pack.

The same sort of fatherly concern towards subordinates that sat so oddly and yet so warmly on Jo Holland was apparent in 'Pug' Ismay. Liftmen, messengers, shorthand typists, clerks, junior officers, cleaners – all felt free to speak to him and be sure of a hearing, a reaction, a joke, or an enquiry about their families. A great supporter of women workers, he treated us all with teasing courtesy, demanding from us at the same time a high standard of real labour.

'Whether in food or drink, work or people, "Pug" just isn't interested in anything but the best,' said Colonel Hollis.

Standing beside his desk while he amended my drafts of the COS(D) telegrams – amendments made in such a way as to make me feel I had thought of them – I looked at this apparently simple, inwardly complex, pugnacious officer and fell finally into his trap. It seemed then even more difficult to feel I was doing a full-time job of work; at the end of the day to report the visit of one, perhaps two or three, commanders-in-chief did not make my contribution to the war effort seem particularly momentous.

Except, perhaps, on the day that General Wavell came. It was September, and he had just been appointed Commander-in-Chief India, his command in the Middle East now belonging to General Auchinleck – an arbitrary change which had followed the disasters of our military aid to Greece. His voice was dry and grating, and he was sparing in its use. Vice-Admiral Sir Hugh Binney, Commander-in-Chief Orkneys and Shetlands, was already reading at the table. 'We've met before,' said Sir Archibald and sat down. No more was said, and I clucked round. Wavell wanted to see the state of our anti-aircraft defences and fighter strength, and then sat silent, making quick movements as he turned the pages but not seeming to be particularly interested in them. Now and again a beady eye was fixed on me, its stare accentuated by the monocle in front of it. He left without a word, came back a day or two later and asked for statistics on tanks. This time there was a twinkle. I took advantage to make good a promise to my old colleagues in the Joint Planning Staff and Map Room.

'Would you mind coming down below?' I said. He seemed pleased to be needed anywhere, and we were soon surrounded by officers from all three Services whose respect for him was strengthened by their dislike of his summary treatment by the Prime Minister and War Cabinet.

He invited me to lunch, which he ate silently at the Senior United Service Club. Walking back through St James's Park, he asked me: 'Why does Winston dislike me, Joan?' I was not then, nor ever have been, in a position to answer that one, even if it were true. What was obvious at that particular time was that this quiet soldier, so lately a great victor in Africa and Egypt, was feeling out on a limb, shut off from the inner circle of affairs. In April he had known from his Intelligence sources that strong reinforcements were reaching Rommel's Desert Army across the Mediterranean. His reaction to repeated enquiry from Prime Minister and War Cabinet as to whether these would interfere with the need to help Greece, by pinning down forces for the defence of Egypt, had been equivocal – almost a shrug of the shoulders and a 'Oh well, if you say we must help Greece, then we must'. He had, since the early days of the war, worked miracles of conquest in the Middle East with very few forces and little equipment and was apt to regard any extension of operations as 'just another chestnut to be pulled out of the fire'.

It was a tragedy that Mr Churchill had lost confidence in Wavell but more of a tragedy that Wavell was so inarticulate, so unable to make out a case for himself. He was a soldier's soldier, a poet, a philosopher, but he was not astute when it came to dealing with his brilliant Prime Minister. He called himself lazy; perhaps he was, perhaps this was why he sometimes found himself cornered. He was tolerant of his dilemmas, regarded them as 'just another baby for me to hold' when he should have foreseen the birth and prepared for the accouchement. At the time when an invasion of Britain seemed certain Mr Churchill took grave risks at home by sending him men, tanks and guns, committing them to the perils of the sea for convoy at great cost through the Mediterranean and round the Cape. Mr Churchill had to defend himself and his Cabinet against serious criticism in a Parliament rightly fearful for the safety of the country. In his messages home Wavell failed to give the impression that he recognised the sacrifices that were being made: what was worse, by striking a minor, pessimistic note without any accompanying chord of appreciative understanding, he could sound petulant and ill-used. Mr Churchill liked to be tuned-in to his commanders abroad; his personal messages to them and those he received in reply were important to him. Wavell never found the right wave-length; it was this failure to reach back to the man who held the life-line of our affairs in those dangerous days, to get into his heart and thought, that did as much as anything else to lead him to St James's Park and his question to me.

'Good generals, unlike poets, are made rather than born', he wrote, 'and will never reach the first rank without much study of their profession; but they must have certain natural gifts – the power of quick decision, judgment, boldness, and, I am afraid, a considerable degree of toughness, almost callousness. . . .' In General Wavell's case the toughness which was apparent to his troops, who loved him for it, seemed more like pique to his decisive, bold and tough Prime Minister.

His failure to be articulate was unfortunate in a man who could express himself so ably and smoothly on paper. He said his mother had put words between his childhood thought and utterance, had in fact taken the words out of his mouth. But this seems too ordinary an excuse – there are few mothers who do not do this for their children – and perhaps the indolence which he said was so large a part of his nature was the real cause. If only he could have communicated with Mr Churchill with energy and a presumption of equality, the two men might have fused. They never did; the one rejected, the other admired and felt ill at ease.

General Wavell left for India at the end of September, his link with me in the Special Information Centre becoming a continuing thread of letters, which showed that this silent commander had a deep interest in literature and poetry and a philosophic power of detachment from the events in which he played a key part, that he was as much at home with a pen as he was with the sword.

By the turn of the year, my carpet, polished table, easy chair and official secrets were being used by a small but regular bunch of commanders-in-chief: General Sir Bernard Paget, Commanding

Home Forces, whose office was in the same building and whose bright eyes held no clue to his stern, uncompromisingly honest and Cromwellian character; Admiral Sir Bertram Ramsay, in active and constant charge of naval forces at Dover, and a lynchpin in the Dunkirk evacuation; General Franklyn from Northern Ireland, Admiral Lyon from Chatham, and Air Chief Marshal Joubert, Coastal Command. He was the only airman who paid more than one visit. Funny, I thought, but perhaps the fliers still do feel that strategically they are a service apart and unconcerned with the Army and the Navy who have shared the same skin for so many generations.

The two most faithful were Admiral Ramsay and General Paget, two men with a characteristic which I can only describe as 'alive'. Each was keenly interested in the whole sphere of the war, right round and outside their own particular command; they liked talking, they liked criticising, they were human and they were kind; they were not pompous and they were not self-important. Another human being entered my room when Admiral Sir James Somerville, recently appointed Commander-in-Chief Eastern Fleet, began a series of daily visits which lasted until the end of February 1942 when he left to take up his post and join Wavell in South-East Asia. He was a delight; gay, uninhibited, immediate in his reactions, the teller of stories *par excellence*, and no respecter of persons. A bird-like face peering round the door with a 'Hello, Joanie!' was followed by a sea-dog figure encrusted with gold and a warmth which not only filled the small room but spilled itself out into the intellectual corridor outside. Of him, later, Wavell wrote: 'a refreshing person . . . like champagne . . . thoroughly competent and sensible'.

Admiral Mountbatten visited the Centre once, but the next year he became Chief of Combined Operations, drew all the secrets to him and was as much part of the frieze of Whitehall as the other Chiefs of Staff. Except for his extreme good looks, he was not a person it was immediately easy to like; he seemed too successful and sure of himself to be bothered with juniors. I met him during the conferences and changed my opinion, realising that what seemed like loftiness was in fact a combination of rapid and concentrated thinking, and rapid efficient application of his thoughts.

From Buckingham Palace Sir Alexander Hardinge, Private Secretary to the King, came half a dozen times, the only civilian with seniority equal to a commander-in-chief's allowed to do so, but, here again, any information the Special Information Centre could give him was already his.

A self-effacing caller, Colonel Buxton, began appearing from the Map Room below. He was bald-headed, with a lanky moustache, a brewer in private life. From his kind heart he wished to add grace to the drab harness of war, and began bringing offerings, not only to me but also to the girls on the telephone switchboard, and sometimes to Miss Brown, head of the typing pool. Colonel Edward Buxton had a garden at his home in Epping Forest and from it regularly, till peacetime, he brought the flowers and shrubs natural to the season. A tall blue glass vase on my table was never empty of great sprays of wintersweet, fruit blossom or summer flowers. Grown and tended with the real difficulties of any garden possessor in wartime, when gardeners were scarce as face tissues, hair-combs and toothbrushes, they were picked, sorted, tied, wrapped and carried by him in overcrowded, standing-room-only railway carriages, whose jostling and harried occupants did not in the least feel ready to make room for beauty – either of character or of nature.

The Prime Minister's Special Information Centre had settled itself into an available perquisite for those who could use it, but as far as I, the incumbent, was concerned, it still did not give me a full-time job.

I began thinking that a natural development would be for me to take in the central filing system of the Chiefs of Staff Committee Secretariat. One existed, of course, within the Private Office of Colonel Hollis and his Assistant Secretaries, but their staff had more than enough to do in seeing to the production of minutes, the preparation of papers for meetings, and the constant telephonic and personal contacts with other departments. A centralised registry would not only be a contribution to the whole but it would take from them the massive day-to-day filing of papers. I tentatively suggested this to General Ismay, who was, as always, pleasantly interested but not particularly enthusiastic. Disappointed, I returned to my room. I should have known that underneath the social pleasantry a shrewd mind was summing up the situation and, after consultation and thought, coming to a decision.

Things began to move. I was asked what staff I would need.

'Three girls,' I said, 'who can type.' What rooms? 'Two – mine and the large one next door.' Within a week the occupants of the next-door room were sent elsewhere, Joan Umney-Gray, Laura

Cooper and Winnie Spearing appointed to the Special Information Centre and the communicating door from mine to theirs opened. About two hundred files, piled high in laundry baskets on wheels, were delivered to us. We set to work on the daunting but enthralling task of forming them anew into a complete set covering all subjects which came before the daily meetings of the Chiefs of Staff Committee. It took time because, apart from the fact that they were in current use, they were also spread around amongst each other, few of them containing a chronological story. Basing the system on my original Joint Planning Card Index, we ordered files of the different colours and were soon hole-punching and tagging-in the papers relevant to the green, blue, pink, white, orange and mauve. To fill in gaps and cross-references, we copied, filched and begged. I became adept at reading upside down. Waiting for something beside someone's desk, I would see a paper, take a quick look and think, Oh, yes, that's okay, we've got that one, or make a mental note to get hold of it if we had not. Eventually we achieved a place on the circulation list of minutes, memoranda, telegrams, reports, letters and comments; once the basis was up to date, it was comparatively easy to keep the files fed regularly. Like most other departments, we gave a twenty-four hour service from the day we started the section until the end of the war, one of the three girls coming in at teatime and staying on duty at night, with me, floating, as a fill-in. Winnie, Joan and Laura were ideal: they were conscientious, quick, loyal and always ready for a laugh.

We became an integral part of the War Cabinet Offices, the two sides of our work complementing each other. In the larger room was the filing section while my room remained tidy in case of visits from commanders-in-chief, when it was easy to find and spread out, on the reading table where the flowers stood, the material they needed.

The big armchair and sitting-room atmosphere attracted other visitors – friends from the past, co-workers of the present – and I now felt confident enough of my place in the hierarchy not to be shy and hasty when they dropped in for a gossip. One such was Peter Fleming. He was back from service in Greece when he walked in as imperturbably as he had walked out of MI(R) for Namsos that evening many months ago. It was always good to see his square face with its wide smile and to straighten out one's own fevers and uncertainties against his calm acceptance of events and tolerance of human frailty. He was a four-square, basic, solitary sort of person, immune to luxury, to heat or to cold, with a rock-like quality which made him the most staunch of friends and a kindness which made him the least vindictive of enemies. He was in his way a famous figure, not only because of his early and romantic success as explorer and writer and his marriage to one of our best actresses, Celia Johnson, but also because he kept his own brand of personality intact and dignified, dealt with all men as equals, and used his pen honestly and well, based on logic and spiced with satire.

My life settled into a winter pattern of two-thirds work and one-third play. The pleasures lay in dining, talking and dancing, for which there was no lack of men or gaiety. With the finish of the Blitz – there was only one raid on London during the autumn – we were free to pick and choose the restaurants or night-clubs we wanted to visit. Their *maîtres d'hôtel* were delighted to see us fill their tables and partake of their efforts to present the strictly rationed food in attractive guise. The weekly ration per person had sunk to its lowest level:

4 oz. bacon or ham
8 oz. sugar
2 oz. tea
8 oz. fat (of which 2 oz. butter)
2 oz. preserves
1 oz. cheese
1 egg (if lucky)

For those like me who lived in hotels and ate out, the hardship was negligible, but when, for instance, I went home for a weekend with my mother and saw the eking out she had to do on her one ration, I fully realised how lucky I was to have my time filled with files and friends instead of an empty larder and stomach.

The undamaged basement of the bombed Carlton Hotel in the Haymarket became a haven for many leading Whitehall figures. General Ismay preferred it to his club 'because,' he said, 'I don't have to put on a cheerful face and look confident when my fellow-members ask me how the war's going'. Each to his table could be sure of swift, quiet service and no need for dissimulation before returning to long nights of work.

Mr Shaw had moved from London to a hotel on a hill outside the city of Bath. When I went home in the cold, crammed, blacked-out trains to see my mother in nearby Freshford I usually managed to see him as well. I had been caught there one night by a surprise air attack on Bath and saw from above it the bombers going in and the brilliant explosions and fires, feeling sick that such things could happen to an undefended town. It had not been quite so bad in Bristol when I had spent a weekend with Nancy and there had been a severe and long-drawn-out Blitz; but bad enough to make one realise that the tightly packed 'box' of anti-aircraft defences in and around London had given us who lived there a greater sense of security than would be felt by people living in the more 'open' towns.

The pattern of personal life continued against the vast and shifting background of world events. The Germans and Russians were battling at the gates of Moscow while relatively as great a struggle was going on in Cyrenaica where Rommel's reinforcements were making the Eighth Army fight for each mile of territory. At sea, no respite, though our shipping losses between July and October had dropped from two million to three-quarters of a million tons. From the air the Royal Air Force bombed targets in Germany and north-west Europe but only at night. General Wavell wrote:

> 1941 has on the whole been a better year than we had any right to expect with our backwardness of preparation. . . . I hope that whatever happens the P.M.'s position will remain untouched, his courage and drive and leadership are indispensable. A very great man, if he had a better balanced judgment and chose men with his head rather than his heart he would be almost superhuman, and how unpleasant people approaching the superhuman are! . . . Man is a greedy, stupid, short-sighted animal, however he is governed, and as a writer rather aptly remarked in the last war: 'I see no reason why the human race, so inefficient in time of peace, should suddenly become efficient in time of war'. . . . If we devoted all our attention to war for 8 or 10 years, God forbid that we ever should, I think we should on the whole make a better job of it than the Germans. . . . Only two things really matter, as a poet said just before getting killed in the last war
>
> The beauty of this green earth
> And the gallantry of man.
>
> Courage and kindliness are the only two qualities that excuse human existence. A people like the Egyptians are kindly but not brave, so we despise and rather bully them. The Germans are brave

but not kindly so we hate them and fight them. Can we claim as a nation to be both brave and kindly?

On 6 December I had dinner with Peter Fleming at the Carlton Grill. It was Sunday and there was no work to go back to. He walked with me across St James's Park to the St Ermin's Hotel, and I went to bed. It was a night to be remembered – not for itself but because early next morning I turned on the radio and heard astounding news. The Japanese had bombed US naval, military and air bases in Hawaii, including Pearl Harbour, and had destroyed many units of the US Navy. It was incredible, and remained so to me until I got myself quickly to the office and could share in the feelings of anger and sympathy, tinged with relief that at last the United States of America were in the war with us.

Almost immediately Mr Churchill left for Washington, taking with him Lord Beaverbrook, the three Chiefs of Staff and, from our office, Colonel Jacob and Colonel Hollis. He also carried a bitter load in the knowledge that on 10 December the Japanese had sunk two of our largest battleships, *Prince of Wales* and *Repulse*.

It was eleven months since Colonel Cornwall-Jones had accompanied the Anglo-US Technical Conversations delegation to Washington, and four since Prime Minister and President had met at Argentia and issued the eight-point declaration of peace aims known as the Atlantic Charter.

Mr Churchill spent Christmas with President Roosevelt at the White House, their friendship becoming a factor which worked for great good in the new relationship which now existed between the two countries. Smoothly, because as yet the Americans were the 'new boys', the machinery for combined action slipped into gear as the agencies already set up expanded to meet the demands of global war.

The crisis sent General Wavell from India to become, briefly because events moved too fast, Supreme Commander of the South-West Pacific Area, and brought my family affairs right into the War Cabinet Offices. I saw copies of telegrams coming in to the Foreign Office from Godfrey Phillips in Shanghai, asking for guidance as to the line to be taken by allied nationals in their relations with the new enemy, Japan. There was no clear answer, there were too many civilian families in the International Settlement, and all they could do was to tread delicately until, in the autumn of 1942, an exchange of some hundreds of British against a similar number of Japanese internees brought some of them home – among them Godfrey, Betty and their two young children. They brought nothing with them except their clothes and a very few personal belongings.

CHAPTER 6

The Royal Navy relents (1942–1943)

AMERICA ROSE IN WRATH AFTER THE SUDDEN, flaming attack which would be known for ever as 'Pearl Harbour', and set about the business of beating the Axis. The issues to be fought for were clear, the partners in the British Commonwealth experienced, the newcomer energetic and strong; one partner, Canada, secured the border to the north; to the south, America's 'Good Neighbour' policy of the 1930s yielded at any rate an inactive neutrality in the countries of Latin America. If the main aim was to kill Germany before Japan, then the sooner the Allies mounted an invasion of the Continent of Europe the better – the better for hard-pressed Britain, for enslaved Europe and for the battling Russians, who, ignoring the fact that a bitter struggle was going on in Cyrenaica between Rommel's forces and the British Eighth Army, clamoured for the opening of 'a second front' in Europe.

The collapsing pattern of Allied control in the Far East as Hong Kong, Manila, the Netherlands East Indies, Singapore, Java, Rangoon, fell to the fast-moving Japanese, caused many people in America to feel that Japan should be dealt with first.

In April 1942 Mr Harry Hopkins, personal representative of President Roosevelt, and General George Marshall, Chief of Staff US Army, took to London a memorandum, prepared by the American Joint Staff and approved by the President. This called for planning and preparations to begin immediately for a major invasion of Western Europe in 1943, with at the same time a plan prepared for an emergency landing on a smaller scale in 1942 if there should be signs of disintegration in Germany or of collapse in Russian resistance.

The British, pleased that their American opposite numbers were marching so directly along the road to Europe, overdid their approbation and failed to make it clear to Marshall and Hopkins that they had reservations about the possibilities of the earlier landing.

When, after further examination of the American memorandum, their views reached Washington there was alarm and despondency.

The British views were that, though they fully approved plans for a 1943 – or 1944 – large-scale invasion, they were against a 1942 small-scale one, and thought that a landing in North Africa in 1942 – with, by then perhaps, hopes of a link-up with a victorious Eighth Army – would yield a better chance of bringing American and British forces successfully into action against the Germans.

The Americans, who were proceeding urgently to implement their planned build-up of troops and supplies in the British Isles, were puzzled, critical of this apparent lack of resolve. Feelings of admiration and respect for Mr Churchill and the nation and Commonwealth which he led were tempered by suspicions that the British were chary of crossing the Channel – in 1942, 1943 or ever. Some felt strongly enough about it to recommend that the main American effort should be transferred forthwith from the Atlantic to the Pacific.

At a time when many combined boards and committees were being set up in London and Washington, to work with mutual co-operation and goodwill for the duration of the war, it was sad that doubts as to British intentions should have arisen within the area of relationships between the Combined Chiefs of Staff; they were to be responsible for further misunderstandings in the future.

Now as always, however, mutual agreement was reached. In June, meetings in Washington between Mr Churchill and Roosevelt, between the Chief of the Imperial General Staff, General Sir Alan Brooke, General Ismay and the three American Chiefs of Staff, were followed in July by a visit from the latter and Mr Harry Hopkins to London for consultation with General Eisenhower and the British Chiefs of Staff. The decision was taken to mount a full-scale invasion of north-west Europe at the earliest opportunity, and in 1942 to concentrate on a November invasion of North Africa – code name Operation *Torch*, Supreme Commander General Dwight D. Eisenhower.

General Eisenhower, Commanding General of the European Theatre of Operations, US Army, had set up his headquarters in London in June and, with his Chief of Staff Major-General Bedell Smith, was soon to achieve a highly successful integration of Allied staffs for the planning and carrying out of *Torch* and the major operations of the future. I never met General Eisenhower, but I knew that General Ismay had a great regard for him, not only as a friend but as the model of a man able to combine the handling of a diverse international staff and a trusted relationship with men at the top of affairs. 'Bedell' – his direct approach, his rugged bulldog face – was a familiar to us all in the War Cabinet Offices and a real friend of Ismay, Hollis, Jacob, and any other members of the Secretariat with whom he had dealings.

On the other side of the Atlantic we were lucky in our Chief of the British Joint Staff. When in December 1941 the Combined Chiefs of Staff were set up to be responsible for the strategic direction of all Allied forces and for the allocation of manpower, munitions and shipping, Field Marshal Sir John Dill had been appointed as head of the representatives of the British Chiefs of Staff, the Planning and Intelligence Staffs and the Secretariat. He had just been succeeded by General Sir Alan Brooke as Chief of the Imperial General Staff, and was about to become Governor of Bengal in India, when the happy change was made and he was sent to Washington. Dill was typical of the best type of English officer – modest, honest and quiet – with long experience of competent command. He was frail in health but upright and strong in character. Between him and General Marshall there grew a sincere and true friendship, the fruits of which hung ripe on the boughs and sweetened relations between the two countries. The Field Marshal died at the end of 1944; Vice-President Truman went to his funeral in Arlington cemetery and the American Chiefs of Staff were his pall-bearers.

When in London during the summer of 1942 I met Colonel Frank McCarthy, military aide to General Marshall, he told me a story which showed the sort of courtesy extended by his chief to Field Marshal Sir John Dill. Marshall was invited to take part in an official review of troops; knowing that Britain's chief military representative had not been asked, he regretted but he could not accept owing to a previous engagement 'with Field Marshal Dill'. Result: Dill invited, sat in the official box with the President, Mr Harry Hopkins and General Marshall just the four of them.

General Wavell had gone early in 1942 to the south-west Pacific area as Supreme Commander of all American, British, Dutch and Australian forces with, as his Deputy, Major-General G. H. Brett, US Army. It was a lost-cause command; the Japanese literally took the ground from under them; in six weeks he was back as Commander-in-Chief India and General Brett in Australia as Deputy to General Douglas MacArthur, newly appointed Commander-in-Chief of Allied Forces in the Far East. At this same time General Sir Harold Alexander was sent to command British forces in Burma and General Joseph Stilwell, US Army, to be Chief of Staff to Generalissimo Chiang Kai-shek and Commander of the Fifth and Sixth Chinese Armies in areas which included Burma, Indo-China and Thailand. It was a strange mixture that brought these two outstanding and dissimilar characters together for a few weeks, to fight a bitter and losing battle against the Japanese in Burma. It ended with part of Stilwell's forces withdrawing into China and the rest following him over the mountains into India, while Alexander marched north-west to guard the eastern frontier and bar the road into India. Alexander, distinguished for his courageous handling of the Dunkirk retreat, was calm, good-humoured and unhurried; he was always impeccably dressed and had a 'feel' about him which gave confidence to the men under his command. Stilwell, who spoke perfect Chinese, was gruff and resourceful, 'quite a character', wrote Wavell. 'He says very little and, I fancy, thinks quite a lot. I like him and we get on well.' Admiral Somerville wrote much the same but added that 'he sits there immobile and suddenly ejects a remark – always straight on the target and to the point. I was very favourably impressed.'

In April General Ismay had a cable from General Wavell asking whether I could go to India and help in setting-up a secretariat on the War Cabinet Offices model. The answer was 'no' – but it was nice to be asked for. I wrote and sent him a copy of a memorandum about our organisation.

> Many thanks [he replied] for the papers and cuttings on Joint Planning, a very complex subject on which I will not bore you, or myself, with my views. . . . Alex goes home tomorrow (do you know him, a really high class commander, and we have very few of them?)

General Alexander was returning to be a Task Force Commander in the North Africa operations, but the retreat of the Eighth Army and the presence of Rommel's forces on the borders of Egypt at El Alamein convinced Mr Churchill that new blood was needed in the Middle East command if an autumn offensive was to succeed in taking back all the lost territory, and more. In August, with General

Sir Alan Brooke, he went to Cairo to see for himself, and decided to appoint General Alexander Commander-in-Chief Middle East and General Sir Bernard Montgomery Eighth Army Commander. He then proceeded to Moscow to break the news to Marshal Stalin that North Africa and not north-west Europe would be the invasion ground for 1942. General Wavell, who had been called to Cairo for consultation, went to Moscow with him. He spoke some Russian, and, better still, would be able to fill in the gaps of his knowledge of events about which he had complained to me in a recent letter.

> You know more about the war than I do (even if the CO S(D) telegrams arrived regularly and punctually!) and I feel you know almost my daily mood from my telegrams home, rather caustic and petulant lately – partly hot weather, partly impatience with the methods and ideas of the War Cabinet. I make a fuss about not being kept in the picture and they ordain a fortnightly (or whatever the period is meant to be, the intervals are long) telegram, rather in the spirit of giving the tiresome child a toy to keep him quiet. They don't seem to realise the necessity to keep commanders informed of events and ideas that concern them as and when they happen. For instance the flank of India, in Iraq and Persia, was skinned of troops without one single word being said to me. I won't enlarge – but I should hate to treat my commanders that way. . . .

He was probably right about the information telegrams. But it had been a difficult summer, we were all tired, and there had been little news to tell that was not already making headlines of disaster in the world press. The discussions and divisions between the Americans and ourselves had been too delicately balanced to give General Ismay the feeling that he wanted to expand them into a secret situation report.

General Wavell's comments on the changes in command in Cairo were that,

> The P.M. is in his most Marlburian mood, and sees himself in the periwig and red coat of his great ancestor, directing Eugene (for which part Alexander is now cast) to begin the battle of Blenheim. Heads are falling so fast that the supply of chargers to put them on must run short soon, and the 1st Reinforcements Camp of Superior Commanders must be almost empty.

We were lucky to have as Prime Minister a man of action rather than one like a fellow naval officer of Admiral Somerville's, 'who', he said, 'they told me was a sound fellow, never puts a foot wrong. Of course he doesn't; he never bloody well moves!'

The fatigue many of us were feeling was compounded of what Mr Churchill called 'the inward excitement which comes from a prolonged balancing of terrible things'. For those who had to deal with them, the months between Pearl Harbour and the realisation of the plans for attack in Africa had been exhausting and worrying, above all for the British who had already borne so much. The welcome entry of America had brought its own problems, which, at the low ebb of our fortunes all over the world, added to the general depression.

I had two material lifts of the spirit. I was lent a small and delightful house in a mews near Sloane Square by a friend in Military Intelligence. 'You can live there,' he said, 'so long as you are prepared at any hour of the day or night for the arrival of one of our agents coming secretly to London.' As not one appeared during the year I was there, I felt I had it under false pretences. But it was so nice after the one room in the St Ermin's Hotel that I stifled my conscience and filled the spare room with members of my family and my friends. My sister Felicity, gay and smart in her Women's Royal Naval Service officer's uniform, came on her way to Gibraltar to be part of one of the many units going there in preparation for the landings in North Africa.

The second lift was a rise in my salary to £500 a year. An announcement in the House of Commons at the same time, that Britain was spending £12½ million a day, did not cause me nearly so much surprise. I wrote at once to Mr Shaw to tell him that I could now live on what I earned and would have no more need of his much-appreciated allowance; I went to the Elizabeth Arden Salon for a steam bath, massage and face treatment; and ordered myself a new suit.

By December 1942 the world looked a better place. The great American naval battle at Midway in June was proving itself, from studies of Japanese dispositions, to have been a turning-point in the war in the Pacific; the Russian armies were slowly but surely turning from defence to attack; the Battle of Alamein, which opened on 23 October, had been so successful that in November the church bells were rung all over Britain to celebrate victory in the Battle of Egypt; and in North Africa the Allies had completed successfully the first combined landing of the war. It was a happy time.

* * *

'Monday, 4th January, 1943: a flap at the office.' This is all my pocket diary says about the meeting which took place ten days later at Casablanca between President Roosevelt and Mr Churchill and their military staffs. On ground which their two nations had so recently cleared of the enemy they agreed that future military strategy would include the occupation of Sicily, intensification of the air offensive against Germany and of the build-up of invasion forces in Britain. In the Far East pressure would be maintained against Japan and would include plans for the recapture of Burma in 1943 and for operations against the Marshalls and Carolines.

'Civilian women must not go in battleships' sang the Board of Admiralty. Behind them swelled in harmony a chorus of generations of men of the British Navy who had guarded their ships as jealously as they had guarded our shores. The *Bulolo*, a liner fitted out as a headquarters ship for amphibious operations, would be used as a communications centre by which news and views would go from London to the staffs at Casablanca and their replies pumped back again. Aboard her to do the work would be girls in the uniform of the Women's Royal Naval Service (Wrens), Auxiliary Territorial Service (Ats) and Auxiliary Air Force (Waafs). In our civilian clothes we typed, flagged, tagged, filed, slapping the papers into folders, and feeling nasty about the girls in khaki and blue who would do the same at the other end. We managed to force a smile when we said goodbye to our sheepish officers.

Senior officers should not go in bombers, but they did. The First Sea Lord, Admiral Dudley Pound, the Chief of the Air Staff, Air Chief Marshal Sir Charles Portal, the Chief of the Imperial General Staff, General Alan Brooke, the Chief of Combined Operations, Admiral the Lord Louis Mountbatten, and the Chief Staff Officer to the Prime Minister and Minister of Defence, General Sir Hastings Ismay, done up like parcels in their parachute harness, climbed into their Liberator aircraft and lay side by side in bomb bays. They arrived dirty, hot and tired at Casablanca to see their American colleagues emerge, spruce, shaved and fed, from comfortable aircraft into the Moroccan sun.

Mr Churchill met them and after one look at their flushed faces was most ready to agree that the first item on the agenda of the next British Chiefs of Staff meeting should deal with the question of providing a more suitable machine for the future air journeys of his military advisers.

They returned. After praising the smart look of such a Wren or 'At' or Waaf and assuring us that 'the Americans never have anyone with them who is not in uniform', they gave us bottles of scent and nylon stockings, and we settled back once more to our work.

Colonel Ian Jacob was one to follow through, however. Sure that the Casablanca Conference would be the first of many and that the American system would contribute to the right mixture of efficiency, discipline and concentration, he searched for a uniformed male secretary to replace his own witty and Scottish Miss Wendy Wallace. He found one, an Army corporal, of meagre literary attainments and no keen feeling about the freshness of his person.

'Have you told Wendy?' asked General Ismay.

'Oh no – no need,' said Colonel Jacob. 'She'll be all right, she'll get promotion.'

Colonel Jacob did not share the view of Fritz Bieler, the pilot in Mexico, who had once remarked that 'Wimmens wizout complications is a nonsense': he had reckoned without his Wendy, who, later that day, was seen by General Ismay rushing down the passage in floods of tears, secure in her knowledge that every civilian girl on the second floor was on her side.

Proximity to his military clerk and a series of disasters to his succinct and intelligent memoranda caused the surrender of Colonel Jacob. Miss Wallace returned triumphant and remained with him for the rest of the war.

The austerity which had marked Colonel Jacob at my interview with him misled me for quite a time. I held him in awe, his efficiency and powers of concentration setting a curtain between his humanity and my natural sense of being a subordinate. The warmth and humour of men like General Ismay and Colonel Hollis, with their rich sense of the ridiculous and their ability to descend to the level of their juniors without losing their respect, did not sit easily on the compact and smoothly working Royal Engineer. He was shy and he was matter-of-fact; his clear brain felt no need for bothering too much about personal relationships in the office. He gave and he expected to receive cool and effective service, becoming genuinely surprised if his own straight dealing came back at him knotted with the strains and misunderstandings of more complicated minds. His desk was always tidy, his in-tray systematically emptied and his brain clear and uncluttered.

His office was next to mine. As time went on, his smile broadened warily, and one day he actually opened the communicating door and came into my room for a social chat. From then, for the rest of the war and beyond, I found him most approachable, most sensible in his solution of any problem, and one of the most delightful characters in the War Cabinet Offices.

The winter months of 1943 flew towards spring, my time filled with work and the same calls of social and off-duty obligations. Because of complaints, like General Wavell's that our information telegrams were dull, General Ismay and I agreed to start a two-tier system: in one telegram, which we called the *Sictel*, we would give news of the strategic picture as a whole and generally unknown items of interest: in a *Chieftel*, with a much restricted circulation, for the more senior commanders-in-chief only, we would inform about forthcoming operations and future plans. This last became quite a status symbol to those who received it.

'The *Chieftels* are first-class', wrote General Wavell. 'I hope we shall get plenty of them.'

For the past year I had never felt completely well, seemed always to have a rotten cold in the head. My friends became concerned and I was sent to a doctor. He diagnosed badly infected tonsils, so off I went to hospital to have them out. I was away a month and received so many kind messages and enquiries that I returned to the office like a homing pigeon.

Very soon it became obvious that there was going to be another meeting like Casablanca – this time in Washington – 'and', said the girls, 'we are going too'. The need for continuity, the difficulty of using clerical staff unaccustomed to the format of committee papers and the risk of increasing the numbers who knew the secrets, had won them their emancipation. The Board of Admiralty had yielded, with a compromise. As it was to be a merchant ship – in fact the *Queen Mary* – which would carry the delegation across the Atlantic, restrictions against women in warships could be ignored. In time they were waived altogether and civilian women travelled in anything that came to hand.

'You don't put your girls in uniform then?' remarked General Eisenhower one day.

'It wouldn't make them any more reliable if we did,' said Colonel Hollis.

I could only share in the excitement; there was not a chance that I would go. The Special Information Centre files were basic, central, sitting heavy in their steel filing cabinets; commanders-in-chief were mobile and likely to call in at any time. Three did, on the day after my return from sick leave: two old friends and one new one came beaming through the door. General Wavell, Admiral Somerville and Air Marshal Sir Richard Peirse, Air Officer Commanding-in-Chief India, were home and due to go to Washington as part of the delegation.

'Pity you can't come with us, Joanie,' said the Admiral. 'It would be a nicer, happier party than having some egg-bound C.-in-C. sitting in clammy silence in your room.' Pity indeed, I thought.

'A pity,' I said to Joan, Laura and Winnie, 'a pity for the four of us.'

The door opened again.

'Would you like to go to Washington?' I stared at the beautiful face of General Ismay. My mind whipped about: what job would it be? Not belonging to someone else? That would never do – those hard-won friendships.

'Well, of course,' I said. I did not know then that it was work which would ensure my being on every future conference of the same kind.

The excellent administrative arrangements made by the United States delegation, who were hosts at Casablanca, had brought home to our delegates that the British would need an administrative section for all future meetings. Because the War Cabinet Offices worked on an inter-service basis, it was decided that this was the department to be made responsible. The head of General Ismay's Private Office, Paymaster-Commander Maurice Knott, was told to form an ad hoc section and it seemed that I was to be part of it, with special responsibility for the distaff side.

We could not believe our luck. Like many, many others, we had been shut up inside the fortress of Britain, blacked out, bombed out, conditioned to austerity. Now we were to sail away from it all on a top-secret, top-priority meeting. From now on, in our coupon-valued clothes, we would join the ranks of khaki and blue, pack our bags and climb into special trains, aircraft, ships and staff cars. We would be carried from one place to another to open our typewriters, shorthand notebooks, duplicating machines, and try to produce the same standard of work as was expected – and received – in the London office.

From the moment that General Ismay closed my door until we slipped quietly out of London during the night of 4 May, we had four days to get ready. Commander Knott went ahead to the *Queen Mary*, waiting in the Clyde, a hive of rumour as to the reasons for the delay. So well had the secret been kept that a group from our own office, going to the Hot Springs Food Conference, had no idea, until they saw us come aboard, that we were part of the cause of the hold-up.

Such security was not peculiar to us but was common in all departments; it was surprising, among the large numbers of people involved, that there were no leakages as to departure date and destination of the wartime conferences. Each person had to make his or her own 'cover plan', decide on a suitable story for relatives and friends. It became more and more difficult, almost ridiculous, as conference succeeded conference. I would really be going on holiday and my friends thought, Ah, yes, another meeting of heads of state. I would be really going to such a meeting . . .

'You went to Casablanca, of course,' said someone to me.

'Yes,' I replied, imagining they meant the film of that name which had been on in London during the same period.

I tied up the ends for Commander Knott, sending out instructions, labels, accommodation lists, to seventy members of the British delegation, sixteen Royal Marine orderlies and sixteen Wren signals officers. Each had to be told what they had to do to be where they had to be; how much luggage they could take; what they should do with their working papers, typewriters, duplicators; what the climate would be like, what currency allowed.

The special train in which we travelled left most secretly from Addison Road, a goods station in the west of London. It was dramatic, sliding through the darkness past stations where a solitary official stood watching the blinded windows, aware – or perhaps not aware – that the Prime Minister was behind one of them. Equally dramatic was the arrival of the tender alongside the towering grandeur of the *Queen Mary* carrying, in the bright morning sunlight, a posse of senior officers radiant in scarlet, gold and blue.

'Winston's aboard!' The great bows headed out towards the U-boat-infested waters of the Atlantic.

The Administrative Office on 'M' deck became a bedlam of travellers, demanding this and complaining about that. No one wanted to share a cabin, but it had to be done. The girls suffered the most; they always shared, four, eight, ten, unless their rare seniority rated them a double. And furniture – everyone wanted furniture. Thinking they were still in Whitehall, perfection-prone officers flew to their office cabins, rushed out, called for more tables, more chairs, more lamps. It was a day of sound and fury which ended in the early hours of next morning as the Administrative Staff – Maurice Knott and I – sat silent and ate our supper.

Except for the fact that I sensed an inner resentment against my inclusion in this preserve, I liked working for Commander Knott. He was a gentle person, with quiet authority, and did not let himself become involved in other people's hysteria. He was not one to delegate and when I worked with him on administration I was not given direct responsibilities. However, he had a good sense of humour – here there is always common ground – and he served General Ismay well for the three to four years he was with him. His heart lay at sea and not in the bureau.

To bring from America the troops needed for the invasion build-up, the *Queen Mary* had been stripped to the bone and made capable of accommodating fifteen thousand souls, most of whom would be servicemen and the rest official passengers and crew. As on her westward voyages she was nearly empty, it had been comparatively easy to fix up the special needs of the conference delegation. A large part of 'M' deck was roped off, and here were the offices and the suites for the VIPs. We had a lot with us: the Chiefs of Staff, the three commanders-in-chief from India, Lord Leathers, Minister of War Transport, Lord Beaverbrook, Lord Cherwell (or 'Prof' Lindemann as he was called), Mr Churchill's personal scientific adviser, and, of course, General Ismay. Attached to his suite the Prime Minister had his beloved Map Room. Wherever he went he was sure that Captain Richard Pim, RNVR, who was in charge of it, would manage to set it up quickly and completely. This one was particularly nice, with good lighting, a soft carpet and plenty of space for maps showing the progress of the war at sea, on land and in the air. During the voyage the one most looked at, needless to say, was that which showed by little black coffins the movements of U-boats. Some looked perilously near to the great ship, as she heaved herself through the water at thirty knots, twisting and turning, going south, going north, her escort of four destroyers (or two cruisers) digging deep into the sea on either side.

Besides the VIP suites there were twenty-one offices: Administration and Finance, Admiralty and Ciphers, War Office, Air Ministry, Combined Operations, Ministry of War Transport, Movements, General Ismay, Chiefs of Staff Secretariat, Joint Planning and Intelligence, Typing Pool, Cipher Office, Conference Rooms. For five days a miniature Whitehall rode the waves, self-contained, free from outside interruptions, well fed and therefore good tempered – the arrangements showed themselves to be ideal.

On the sun deck above and on 'A' deck below slept the rest of the delegation. In the special dining saloon a high table was reserved for VIPs, but towards the end of the voyage they broke up and joined any table they liked the look of. This friendliness was in no small measure due to the presence of Admiral Somerville; he was without any kind of self-consciousness and could see no reason for having to sit with his equals when he could have a giggle elsewhere. He, Wavell and Peirse were thoroughly enjoying themselves, Wavell in his own way because he was busy compiling an 'Anthology of Remembered Verse', which was later published under the title of *Other Men's Flowers*. I offered to type it for him but never got around to it.

The ship was 'dry' but the Special Party was not – a privilege we owed to General Ismay. When he had heard about the prohibition rule he had risen from his chair and cried,

'What! You are not suggesting we should cross the Atlantic without a *drink*?'

I was having one in the bar one evening when Mr Churchill appeared. We all stood up. He walked round and, seeing me, stopped and stared. Sir Charles Portal broke the silence by introducing me as the caretaker of his Special Information Centre for Commanders-in-Chief. A shake of the hand, a growling question,

'Does *she* know all about *Peradventure*?' and he was gone. After two and a half years in his office it was the first time I had met him hand to hand, and I was very pleased. But also puzzled. What was *Peradventure*? I had never heard of it, and I thought I knew all the secrets. I felt shy about asking anyone, and to this day I do not know what he meant.

Strict instructions had been issued about the disposal of 'Secret Waste' (worn-out carbons, 'doodles' from meetings, any discarded notes or drafts, all office rubbish, in fact). It would be collected each evening by Royal Marine orderlies and taken under guard to be burned in the belly of the *Queen*. The first night out, the eyes of the 'Watch' had scanned the dark seas and sky. All portholes were sealed, the decks out of bounds to passengers – even a cigarette smoked in the night was a danger, a beacon to U-boats – when, from the funnels there belched a bright cloud of burning paper. On the bridge there was consternation, bells rang, and the further firing of secrets was hastily stopped.

There was a pregnant moment when we lay off Staten Island. The Chiefs of Staff, the generals, air marshals and admirals, their chests resplendent, were waiting on deck for the launch which was to take them ashore. Past them came a file of three hundred German prisoners of war who had also been passengers on board. The two groups stared across the gap, steadily and in silence.

The Special Party left the ship by boat and proceeded to the jetty at The Anchorage, where lines of sailors and marines stood stiffly at attention. Machine guns bristled as the motorcade swept past to the special train onto which our baggage was being loaded by the US Navy. During the journey representatives from the British Embassy in Washington gave us currency, room lists, instructions and special passes. Maurice Knott and I sat back and enjoyed the freedom from responsibility while we ate a fabulous lunch which included steaks of a size to equal a month or two's ration at home.

The delegation dispersed in Washington, the Prime Minister and his party to the White House, others to the Embassy and the rest of us to the Sheraton and Statler hotels.

'The main ethical objection to war for intelligent people', General Wavell had said in a letter, 'is that it is so deplorably dull and usually so inefficiently run.'

For us this was not so. We were comfortably, even luxuriously, looked after during the nineteen days we were there. Washington was a whirl, a blur, a burst of vivid colour and, at night, street lights shining under green trees. We had forgotten what it was to see a lighted window bare to the night or a woman with a flower in her hair. A handsome blonde behind a desk in the hall of the Statler had two large pieces of artificial wistaria hanging on each side of her face.

I was kept busy with the personal needs of members of our delegation, with times of cars from hotel to conference room, with arrivals and departures of despatch riders and King's Messengers.

There was nothing concrete to catch hold of, but it was all so surprising to me that I never really touched ground. When I had time to think about it I missed my own 'war' work and felt it odd not to know what was going on. I found, when I was doing administration, a reluctance, even a refusal, on the part of my normal working colleagues to show me papers and telegrams or to tell me anything concerning the progress of affairs. It was odd, but it was human, a sort of possessiveness, a feeling that the curiosity of an 'admin officer' should be discouraged and that 'in her job she shouldn't know about this'. Accustomed to being a 'know-all', I felt resentful, which was silly because General Ismay never minded being asked and always treated each one of us as being worthy of confidence.

The American Chiefs of Staff, in a graceful gesture, invited the British Chiefs of Staff and the three commanders-in-chief to be their guests at Williamsburg in Virginia for the first weekend of the Conference. General Ismay said afterwards that it had been beautifully arranged, had given them all a chance to get to know one another, and that there had not once been a mention of the war.

Otherwise, during a fortnight of meetings, discussions had been frank, at times bitter. It was, of course, obvious that there would be no cross-Channel assault in 1943, but the same serious divisions of opinion were still there: the Americans wished to turn from further operations in the Mediterranean area and concentrate on action in northern Europe; the British wished to keep in action the million and a half troops in North Africa by exploitation from Sicily to the Italian mainland aimed at knocking the weakest of the three Axis partners out of the war. Eventually it was agreed that General Eisenhower's Planning Staffs should study plans of exploitation most likely to eliminate Italy and at the same time contain as many German forces as possible.

Mr Churchill, with General Marshall, General Alan Brooke and General Ismay, flew to North Africa to meet General Eisenhower and his commanders. Since the link-up between the Eighth Army and the *Torch* forces, General Alexander had become Deputy to Eisenhower in executive command of all Allied armies on the Tunisian front; Admiral Sir Andrew Cunningham was the Naval Commander-in-Chief and Air Marshal Sir Arthur Tedder the Air Officer Commanding-in-Chief. General Montgomery continued as Commander of the Eighth Army. Further meetings on the follow-on after Sicily led to the narrowing down of future planning to two alternatives – the capture of Sardinia or a landing in Italy across the Straits of Messina. Mr Churchill left for England, satisfied; he was sure that the second alternative would be the one.

When all the senior members of the delegation had flown from Washington, the rest of us junior officers, clerical and Wren cipher staffs, Royal Marines – waited for the *Queen Mary*'s sailing date from New York on 1 June. Peter Fleming and his brother Ian were both in Washington at the same time, and suggested I go to New York with them for Saturday night. Peter had come from India, where he was on Wavell's staff, running a section which planned ways of deceiving the enemy. Ian was Personal Assistant to the Director of Naval Intelligence in the British Admiralty where his acute sense of adventure and clever brain were being used for all sorts of unusual schemes and operations. They were an attractive pair, amusing, good-looking, sure of themselves, and devoted to each other. The detachment from his surroundings which was part of Peter's character was also present, in a different way, in Ian's. Ian was more persuasive, had more apparent and vocal concern towards the people he liked, wanting them to do what he thought would be to their advantage; but he could also detach himself from them and temporarily but summarily dismiss them from his thoughts; he would return to them – or not – later, depending on how he felt, knowing they would be glad to have him back. We who were fond of him always were.

Ian disappeared when we got to New York, but Peter took me to see Ethel Merman in *Something for the Boys*; after dining at the '21' Club we ended the evening at the Vie Parisienne. It should have been such an enjoyable evening – it was really – but the city was hot, my feet swollen, and it was agony to hobble along in my shoes.

After returning to Washington on Sunday to pack up and collect myself along with the others, I was back in New York by midday on Monday, 31 May. We boarded the *Queen Mary* in circumstances which were very different from the shining arrival on the shining waters of the Clyde – different and far more real. There were no VIPs, no special guards, no roped-off quarters just fifteen thousand people, most of them American troops. Within their power the ship's officers did their best for us and, relatively speaking, their best was *the* best; they had managed it so that one of the eight-berth cabins allocated to us slept only two, which meant that we could use it as a sort of club room, an escape from the crowded ship; Mr John Pearce, the chef, saw to it that the gap between the two-meals-a-day routine was filled with delectable sandwiches brought discreetly to the cabin. For the rest, we were part of a great experience. To make use of the maximum space there were no doors; GIs were crowded in every passageway; our twice-daily walk to the dining saloon was accompanied by cat-calls, whistles, sighs – 'Look out! dames coming!', 'Whew-w-w!', 'Watch your talk!' – and our sleep by the click of the dice in their eternal crap games. They were a cheerful lot, like most soldiers philosophically making the best of things.

As we neared England and dried eggs on Sunday, 6 June, loudspeakers warned us against crowding to one side of the ship because she was now top heavy, the lighter by thirty thousand meals a day and hundreds of tons of fuel.

CHAPTER 7

Canadian hospitality (1943)

FOR THE GIS, England was a strange landfall; for us, it was home. We were welcomed back with unselfish interest, and I think none of us felt complacent at having been the lucky ones, just excited and pleased to have been among them. In my section the files had grown fatter and I was able to read for myself the minutes of the Washington meetings. General Wavell had not returned to India with Somerville and Peirse but had stayed in London because he had been offered a change of job, which, he said, 'means doing all the things I hate doing most – pomp and circumstance, politics. I may not be a very good soldier, but it is the one subject I do know something about.' The Prime Minister and War Cabinet wished him to be the next Viceroy of India; after hesitation, and consultation with Lady Wavell, he agreed to be so.

Colonel Holland rang up suddenly, and I lunched with him. He was the same heavy-smoking, unpredictable person, shy in his questions, quietly pleased that I was working for General Ismay. General Paget sent a car for me to go and dine at his Home Forces Headquarters, which were no longer in our office building but on a country estate outside London.

'If I am not able to go so often to the Special Information Centre,' he said, 'the Special Information Centre must come to visit me.' I went home for a long weekend with my mother, where my sister Betty and her two children were living, and I saw Mr Shaw in his hotel near Bath. There was only one change in my private life. The lease of the mews house had ended and I was room-hunting, most difficult in a city full of bomb gaps and visitors. Lady Ismay suggested I should move into their flat in Lowndes Square until I found something, or at any rate until the next conference – due shortly at Quebec – was over. I did – and remained there for three and a half years.

General Ismay wore his wife Darry in his 'heart's core'. She was a warm, generous and necessary person, giving him, whether in the comfort of their London flat, or during the few days he could spare in their country home in Gloucestershire, a base from which he drew strength to meet the heavy demands made upon him. She matched his with her own good brain and perceptive intelligence, and her sense of the ridiculous kept him well below the line at which many men become pompous. A part of their happy marriage was the fact that they were great friends, and able to laugh at each other's foibles; and the happiness that they shared together radiated outwards and included in it their friends and working colleagues, most of whom were frequent visitors to the large and attractive drawing-room on the top floor of 10 Lowndes Square. General Ismay had a high regard for his wife's judgment and it rarely let him down.

The war for Lady Ismay – as indeed for many others like her – was not glamorous; part of their country house, Wormington Grange, was being used as a refugee children's home; she had three daughters in their teens, two of them at boarding-school; and she could not escape from the dull grip of petrol rationing, food shortages and other difficulties of housekeeping in wartime.

Between the Quebec Conference in 1943 and the Potsdam Conference in 1945 I did six journeys abroad as part of her husband's staff; she never showed envy or made me feel embarrassed that I was going and not she, and she never failed to give me a warm welcome back to Lowndes Square.

The flat was looked after by a Belgian butler, Félicien, whose wife did the cooking, and nearly always General Ismay took me to the office in his official car. I made sure he got into it first; I could not have borne it if the reverse had happened; I felt guilty enough as it was to be in the luxurious state of not having to think of either food or transport. The years of my mother's strict upbringing did not sit lightly upon me. Sweeping into Belgrave Square we sometimes saw an officer friend of his tramping steadily to the War Office.

'Poor old Musgrave!' said the General. 'Look at him, he's ageing.'

My reply 'So would you if you had to walk to work' was greeted with a shout of laughter. He loved to laugh and, so long as the distinction of rank was not forgotten, he loved to be teased. He had a huge fan mail – from retired Indian Army officers, elderly ladies spry enough to appreciate the job he was doing, from all sorts of people all over the world.

'Here's a good letter, do read it,' he said. I began at the beginning.

'No, no, over, turn over; it's far more interesting at the end.' He waited. When I got to such sentences as 'without you this war would never be won' or 'I pray for you, the one on whose shoulders . . .', I looked up and laughed. He laughed too, not at the writer, never that, but because he so enjoyed his own pleasure in flattery. It was not vanity, it was a genuine and surprised delight. Beneath the broad shoulders and the seeming imperturbability lay a sensitive and humble spirit: if it had guile, it was used for good; if vanity it was a redeeming feature in a self-effacing man.

The conference at Quebec in August so soon after the one at Washington was felt to be necessary for three main reasons. The landings in Sicily on 10 July had been successful and operations were proceeding towards complete possession in a matter of weeks. It now looked as though a landing in Italy would be the right choice, and the resignation of Mussolini on 25 July lent support to this view. Next was the need to study the outline plan for the invasion of France in 1944 – code name *Overlord*. This had been prepared by British General F. E. Morgan, Chief of Staff to the Supreme Allied Commander (COSSAC), and his Anglo-American staff in the London headquarters set up for the purpose after the Casablanca Conference. The target date – early May – was only ten months ahead. Thirdly, the Burma–Chinese theatre needed a push towards a more positive future and a better system of co-ordination for the British, American and Chinese forces.

Commander Knott went ahead to the Château Frontenac Hotel, the fine venue in Quebec which would house the delegations. Mr Ronald Harris, from Sir Edward Bridges' office, was to see to the London end, and I was assistant to them both. Ronald Harris was an engaging character, highly intelligent, and much amused by the work we had to do. Lists from participating departments, allocation of cabins, and the composition of administrative instructions, were the three fences we had to ride over. First, the lists. Extracting them was like trying to seize the cards of a group of poker players; each department held its hand until it saw its opponents'; if the War Office decided to take ten officers instead of, say, six, the department which had kept its hand hidden the longest could step up the bid and fill in the gaps. If one department overdid it and had too many on its list, there was a rustle of disapproval from the others. When at last the final count came through to us, our remarks were automatic: 'Of course, I knew she would come', 'Oh, that awful man again', 'What on earth will five brigadiers find to do?'

Meanwhile, the game would have begun with the Americans. A cautious cable from London to the Joint Staff Mission in Washington would say: 'Please find out size of US delegation.' Reply: 'Have not been very successful. Can you give an idea of size of British?' 'Quite small', was the quick response, 'only Chiefs of Staff, personal staff officers, usual clerical staffs and Prime Minister's party.' 'Same here', from Washington. Eventually, a pocket size in delegations was ready to sally forth from London and from Washington, numbering some two hundred and fifty persons each, including, besides the actual delegates, cipherers, typists, orderlies, photographers, clerks. For the same sort of reason which makes those who 'feel the cold' feel inferior to those who do not, it was a matter of shame if one delegation was much larger than the other. Usually, the game equalled out and both met in amicable and numerical equality.

Allocation of cabins was the next headache – for this Conference again it would be the *Queen Mary*. Carrying our lists, Ronald Harris and I went up to Berkeley Square to the Ministry of War Transport and sat with their representatives before a huge plan of the ship. After Washington I was a little more familiar with the idiosyncrasies of delegates. Later on, with experience, I reached the point at which I could get on to the telephone and ask Group-Captain A whether he liked his colleague in the Air Ministry well enough to double up with him, or warn Commander B that he might find himself sleeping on a very low deck. But not yet; we were still making mistakes. In Quebec Commander Knott had not had time to do more than allocate rooms from the hotel's own list and had only seen the main ones. He earmarked a double room for two officials from the Ministry of War Transport. One of them, wild-eyed, met me on the train between Halifax and Quebec, his hand clutching the accommodation list.

'Look!' he cried. 'Knott has put me to share with D and I can't stand him!'

'Leave it,' I said, 'until we reach the hotel and then we'll see what we can do.'

I forgot all about it. Walking down a passage later in the day, I met him, his face ashen. He rushed at me, saying desperately: 'But this is the last straw. Not only am I sharing a room with D but a bed as well.'

We became wiser, but the problems of accommodation were always thorny; few believed that the mistakes we made were unintentional or that we were not guilty of favouritism. The VIPs were all right, they had no reason to be otherwise with the pampering they received. 'My' commanders-in-chief were always content; I do not think Wavell, Paget, Ramsay or Somerville would have minded a bit if they had been put into hammocks. Next below, the directors, major-generals, rear-admirals, air vice-marshals, was a delicate balance, sensitive, easily upset. The biggest question mark hung over the ranks of group-captain, colonel, commander, the civilian counsellor rank: here it was the personality itself which gave the answer – whether a man was meek, vain, arrogant, or contented; some were accommodating and appreciative, but, generally speaking, they cared a lot about getting value for rank. The Wren officer cipher girls were usually easy and nice, though some were spoilt; two complained to me on a station platform, within ten minutes of finding their first-class sleeping compartments, that there were no face towels in it. Civilian clerks and civilian girls were the most reasonable and, being so, deserved better than they got. The girls, particularly, shared cabins, eight, ten, at a time, and were treated as a crowd. I thought to myself more than once: How actually would these men in their comfortable quarters get on if they had no shorthand typists? Does it ever occur to them that the girls are not working less hard but that they are certainly less well provided for?

Finally, the compilation of administrative instructions. The language we used for them was in poor taste; try as we might, we could not avoid using such terms as 'Members of the delegation will . . .', 'It is recommended that . . .', 'You are requested to . . .', 'lounge', 'ladies' room', and so on. It would have been so much better if we could have sent out something like, 'Believe it or not, we are off again', 'Don't forget to bring your passports' or that 'You can't take more than £10 out of England', 'Bring a waterproof, the weather is likely to be lousy', 'For goodness' sake hurry up and let us have your final list'. The status of administrative officer, neither dictator nor friend, was ever invidious; such familiarity would bare another piece of quivering flesh to the barbs of all delegates, high and low.

On the evening of Wednesday 4 August, Ronald Harris and I, with the feeling that things were more or less under control, climbed aboard the special train. On the journey north, like couriers with a tourist group, we passed up and down the carriages containing the main part of the delegation. It was unnecessary to fuss about the VIPs; they had their own staffs who would be immediately explicit in complaint to us but thought, as it was too late to change very much, we might as well show ourselves ready to please. Because the boarding of the *Queen Mary* for the Washington Conference had been glittering and public, the Ministry of War Transport had decided to use Faslane, a lonely port north of Glasgow, built for wartime embarkation and disembarkation of troops, but scarcely used. The giant ship looked incongruous against the dark hills surrounding the stretch of water.

The arrangements on board were, as before, near perfect, but this time there were friends among the ship's company to greet and be pleased to see again; I am sure they enjoyed the brief return to pre-war Cunard Line service which these journeys entailed. There were five guests in the Prime Minister's party: Mrs Churchill, his daughter Mary – looking gay and pretty in the rather drab uniform of the Auxiliary Territorial Service – Brigadier Orde Wingate, DSO, and his wife, and Wing-Commander Guy Gibson, VC, DSO, DFC.

I experienced the wrath of two members of the Chiefs of Staff Committee when we detrained that morning. First, a furious Sir Alan Brooke, Chief of the Imperial General Staff, who told me with sharp clarity *never* again to allocate him a sleeping compartment right above the grinding train wheels. He did not give me time to tell him that in my ignorance I had naturally accorded him Compartment A as being the right letter for his rank. All I could stammer was an apology and a promise to look to it in the future. Minutes later, the Chief of the Air Staff was saying something angrily to me. When I could recover my balance sufficiently to hear what it was, I learned that I had unpardonably put one of the great heroes of the air – Wing-Commander Gibson – into a second-class, instead of a first-class, compartment. As, later, on the train between Halifax and Quebec, we had a hunt for him all through the Pullman bunks because we were not sure that his attraction – as man and hero – had not gone to the head of one or two of the girls, the effects of this attack did not last so long as those produced by General Sir Alan Brooke.

It was the first time that I had been on friendly terms, so to speak, with either of these two Chiefs of Staff, but at Quebec they, and the First Sea Lord, Admiral of the Fleet Sir Dudley Pound, acknowledged me with a smile when we chanced to meet in the elevator or passages of the Château Frontenac. Sir Dudley Pound did not look at all well, and General Ismay told me how concerned he and others were by his lethargy, and the lack of his former crisp grasp of essentials. It became known afterwards that he was fighting his last battle – a lonely and frightening one against the effects of a stroke which he had hoped would pass off. He died on 21 October. We watched in Whitehall as, with full naval honours, his funeral cortège kept sad step to the music of Chopin's Funeral March. He was succeeded as First Sea Lord by Admiral Sir Andrew Cunningham, Commander-in-Chief of the Mediterranean Fleet.

Brigadier and Mrs Wingate were surprised to find themselves aboard the *Queen Mary*. He had been dining with the Churchills on the night before, and she had been on her way south from Scotland to join him in London. The Prime Minister had thrilled to the Brigadier's description of the three months he had spent behind the enemy lines in Central Burma with a Long-range Penetration Group. Knowing that the Burma–Chinese theatre would loom large on the Quebec agenda, Mr Churchill wished him to speak for himself about the use which could be made of such operations. He therefore hijacked him on to the train that evening, sent a message to Mrs Wingate to meet the party next morning at Glasgow, and was pleased to see the unexpected meeting of wife with a husband who was still dressed in the tropical uniform he had been wearing on his arrival in England the day before.

Brigadier Orde Wingate came into the Administrative Office on 'M' deck to ask how he could find a change of clothes. I was interested to see this man about whom we had heard so much, not only as a leader of irregulars in Abyssinia but also as a 'Lawrence of Arabia' type – with the difference that, as a Zionist, he would have led the Israelis against the Arabs. He was slight in build, quiet-voiced, and directed from his strange blue eyes a penetrating stare. Without preamble, from the other side of the desk, he looked searchingly at me and then made the surprising remark:

'We have met before.' After a pause, he added: '. . . in a former life.'

Feeling relieved because during the pause I had searched my memory and found it wanting, I turned to the more immediate need of borrowing for him a coat and slacks from one of the ship's officers.

As he was going out of the door, he turned and stared again.

'Without religion,' he said, 'man will perish.'

Wing-Commander Gibson's heroic qualities were cast in a more recognisable mould. There was not one of us girls who was not dazzled by the five simple but remarkable medals for gallantry on his chest, or softened by his direct masculine approach to each of us. Both of these characteristics were accented by the glory and personal courage of his most recent exploit. On 16 May he had led sixteen Lancaster bombers which, from a height of sixty feet, had dropped air-mines and destroyed the Mohne and Eder dams, feeders of the industrial areas of the Ruhr. With half his aircraft shot away, Gibson had remained in the holocaust directing the others till the end. A dramatic and, in its consequences, terrible feat. I asked him what he had felt at the time.

'Nothing much,' he said, 'but I let loose vile oaths – "Here it is, you . . . s, take it, you . . . s, I shouted".'

He was not happy to be with us, felt he was deserting, dreaded the lecture tour ahead of him, 'and', he added, 'what's more, they've taken away my name. It's "dam buster" here and "dam buster" there.'

The voyage was depressing, partly because the weather was dull and stormy, with bad visibility, but mostly because it was certain that ahead lay reefs of argument between the two allies about the next stage of the war.

A tremendous reception for Mr Churchill when we reached Halifax on Monday afternoon, 9 August, came as such a surprise that dullness slipped away. Soon everyone was smiling, waving at the crowds on the quayside, who, behind the red hem of Canadian Mounted Police, looked up, cheered and waved back.

Along the route of the 24-hour train journey to Quebec there were knots and groups of people waiting through the night and the next day to see the Prime Minister pass by – their Prime Minister from Britain and the people he had brought with him.

As a meeting-place the Château Frontenac Hotel was perfect. Both delegations could live and work under one roof, an important factor in the smooth running of any conference; and up at the Citadel, summer residence of the Governor-General, President and Prime Minister were housed in comfort and dignity. If satisfactory agreement could not be reached here it could not be reached anywhere.

The kindness and hospitality of our Canadian hosts from first to last was notable. Nothing was too much trouble, nothing too good for us; we were treated as though we had come straight from a slave-camp, with a thoughtfulness and consideration which remained in the memory long after the flag-waving and speechifying had been forgotten. The Under-Secretary of State, Dr E. H. Coleman, was Chairman of the Canadian Co-ordination Committee and responsible for the arrangements; with his own high-class staff and Mr B. A. Neale, manager of the hotel, and his trained employees, the living and eating conditions were set at as high a standard as any comparable *hôtellerie* could provide anywhere in the world.

I found Commander Knott sitting at a desk in the corner of the entrance hall, so busy he could do no more than say 'Hello' and tell me to stand by. I did – and watched the fun. Some of the arrivals – so recently calm aboard the *Queen Mary* – were tearing about, up and down the main staircase, in and out of the elevators, hunting for lost baggage, gesticulating, bumping into each other. One or two stood about, looking uneasy, as though they wished they had never come. The usual complainers were looking for someone to complain to, and a few, the very few, stood satisfied and smiling, waiting for the commotion to subside.

Lord Moran had lost his hat, and I joined rather half-heartedly in the search. As physician-extraordinary to the Prime Minister, he had no particular niche, was as absent-minded as an absent-minded professor, and managed to lose something at each conference.

Mr D's threatened bed-mate passed me four times, but happily, since he now had a bedroom to himself.

Mr Churchill had gone to visit President Roosevelt at his country home at Hyde Park and the American delegation were not due to arrive for another two days, so a holiday was decreed for Thursday. The Chiefs of Staff went fishing – their favourite sport – and General Ismay took some of us for a picnic near Montmorency Falls. It was a surprise when a few of the officers came in to dinner in civilian clothes; so used were we to uniforms that it seemed all wrong to see General Sir Alan Brooke and General Ismay in grey pin-stripe, and Sir Charles Portal in a pinky-beige tweed suit. They looked more human and less splendid.

I looked after office accommodation and equipment, kept the telephone directory up to date and saw to the pass-lists. The Royal

Canadian Mounted Police, who were in charge of security, had issued five different colours ranging from pink – bearer admitted to hotel but not to conference rooms on third floor – to a restricted white which gave access to anywhere in the area including the Citadel. The right to the white pass was craved by those who did not warrant one.

There were the usual orders and counter-orders for the disposal of secret waste. First:

> As there are no locking steel cabinets, all officers must keep their papers locked in the clothes cupboards in each room, the keys of which should be left when not required in Room 4304 each night and the rooms locked when unoccupied.
>
> All waste paper baskets may be regarded as secret and arrangements will be made for the waste to be collected and burned under proper supervision in the furnace of the hotel. In order to allow this waste to be collected from locked rooms, a master key is held by Mr Charman (4304).

Then, the counter-order:

> Secret waste will not be collected from individual rooms and should be deposited with Mr Charman in Room 4304.

People carrying waste-paper baskets along the passages was an inspiring nightly sight.

Under another dreadful heading – 'Refreshments' – came the news that there was 'a lounge on the main floor just off the lobby . . . for senior officials and officers of the equivalent of field rank and above', and a 'general lounge for officers and civilian personnel on the Terrace Floor overlooking the river'. There was 'severe liquor rationing in Canada owing to shortage of supplies' – a monthly quota for spirits of two bottles a person – and, though the Canadian authorities wished to do us very well, 'it must be remembered that there are a good many Canadians in the Château Frontenac, and those running this party could quite easily lay themselves open to considerable criticism if the special concessions they have made were abused in any way.'

The standard of comfort and service was so high that it was only too easy to forget the fact that we were guests of the Canadian Government and living in the hotel by courtesy of its usual visitors.

Calls for room service during the long hours of work reached such proportions that from the patient and kind Dr Coleman came a cry reminding us that 'the Hotel Staff, owing to war conditions, is very short-handed and cannot be organised so that every room can have individual attention at the same time'. Commander Knott circulated this, adding his own note to say that 'at 4.30 on Sunday afternoon, the 15th August, there were more than fifty separate orders for tea outstanding and at noon on the same day there were no less than twenty orders for tea or coffee'. We had slipped too easily into luxury living. We drank orange juice for breakfast each morning without giving it a thought. In London afterwards I had a letter from Dr Coleman telling me that, especially in Quebec, there was a real shortage of oranges in Canada. 'Mr Neale,' he wrote, 'the incomparable manager of the hotel, recognising how keenly the delegates from Great Britain enjoyed the orange juice, had the oranges flown in from New York at very considerable expense, and it was not until after you had gone that the breakfast orange juice disappeared from the menu.' This, too, we had not realised, had forgotten that others suffered rationing besides ourselves.

We were spoiled – even to a running buffet being set up in the foyer of the dining-room for all those who could not forgo their tea and coffee breaks.

Commander Knott had made a happy room allocation when he allotted to two of the three Directors of Plans an elegant 'Chinese Suite'. It had two bedrooms and a sitting-room, curvaceous Oriental furniture and delicately coloured silk hangings. The Director of Plans (Air), Air-Commodore William Elliot, and the Naval Director of Plans, Captain Charles Lambe, were not only great personal friends but they shared the same intellectual and artistic tastes. Captain Lambe was an artist – a painter and a gifted pianist; Air-Commodore Elliot was a lover of poetry and literature, a dreamer. At the conference table they were men of decision, certain of their facts, with long experience in their Service. This ability took each of them to high command in the future; for the present they were content to share a leaning in their political views towards socialism, a common interest in pictures, music and drama, and to keep separated the exigencies of war planning and the arts of mankind.

The exigencies of war planning at Quebec had been resolved after long, sometimes heated, but always reasoned and fair, discussions between the American and British Chiefs of Staff. Just before their final conclusion there had been a 24-hour break. The Canadian Chiefs of Staff invited half of each delegation to make a trip up the St Lawrence on the steamer *Taddoussac.* 'The cruise will be treated as a military operation, and will be given no publicity,' we were told, but as the ship drew away from the jetty, on the main deck stood Admiral King, General Marshall and other distinguished officers, deafened by the trumpeting of a military band and looking embarrassed by the waves and cheers of a large crowd of people who had come to see them off.

The British decided not to take civilian clothes because they felt sure the Americans would not have theirs aboard. Envious eyes were fixed on General Marshall when on Sunday morning he appeared looking relaxed and comfortable in a lounge suit.

On Monday the last meeting took place and agreement was reached that Operation *Overlord* – the invasion of the Continent – should have priority, target date 1 May 1944, and that its implementation should be based on the plan produced by General Morgan and his staff. The exploitation of the Sicily operations by landings on the mainland of Italy were accepted. Admiral the Lord Louis Mountbatten was appointed Supreme Commander in the South-East Asia theatre of war, to direct all future operations, among them the reopening of land communications with China. The British felt that the setting-up of a command headquarters similar to General MacArthur's would give the right weight to their contribution to the war in the Far East. They wished to establish the fact that they had long had special responsibilities in the area, and that, when the war against Germany was ended, they had no intention of leaving their American allies alone to fight Japan.

With the agreement of the Americans the Prime Minister made two personal appointments. Major-General Adrian Carton de Wiart would go to Chungking as his representative with Generalissimo Chiang Kai-shek, and Lieutenant-General Herbert Lumsden to General MacArthur's headquarters. Both were ideally chosen. General Lumsden had the right mixture of 'an English officer and gentlemen' to suit MacArthur, with whom he got on well. General Carton de Wiart was a special sort of person; he carried the signs of past battles on him – the Victoria Cross, one eye and one arm – and in him a personality full of humorous corners and unexpected reactions which appealed to the Generalissimo and Madame Chiang, who wished him to stay on after the war was over.

Always operational decisions depended on available shipping – this was an overriding factor. The American War Shipping Administration, headed by Mr Lewis Douglas, and the Minister for War Transport, Lord Leathers, and his staff, at Quebec, worked harder than anyone else to find the sinews on which the future depended. In all-night sittings they wrestled with estimates of the amount and kind that would be needed and the possibilities of providing it.

Through his cousin Naomi, a friend of mine in the Mexico days, I met Mr Douglas. He invited me into the 'field rank and above' bar for a drink, and within minutes had me charmed. He was one of those people who did not talk about himself but was genuinely interested in what the other person thought and felt. His origins were Scottish, his upbringing in the pioneering days of prospecting and mining in Arizona, where his grandfather had been one of the Grand Old Men of new America. He was not only an experienced and knowledgeable mining engineer and geologist, but he had left Amherst College with a degree in his pet subject – history. To look at, he was a man of the open air, a cattle man, sturdily built, with keen brown eyes, easy manners and a relaxed air. He was whimsical, with a subtle wit, courteous, unpunctual – he had no sense of time – and as hard a business man as a hard life could produce. In politics a liberal, he felt passionately about world problems, and was deeply committed to promoting friendship and understanding between Great Britain and the United States. He had returned to work in Roosevelt's administration, in spite of a major break which had led to his resignation as Budget Director in 1934 and of two campaigns against it in 1936 and 1940. He was powerful and influential, used to getting his own way. An iron will on questions of principle was disguised by a soft and hesitant voice. He moved confidently between the delegations, understood and was trusted by the British.

'All you have seen of Canada, Joan', he said, 'is the inside of the Château Frontenac. One of the bits of Canada that I love is right here in Quebec, down by the waterfront.'

On the last night but one I had dinner with him, and, stifling thoughts of the packing-up I should be doing, walked with him through the ancient narrow streets of the real Quebec. He spoke not at all about the paper ships in the files of the War Shipping

Administration or the close bargaining which had been his share of the Quebec Conference. Instead he told the history of the port, of the great St Lawrence waterway, and the Canada into which it flowed.

Our hosts laid on a dance for us all in the hotel ballroom the evening before we dispersed. General Ismay had a table for dinner, and made us laugh, nervously, when in a loud voice, with waiters within earshot, he hoped we would 'have a smooth voyage' when we sailed 'tomorrow in the *Queen Mary* from Halifax'. The date of departure of any ship was one of *the* most closely held secrets; we told him,

'You're all right, you're going to Washington with the Prime Minister' – and hoped it would be all right for us.

It was – though we thought of him one night, when we were told to sleep in our clothes because of an attentive U-boat.

Mr Averell Harriman's daughter, Kathleen, was travelling with us. Her father had just been appointed US Ambassador to Russia, and she was meeting and going on to Moscow with him. She was dark, slim, vital and attractive, easily and without pretensions fitting in to the homecoming bits-and-pieces of the British delegation. We were back to the two-meal, no doors, austerity run, carrying thousands of Canadian troops this time, no GIs. Unlike the previous trip, when boat-drill had been a muddle and none of us got anywhere near the life-boats, this time we did. As though a giant skein of wool was being unravelled, fifteen thousand people weaved through the passages and up the stairs to the deck.

Trevor Bright

Mia Bright

The Bright Sisters

Jo Holland

John Walter

Millis Jefferis

Colin Gubbins

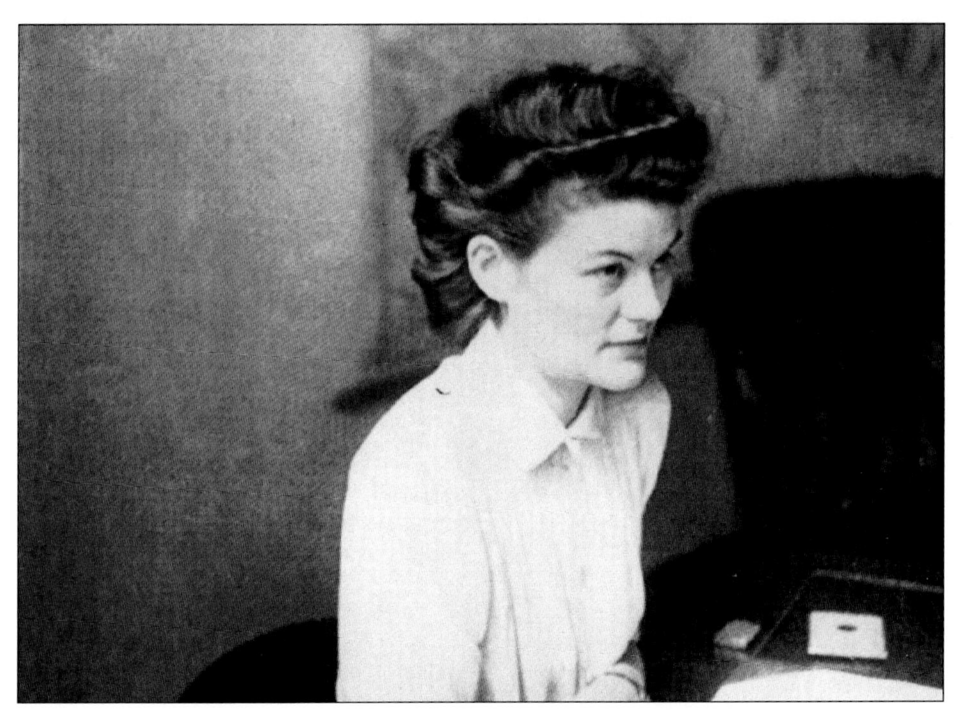

Waiting for business

The Williamsburg weekend

Churchill's birthday dinner, Tehran 1943

The garden of the British Legation, Tehran

The P.M. and General Ismay

J.B. welcomes
Field Marshal Sir John Dill

Saki airfield

Centre of communications at Saki airfield

General Karanadze and J.B. at Potsdam

After the Investiture at Potsdam

Lewis Douglas

Ian Jacob

Chapter 8

Journey to the Summit (1943–1944)

THE PRESIDENT AND PRIME MINISTER at Quebec had decided that a meeting with Marshal Stalin was essential. They had failed to achieve it at Casablanca but this time his reply to their invitation had been an acceptance for November or December. As a prelude it was agreed between the three leaders that their Foreign Ministers would meet in Moscow in October. Mr Anthony Eden asked that General Ismay should go with him to explain to the Russians the military details of the Quebec decision to carry out the *Overlord* invasion in 1944.

The preliminary meetings went well. The Russians were friendly and in good spirits, pleased about *Overlord*; there were frequent firework displays in Red Square to celebrate the victorious advance of their armies along all fronts. General Ismay and Colonel George Price, who went with him, found old friends there: Mr Averell Harriman, and Major-General J. 'Russ' Deane who had been Joint Secretary to the Combined Chiefs of Staff and was now Head of the US Military Mission in Moscow.

The pleasant atmosphere throughout augured well for the meeting of the 'Big Three'.

The choice of a meeting-place had been as difficult to agree on as a mutually acceptable picnic place for a carload of people, but at last Teheran was chosen, the date 28 November. The Americans and British decided to meet together in Cairo first to agree on their common approach to the Russians; then, after Teheran, they would return to Cairo for discussions with Generalissimo and Madame Chiang Kai-shek.

For the Cairo part of the proceedings, the British Government was host and Mr Lawrence Burgis, a senior member of Sir Edward Bridges's staff in the War Cabinet Offices, in charge of the arrangements. Commander Knott went ahead to liaise with the British Army Headquarters, Middle East, and I became part of Mr Burgis's staff in London. With cool efficiency he and his Civil Service officers proceeded with the financial, catering and travel problems of our hospitality, while I typed the lists and sent out the administrative instructions. These were complicated by the varied means by which the British delegation were to reach the venue. The Prime Minister sailed from England in HMS *Renown*, taking with him his daughter Sarah, Mr John Winant, the American Ambassador in London, Admiral Cunningham, the First Sea Lord, General Ismay, and his own staff. Some left *Renown* at Malta and flew to Cairo. Another party sailed in HMS *London*, a light cruiser, all the way, stopping at Malta to pick up people from *Renown*. Others flew the whole way. Instructions went out of my office into Whitehall:

> Yellow labels for *Renown*, white labels with red band for *London*. Red labels, as usual, for Prime Minister's party. No passenger's name to be written on label but code number provided . . .
>
> Departments to take documents needed for own use, War Cabinet Offices taking complete set of all War Cabinet and Defence Committee documents and telegrams. . . . No circulation box keys, safe keys, passes, to be taken, or ration books. No rations to be drawn on behalf of anyone during absence from UK.
>
> British Government will be official hosts. . . . Each member of delegation will, when ashore, be entitled to draw a special allowance of ten shillings a day. £5 sterling only allowed to be taken out of country. . . .

Thirty civilian women went from Plymouth to Alexandria in HMS *London*; how far we had gone since the Casablanca days! I looked again at a letter I had had from General Wavell, containing a poem which, he said, was his comment on a 'rather pompous Air Ministry wire detailing the arrangements to be made to smooth the passage of VIPs:

> Oh it's nice to be a VIP.
> And travel with a zip
> When you take a little trip
> And be greeted with a 'Hip
> Hip hurrah, here He comes';
>
> While the common sort of CUB*
> (Like the captain or the sub)

* Completely Unimportant Bloke.

Just gets packed in any tub
And goes to the smallest pub
In the meanest kinds of slums.

But I think the CUB does more
To win this ruddy war
Than the VIP, who's just a bore!

The all-the-way-by-air party left London, comfortably in a special train, on 16 November, for Portreath in Cornwall. There were three aircraft loads and, as I had drawn up the lists, I was able to put the only three women into a heated, cushioned Dakota with Lord Leathers, the Minister for War Transport, and the other senior officers. The other two aircraft had bucket seats.

I left my office in a dreadful rush but felt glad that this time only Laura and Winnie would remain behind; their filing section colleague Joan was on her way in the *London* as part of Colonel Hollis's staff. I had hated the fact that, on the last two conferences, none of them had had a chance of coming and would stay to do my office work. For the *Sictel* and *Chieftel* telegrams to commanders-in-chief, however, they were not responsible. I brought the draft of a *Sictel* to finish on the train, which I did, with the help of Group-Captain Earle, Assistant Secretary to the Chiefs of Staff Committee. We sent it back to London by a courier who was taking other papers for our Special Party.

On the journey we were fitted with flying clothing and parachute harness, a hilarious sight in the narrow passage between the seats; swaying off balance, the Minister, the colonels, majors and commanders stepped in and out of assorted sizes, each of us looking incongruous and absurd.

At the airfield, dressed in the heavy flying clothes, we waited for departure. It never came, the weather was bad. We were fed with bacon and eggs, always a treat, and then taken in buses to St Ives where, at 3.30 a.m., we climbed shivering with the cold into our hotel beds. Next day, and the next, we were told we could not leave. By then we were enjoying being suspended from duty and having a seaside holiday, sleeping late, going for walks and to the movies.

We got away at 4 a.m. on the third morning, taking off for Rabat in Morocco where we had a welcome breakfast, American tinned pineapple juice tasting delicious in the Nissen hut Royal Air Force mess, a blazing hot morning outside. We three girls had our first experience of being civilians travelling under military orders. Airfields in distant places were not equipped with washrooms for women – at Rabat they had not expected us – and regulations precluded our use of the men's facilities. An embarrassed Air Force officer led us to a shed and left us.

Biskra in Algeria was our night stopover. It gave me my first taste of 'the East' when I saw a string of camels moving over the desert, with dusty sand kicked up behind it. We stayed at a run-down, once splendid, French hotel. Ian Fleming was with us; in London I often dined with him or went to the cinema, but I never had him as one of my conference 'charges'. He was serious and intelligent over his work, but on the sort of St Ives–Biskra spree we were now enjoying he was a sociable and friendly addition to a party of people who did not know each other on these terms. As a travelling delegate he was the administrative officer's ideal; no matter what happened – whether it be delay or some other kind of confusion in the arrangements – he took a book from his pocket and sat reading, oblivious to all around him until he got the order to move.

He urged some of us to go with him and seek a soothsayer who, he said, he had been told lived in the 'Garden of Allah'. We found the Garden but no soothsayer. In what he called his 'best Goon French' Ian asked a passer-by whether he knew where the prophet was to be found. The Arab sped away promising to find him and return. We waited, watched camels and the sunset, but he never came. I am sure it was an Ian Fleming 'spoof', but he made it all sound so real and true that it was worth being fooled.

The usual 3 a.m. call was no hardship; it was easy to get up in warmth and not to be afraid of the biting cold outside the blankets. The mugs of strong tea at the airfield tasted better under the pink glow of a sky which was beginning to snuff out the stars. The take-off was different; not dark and wet and blind with the blackened-out windows, but light and smooth and free as the machine gathered speed and settled itself at an altitude from which we could clearly see the desert below. We flew over Tunisia and the Eighth Army's battle-ground, slit with trenches and pocked with shell-holes.

At midday we landed at 'Marble Arch' – a huddle of Air Force tents set on the endless sand. We saw some American fighter aircraft re-fuelling on their way to the Persian Gulf. Lord Leathers stepped down from the Dakota into the dry and searing heat, a bowler on his head, his dark city clothes and furled umbrella etching a sober shadow, his lack of emotion making me wonder whether in fact he knew where he was. For lunch the Royal Air Force gave us of their best – corned beef, sour bread, tea tasting of salt water, the whole gritted with fine sand. They said they had only two hours' warning that forty people were arriving – bad staff work by someone at their headquarters in Cairo, someone who probably did not know that water had to be fetched from many miles away and that every mouthful eaten meant less tins of food in the store. Later, I begged from Mr Burgis some Government Hospitality whisky and gin, which we sent to them by a returning flight with our thanks.

When we landed that evening the lights of Cairo blazed up and stunned us. We climbed stiffly, with crumpled clothes, out of the stuffy Dakota into the balmy Egyptian night, and were led into a room where elegant staff officers in freshly laundered tropical uniform pressed upon us a feast fit for kings.

Army cars took us to the Mena House Hotel. I saw Commander Knott and he sent me back to Cairo to my billet in the Junior Officers' Club. I found the other girls from the War Cabinet Offices, who were feeling rather strange and cut off from the centre of events. It was a contrast from the satisfaction of all being under one roof as at the Château Frontenac in Quebec.

Commander Knott and the Army Headquarters had made excellent arrangements under the difficult conditions which prevailed in a sprawling capital city where East met West in crowded and noisy disorder. The Mena House Hotel, near the Pyramids, had been chosen as the conference headquarters because its distance from Cairo made it safer from a security point of view. The President, Prime Minister and VIPs were in villas nearby and the rest of the staffs in the hotel or at British clubs and army messes. The distances between each were linked by well-organised motor transport.

Mr Burgis and his finance and catering staff had established good co-ordination with Army Headquarters, and the bars and dining-rooms in the Mena House were providing all that our guests could want for eating and drinking. 'We apologise for troubling you on so small a matter,' wrote Mr Burgis to the Governor of Gibraltar, 'but would be greatly obliged if you could arrange for thirty dozen bottles of whisky and twelve dozen bottles of sherry to be delivered to the wardroom of HMS *London* as soon as she arrives.' At the start of the conference, unfortunately, few members of either the British or American delegations escaped the discomforts of a 'Gippy tummy'. This digestive malaise made the sufferer feel not so much ill as disgusted by everything.

That the atmosphere during the week in Cairo was unhappy was certainly not the fault of Mr Burgis, Commander Knott or General Headquarters, Middle East. It was due to the early arrival of the Chinese delegation who, by their presence, confused and upset the Anglo-American schedule. This irked the British, who were convinced of the need for joint talks before the Teheran meeting, not only to agree on a common approach to the Russians but also to settle outstanding questions connected with the *Overlord* invasion: a Supreme Commander had to be chosen; operations in its support needed to be discussed. Where these last were concerned the availability of landing-craft was a crucial point which would have a direct bearing on what could be done in South-East Asia. It was no use talking to the Chinese until this was known. The military position in Italy also needed to be discussed. Since the Italian surrender on 8 September, and the Allied landings at Salerno next day, there had been little progress. But the build-up of our forces on this front had been much hampered by withdrawals of units, equipment and landing-craft to the United Kingdom in preparation for *Overlord*. The British felt keenly that opportunities here – and in the Mediterranean generally – were being dissipated and lost. In the Balkans Yugoslav and Albanian patriots were containing substantial German forces, and the Eastern Aegean was still under German control. The argument that a fixed target date for *Overlord* would give the best chance of meeting the enemy and drawing its forces away from the Russians had in it a danger of weakening the Allies in their, at present, only area of contact with the German Army. 'It is certainly an odd way of helping the Russians', wrote Mr Churchill, 'to slow down the fight in the only theatre where anything can be done for some months.' To President Roosevelt and his advisers, however, the Chinese provided an escape from something they did not want to do. The success of the Foreign Ministers' meetings in Moscow had given them a false optimism as to postwar relations with Russia. They regarded prior-to-Teheran Anglo-American consultations as smacking of a 'gang-up', and went so far as to suggest that the Russians should send a representative to 'sit in' on them. Luckily, as the invitation had already been extended to Chiang Kai-shek to come to

Cairo, the Russians did not take to the idea; Marshal Stalin did not wish to upset his relations with Japan by being near a table which included the Chinese. The Americans contributed further to the confusion by circulating a paper shortly after their arrival in Cairo, proposing the formation of a United Chiefs of Staff to include Russia and China.

As Generalissimo and Madame Chiang could not be ignored, the first Plenary Meeting of the Conference included them and dealt exclusively with their problems. President Roosevelt promised that a major operation would be planned and mounted in the Bay of Bengal.

The subsequent Combined Chiefs of Staff meetings, and the Plenaries without the Chinese, did not get down to the fundamentals. Old suspicions popped their ugly heads from beneath the table: the Americans suspected the British of pursuing their colonial interests in the Mediterranean and of being lukewarm about *Overlord*; the British felt that the Americans were thinking just this; the Americans thought the British were pushing South-East Asia into the background; the British that the Americans were bringing it too prominently to the fore; and Mr Churchill helped not at all by expounding on the advantages of attack in the Eastern Aegean.

To put discussions about operations in the Far East even more on the wrong foot, the Combined Planning Staffs were working on a long-term overall plan for the defeat of Japan which could not possibly have been ready until after Teheran.

The five mixed-up days in Cairo were very far from being days of united preparation for the first meeting of the 'Big Three'.

At my administrative level I did not feel I was making much contribution to the material comfort of the delegates. There were plenty of 'admin.' officers from Middle East Headquarters with whom Commander Knott had been dealing from the beginning, so I did odd jobs for people, ran errands and made myself useful where I was wanted. Mr Lewis Douglas was at Mena House, very worried about the uneven and unproductive progress of events. He brought me a new Parker '51' fountain-pen from America with which, he said, he hoped I would be able to write something cheerful about the Teheran meeting.

I was going there! General Ismay saw that I had not got enough to do and, as I could do shorthand, decided to take me as well as his own secretary, Betty Green, and two other girls from the War

Cabinet Offices. The delegation for Teheran was very small and he guessed rightly that he would be busy. It gave me pleasure to be doing real secretarial work for him and to see at first hand the ability and competence with which Betty and the other two turned out top grade work in confined and difficult conditions. They were professionals; they remained calmly concentrated, pleasantly good-mannered and worked together in friendly familiarity, never losing their own personalities or their temper. They were aristocrats among stenographers, and it was a joy to work with them.

Betty Green was a small person, with fair hair, a neat figure and slim hands. She was the best educated of any of us on General Ismay's staff. Instinctively thoughtful for others, she was courteous and kind. In her work she was deft and tidy, and to see her dealing with a pile of papers was as satisfying as watching a ballet-dancer putting her toes into precise positions. Her loyalty to General Ismay was complete.

We left Cairo on Saturday morning, 27 November, a lovely flight with clear views of the painted landscape, and from the airfield into Teheran we drove through ranks of guards and armoured cars to be deposited in the British Legation compound.

Sir Reader Bullard, the Minister, showed remarkable restraint as his Legation filled up with the paraphernalia of paper and people. Mr Churchill, who had a bad cold and sore throat, was staying in the house, as was his daughter Sarah; General Ismay slept at the Counsellor's house, and used Sir Reader's study as his office. It looked out on to the garden, where the tall trees were russet and yellow. I had a bed at a YWCA hostel in the town, but as our working days included working nights I did not bother to use it, preferring to catnap on the sofa in General Ismay's office.

There was general uneasiness about the security arrangements, aggravated by rumours of assassination plots against one or other of the three leaders and the fact that President Roosevelt was living half a mile away in the American Legation, and either he or Mr Churchill and Marshal Stalin would have to pass through the narrow streets of the capital to meet. On Sunday afternoon, urged by Mr Molotov, the Russian Foreign Minister, and by the Prime Minister, he moved in to the Russian Embassy, a low white building surrounded by sycamore trees, next door to the British compound. He was on Russian ground, a wrong balance – in theory if not in practice! But it had to be done, the alternative was too risky, or so it seemed.

All Sunday morning efforts were made to set the hour for the first meeting: the British wanted the early afternoon, the Americans the evening, and the Russians, whose habit it was to go to bed at teatime, aimed for midnight. The solution came at 4 p.m. when Roosevelt, Mr Churchill and Marshal Stalin sat down round an oak table, made especially for the occasion by Russian craftsmen, and within the white and gold walls began their momentous contribution to history.

The fact that a meeting took place at all that day was in no small measure due to General Ismay. Quietly and unostentatiously he worked to reconcile the independent attitudes of the Americans and British, smoothing over their failure, either in Cairo or during the Sunday morning in Teheran, to have reached prior agreement on the line they wished to take when confronted by the Russians. He told me that he thought it was here that the Chief of the Imperial General Staff Sir Alan Brooke came to realise that Ismay's behind-the-scenes role had its uses and that he was not just a courtier-in-waiting beside Mr Churchill's throne. After the war Sir Alan Brooke denied this, saying he had always appreciated the immense debt owed to General Ismay, not least for his ability to be loyal to both Prime Minister and Chiefs of Staff.

At the meeting were Mr Churchill, Mr Eden, Field Marshal Dill, the three Chiefs of Staff and General Ismay; President Roosevelt, Mr Hopkins, Admiral Leahy (who had become Chairman of the American Chiefs of Staff Committee in 1942) and Admiral King; Marshal Stalin, Mr Molotov and Marshal Voroshilov. The respective interpreters were Major Arthur Birse, Mr Charles Bohlen and Mr Pavlov. General Marshall and General Arnold had mistaken the time of the meeting and were sightseeing in Teheran.

I was General Ismay's commander-in-chief keeper, file-keeper and conference housekeeper and now I was one of his private secretaries. In the close quarters of those few days at Teheran, I saw how smoothly, with Colonel Hollis, he was able to pull together the minutes of the meetings and extract from them what it was important to state with clarity. He was never apparently at a loss but always in control in his dealings with other people – gentle with Field Marshal Dill, on equal terms of friendship with Mr Averell Harriman, correctly formal with the Russians, co-operative and helpful with American Committee Secretaries or aides – like Colonel Frank McCarthy – with Major Birse, Major Tom Hankey, who was in charge of the Royal Marine guard detail, or any other more junior person with a job of work to do. If he was bewildered or doubtful, he had a genius for seeming not to be listening or for indulging in personal reminiscence while his mind, like a ray of hot sun, probed, essayed, accepted, or discarded until the right answer came. He had little patience with fools, was obstinate and, at times, pigheaded, but he was supreme in his field.

'One feels the richer for his warmth and wisdom,' said someone: I add 'and his friendship and trust.'

During the three days of the conference, Betty and I only had time to go out once into the Teheran streets where water ran down each side in open channels. Security was complete: the Persians had closed the frontiers, shut down the radio station, stopped all rail and road transport – except for food stuffs – grounded all aircraft. There were armoured cars everywhere, floodlit walls round the Russian Embassy, and Russian tommy-guns among the sycamore trees. Besides the armoured cars at four corners of the British Legation compound, we were guarded by British and Indian Army soldiers, who escorted home anyone not living within it.

We none of us had more than two or three hours' sleep a night. Mine ended at 6 in the morning when three Legation servants came in to rake out and re-lay the fire, bowing politely before they bent to their task. I had one bath, at midday, in the Minister's bathroom. Sir Reader Bullard moved like a ghost through his home, keeping his files in the cloakroom and behind the lavatory door. He was a delightful person, very natural and easy, and took a puckish delight in the goings-on around him. On the last morning, very early, I crept into his sitting-room to fill my new fountain-pen and found him in an easy chair listening to the BBC news. He showed no surprise, just asked me if I would like some tea and a cake.

On Tuesday, 30 November, at the end of the Conference, Marshal Stalin and President Roosevelt came to dinner at the British Legation. Some hours before – luckily not together – we received two visits: the first from a band of Russian officers; the second from a band of Presidential bodyguards. Eyed stolidly by the British guards, they each combed the rooms and the garden, looked behind doors and curtains, under tables and chairs.

Some of us stood in the hall to watch the arrivals. The Prime Minister, whose sixty-ninth birthday it was, paced up and down waiting for them. He stopped and stared at us, asked us whether we were going to wish him 'many happy returns of the day'. We felt foolish and said nothing. The Presidential bodyguard looked foolish too, standing in a row, when they were asked by Mr Churchill to sing a chorus. They were saved by the President, who came in through the back door and down the ramp which had been built for his chair, a long thin cigarette-holder in his long thin fingers. He disappeared into the drawing-room.

Then came a clatter of sentries presenting arms, the bang of a car door and Marshal Stalin was there. He was shorter and older than I had expected, had greying hair and many fine laughter lines running upwards from the corners of his eyes; his face was heavily pitted and he looked like a farmer, but a shrewd and cunning one. He held himself very straight, and the quiet gesture of slow salute as he raised his right arm in greeting was like a rock coming to life. He looked keenly round as Mr Churchill said 'Good evening', and then turned to hang up his coat. The Prime Minister started forward to help and the two fought silently for possession. The Marshal was revealed dressed in a well-cut, tight-fitting, light beige uniform with broad red stripes running down the sides of the trousers.

We left them to their speeches, their dinner and the drama which has been told before but which bears re-telling. A Persian servant came in bearing the pudding – a tall lantern of ice with a lamp inside – his eyes popping as he looked at Marshal Stalin and not the way he was going. The pudding began to slide; Persian and pudding flew round the table at an angle which became more acute with every step. The guests sat transfixed, trying to guess where it would fall. Finally it did, fair and square on to the head and shoulders of Mr Pavlov, who, without hesitation, continued his interpretation: 'Marshal Stalin, he say . . .'

I went to have dinner with Colonel Frank McCarthy at the US Military Camp at Amerabad where he was staying with General Marshall. We ate roast gazelle and then sat talking in a group round a huge log fire, in easy chairs covered by a sort of sacking in gay colours. The walls of the Nissen hut were hung with the same material, and the whole effect was a tribute to someone with imagination and taste.

On returning to my office, where I had a lot of clearing up to do before next day's departure, I found eight Russian security officers sitting around drinking vodka, waiting for the Churchill birthday dinner to end. I sat down at my desk, smiled brightly and pointed to my red box of papers and then at my head. They laughed delightedly and settled down to stare. I gave up, unnerved. With no common language, we spent a couple of hours gesturing, smiling, nipping at the vodka. I fetched a Wren cipher officer to support me:

'*Britanski marine*,' I said.

'*Da, da*,' said they. Another hour passed; I became bored and desperate, I had so much to do. Smelling a party, the White House security men joined us, and the room was packed with people, glasses, bottles, cigarette ends. At last the dinner ended and they left. I had no sleep that night, and did not feel – like President Roosevelt – that the Teheran Conference had 'increased the hopes for a better world, one in which the ordinary citizen could be assured the opportunity for peaceful toil and just employment of the fruits of his labours'.

As we flew off to Palestine next morning, the sun was rising over the mountains and in Teheran three powerful men lay sleeping.

The Palestine interlude was a return gesture of hospitality to the American Chiefs of Staff for the Williamsburg weekend during the Washington Conference. The fleet of aircraft came down at Lydda in brilliant sunshine, the British Chiefs of Staff very content with a new 'York' machine which had just been allotted to them, its comforts making up for the bomb-bays of the past. There were drinks and snacks at the airfield, and then we drove through guarded roads to the King David Hotel in Jerusalem.

Mr Lawrence Burgis had come from Cairo, had cleared the hotel of guests and made it luxuriously ready for the thirty people headed by the Combined Chiefs of Staff, their personal aides, the Committee Secretaries, and including other officers of the military staffs, some Wren cipherers and us girls. As in Cairo, Mr Burgis had had help from the local British Army Headquarters, but his touch was sure in such things as food and wine, in all sorts of thoughtful details of comfort, even to the presentation to each of us of an inscribed olive-wood cigarette-box.

The most thoughtful act, for me personally, was the arrangement he made for my sister Pamela to be given a week's leave from her Military Hospital at Sarafand to join us in Jerusalem and then go back to Cairo with us. Between them, he and General Ismay had kept it a secret, until I arrived in the hall of the hotel when Mr Burgis said: 'There is someone to see you,' and there was Pamela, in her army nurse's khaki uniform, hanging back, typically not wanting to push herself forward. She said she saw me come in, my arms filled with coats and bags, and that I was talking to this person and that person, so she thought she would wait. Wait! When I saw her, the others in the party faded away like mist before the rising sun, and we went up to our bedroom, sat on our beds and talked. It was three years since we had met and there was almost too much to say: our father's death, our mother's life, how were Betty and Godfrey and the two children she had never seen, Nancy and Michael, her husband, their daughter Prunella, and Felicity in her 'Wrennery' in Gibraltar at the other end of the Mediterranean. Pamela, herself an unchanging person, quiet and unassuming, capable and deft in her nursing, was content to be caring for the wounded soldiers of all nationalities, who passed through the 26th (Scottish) General Hospital. The creative side of her character not only found satisfaction in mending broken bodies and spirits, but had now flowed into writing. She had the manuscript of a novel with her, which I took home and asked Peter Fleming to read. It was not good enough, but after the war she wrote, and had published, four good books based on her nursing experiences.

In the afternoon, through cleared and guarded streets, we went sightseeing. Pamela and I joined up with Frank McCarthy and Lieutenant-Colonel Brian Boyle, military aide to the Chief of the Imperial General Staff. Brian, a barrister in private life, was a gentle person, with a good brain, courteous and efficient, who suited his at times irascible but always civilised General Sir Alan Brooke. He was very musical. In the passage of the Joint Staff Mission offices in Washington, I had met him walking towards me, gesturing rhythmically with his right arm.

'What *are* you doing, Brian?' I asked.

'Oh,' he replied, and smiled rather bashfully, 'I was conducting the first movement of Beethoven's 7th Symphony. It helps me a lot when I am under pressure.'

With Frank McCarthy I was on terms of mutual liking and friendship. I had met him when he had come to London with General Marshall in 1942, had been introduced through a friend of mine who had known him in childhood in Virginia. He had not been at the Quebec Conference, but at Mena House, unlike Washington, the two delegates worked in the same building, so we often met. He had a husky voice, blue eyes and a lot of southern charm. Well liked by all who knew him in the British delegation, he was a particular favourite of General Ismay who had a high regard for his character and ability, and appreciated his innate understanding of English humour. Meticulous to a fault in his services to General Marshall, Frank McCarthy was sensitively quick in his reactions, thorough in his work, an ace organiser. In return General Marshall, who treated him on terms of affectionate familiarity and equality, must have thanked Providence for him. They were well matched, the great man and his aide.

When Pamela, Frank, Brian and I reached a bend in the Via Dolorosa, we saw ahead of us a huge crowd, moving slowly up the street. At its head were the figures of the Combined Chiefs of Staff, who were listening gravely to their guide, a Franciscan monk, behind them a line of British soldiers and on the fringe a pushing, chattering mass of Arab families which grew larger at each forward step. We joined the rear and tramped with them through all the Holy Places, the men of war paying tribute to the Man of Peace.

There was a formal dinner that night for the VIPs, and next door a dinner-dance for us. It seemed dull that the glamorous ones were behind closed doors and we hoped they might join us but were not too optimistic. Each one of them might be riotously gay as an individual, but as a combined committee they were rather a formidable and serious package. The door opened; Mr Burgis's choice of food and wine had loosened the wrappings; there was a pause as the group stood and watched us bouncing rather self-consciously around the floor. I was dancing with Frank McCarthy; General Marshall was the first to break ranks and 'cut in' on his aide. 'He is a very nice person,' said the General. And so are you, I thought. If I had been asked which of the Combined Chiefs of Staff would be the first to step on to the dance floor, it would not have been General Marshall. He was a tall and dignified man towards whom awe and respect could be directed but not warmth or lightly felt liking. When I had seen him in any part of the Château Frontenac Hotel, and he had acknowledged me with a nod, I could no more have said something airy and cheerful than I could have turned round and walked beside him. I knew from Frank McCarthy that in private he was delightfully human and teasing, enjoying a crack at some of

Frank's more over-meticulous arrangements. But I also knew that General Ismay and the British Chiefs of Staff – with the exception perhaps of Portal – found him difficult to know as a person, impossible to be intimate with, and were therefore content to leave to Field Marshal Dill the ease of equal friendship. They none of them had any doubts whatsoever about the strength and nobility of his character; his selfless response to the calls of duty; his integrity and the fact that he was an honourable man. With quiet persistence and great organising skill, he had been responsible for increasing the US Army in ten months to a planned strength of seven and a half million men; within the divisions of opinion which existed in the Combined Chiefs of Staff it was he who held most firmly to the view that American forces should cross the Channel with their British allies at the very earliest opportunity. His view was the least open to modification, and soldiers with European experience like General Sir Alan Brooke found its inflexibility difficult to understand. What needed to be remembered was that General Marshall had, as colleague, the Chief of Naval Staff Admiral Ernest King, whose strict concern for his navy and prime conviction that Japan was the major enemy, made him a force to be reckoned with. Any fringe operation which deviated from the straight cross-Channel 'Germany first' route was sure to receive the disapproval of this sailor, engaged as he was on fighting major naval battles in the Pacific against a clever and cunning foe. 'It may well be', wrote General Ismay in his memoirs, 'that [Marshall's] consistency and single-mindedness prevented the postponement of our assault on Europe beyond June 1944.'

General Marshall was courteously old-fashioned in his approach to other people and rarely used Christian names. After the pleasant formality of our dance round the King David's ballroom, on his visits to England, Quebec, Yalta and Potsdam, however, he never failed to bring me a box of chocolates and began, even, to address me as 'Joan'. I have wondered whether he was guilty of trying to promote a union between his bachelor aide and the English Miss Bright, but if he was, it was one of the few things he failed in.

'I want some exercise, too,' said the Chief of the Air Staff, and like a ball I rolled from one pair of arms to the other.

Air Chief Marshal Sir Charles Portal (more familiarly known as Peter Portal) was the member of the three British Chiefs of Staff whose personality was best understood by the Americans. He was cool and detached and did not react sensitively or with anger if his statements were contradicted or his views disagreed with. He looked at the resulting position objectively, with an open mind, and sought to find a middle way without losing sight of the original aim of the discussion. His attitude to life was intellectual and scientific, his mind more curious and interested about a machine or instrument than about the men who made or operated it. He could detach himself absolutely from anything which ceased to hold his attention or seemed unimportant to him. There was a similar disinterest in material comforts; he preferred a bench to a feather bed, a hunk of cheese to a soufflé; it genuinely bewildered Mr Churchill, who appreciated a good table, to see his disregard for the food he was eating. He had an attractive personality and, as Chief of the Air Staff from 1940 until the end of the war, was an essential and irreplaceable member of the Chiefs of Staff Committee, enjoying a good relationship with General Sir Alan Brooke, ten years his senior. The fine brain, with its powers of concentration, lay behind an aquiline face with intelligent eyes and a long nose, a feature inherited directly from his Huguenot ancestors.

A hard worker himself, he drove his personal staff without noticing their fatigue. When he did he was quick to remedy it. His personal secretary, Mr Stewart Crawford, a civilian, at the end of the Yalta Conference was dreaming about returning to Malta in the ship *Franconia* and having a few days at sea before he sat once more at his desk in Whitehall. I felt I knew Portal well enough to tell him this. His reaction was immediate; he was amazed.

'But, of course,' he said, 'of course he can. I never thought of it,' and he rushed off to tell Crawford himself how pleased he was at the idea.

When the holiday evening at the King David Hotel ended the only two who had not danced were Admiral King and Field Marshal Dill.

Admiral Ernest King represented the stern, unyielding, puritanical side of the American character. Few succeeded in breaking through to him. Yet it was this austere figure who bent and picked up my suitcase on Lydda airfield next morning and carried it to the aircraft; who, when he said goodbye and thank you to his hosts, added that 'either we go now or stay for months'; and who, at a last dinner at Potsdam in 1945, raised his glass to General Ismay and paid a special and kindly tribute to him for the part he had played in the war.

General Ismay had never expected anything like that from him, and was pleased and touched.

When we got back to the Mena House Hotel in Cairo, Lew Douglas met me at the door and said:

'Joan, what *have* you done at Teheran? You have set history back many years.'

He was not, of course, referring to Marshal Stalin's firm approval at the 'Big Three' counsels of the *Overlord* invasion in 1944, but more to the threatening clouds which hung over the postwar future in loose provisions – semi-formally discussed and loosely agreed – for the boundaries of Poland, 'zones of occupation' in Germany and Austria, and 'areas of control' in the Balkans and Eastern Europe. Loose provisions discussed between people with democratic principles mean that, in due course, firm proposals are put forward, properly considered and decided upon; to Marshal Stalin and his like, loose provisions, discussions and agreements are regarded as a *carte blanche* for future action.

A supporting operation for *Overlord* was also approved at Teheran. This – invasion of the south of France – was a plan prepared by the American Chiefs of Staff and received with lukewarm acceptance by the British. They felt that at least it would keep badly needed landing-craft in the Mediterranean rather than their being sent forthwith to South-East Asia to fulfil President Roosevelt's promise to Chiang Kai-shek in the Bay of Bengal. But they remained earnestly certain, with Mr Churchill, that the forces and equipment for the south of France should not be earmarked so rigidly as to be at the expense of the armies fighting in Italy. Unfortunately, during the Cairo–Teheran period, the Fifth Anglo-American Army Group under General Alexander and the Eighth Army under General Montgomery were bogged down by bad weather, all hope gone of their reaching Rome in January. But as soon as possible, supported by an amphibious landing, they would push ahead again. Who could tell how far they would get in six months? Options should be kept open to exploit a successful advance up Italy by perhaps turning right northwards to the head of the Adriatic and towards the Danube. At the same time aid to partisans holding down between twenty-five and thirty German divisions in the Balkans should not be forgotten.

Mr Churchill also urged strongly that the Eastern Mediterranean should not be neglected. He felt that the capture of Rhodes, for which there were sufficient troops and air forces in Egypt, would give us domination of the Aegean and this would allow Russia access to Black Sea ports instead of relying on the dangers and difficulties of the Allied Arctic Convoy Route. And if the Turks came into the war, or extended their neutrality, such domination could be achieved without having to take Rhodes.

But Mr Churchill failed in all except agreement that he should treat with the Turks on his return to Cairo. There had been a definite 'two's company, three's none' in Roosevelt's behaviour to him at Teheran. He had been pointedly uninvited to, and uninformed about, the informal parleys which took place between Marshal Stalin and the President in the Russian Embassy, and the President had avoided seeing him alone since they left Cairo. The success of the Three Power Meeting, from a social and war partnership point of view, put blinkers on the eyes of those who were content not to look too far into the future. For those who, like Mr Churchill and Mr Douglas, had a deep regard for history, its results did not look so good.

The last few days of the Cairo Conference were about as uncomfortable as the first. The President was anxious to return home and was adamant over his decision to give major aid to the Chinese in the Bay of Bengal. Mr Churchill and his delegation deplored a rushed dispersal and wished sober attention to be paid to an important statement made by Marshal Stalin at Teheran that Russia would declare war on Japan when Germany was defeated – a factor which could be considered of far greater importance in aiding Chiang Kai-shek than emptying the landing-craft barrel now for a large-scale operation in the Bay of Bengal. They also wanted agreement which would give, if necessary, the May date for *Overlord* an elasticity which could stretch it to June or July.

Some sort of clarity, albeit unsatisfactory, emerged. Rhodes fell away, the talks with the Turks having yielded nothing concrete. Mountbatten's plan for President Roosevelt's 'aid to Chiang' operation estimated for larger numbers of troops and equipment than had been envisaged, and on the last afternoon led to a Presidential decision to abandon it. The Combined Planners' long-term appreciation of the war against Japan was studied and decisions taken for modified action in Burma and future British support for General MacArthur's operations in the Pacific. Finally, and at last, the

Supreme Command for *Overlord* was decided on: it was not to be General Marshall, he was indispensable as Chief of Army Staff; General Sir Alan Brooke had known for some time that it was not to be his, for the same reason but also because the British knew that the larger American contribution deserved an American commander; it would be General Dwight D. Eisenhower.

The Americans left, and we said goodbye to Lew Douglas and Frank McCarthy. The cold and sore throat which Mr Churchill and Lord Moran had kept at bay during the long and anxious days of conference returned to become pneumonia and keep the Prime Minister, as he put it, 'at this pregnant moment on the broad of my back amid the ruins of ancient Carthage'. He remained in Tunis, later convalescing at Marrakesh, until the end of January 1944.

General Ismay retired to bed with an attack of bronchitis. He was a bad invalid, impatient and demanding, but all of us, the members of his staff, were glad to hang about outside his bedroom ready to attend to his wants; we would have felt guilty if we had not. Colonel Hollis and Mr Burgis looked so depressed on one of the evenings that I accused General Ismay of staging a deathbed scene. He laughed, but not very heartily.

Pamela and I shared a room at the Junior Officers' Club and had met, of course, whenever we could during the three days she was in Cairo. Certain she would return to England in time to take part in *Overlord*, she said goodbye to me at Heliopolis and flew off into the sky with an Air Force pilot in a small machine. She had observed us all with interest, had made many friends, had got out of her uniform into clothes borrowed from me, and was now returning to the rows of beds and sick men. We wished she had stayed with us long enough to nurse our General 'Pug'.

The Administrative Office listed and sent off the British delegation in as many different ways as had brought them to Cairo. The ones who were the last to leave were those who would return to England in HMS *London*, among them General Ismay, Major-General Robert Laycock, the Chief of Combined Operations, Junior-Commander Marling, ATS, of his staff, Mr Burgis, Commander Ian Fleming, Miss Jean Crawford from the First Sea Lord's office, Betty Green, me, thirteen other girls, eight Wren cipher officers, ten enlisted War Office personnel and ten Royal Marines. As we drove to Alexandria, we were impressed by the discipline shown in the lines of military convoys, each vehicle keeping well to one side of the road with an exact number of yards between the one in front and the one behind. Near Alexandria they turned off to the left, 'to the Western Desert', down the narrow road which had carried the men of the Eighth Army for miles, disappointed them for months and at last taken them to victory.

In HMS *London* it was a comfortable and carefree squash. General Ismay had the Commander's cabin; separation from his beloved but demanding 'Master', Mr Churchill, and the preoccupations of Cairo and Teheran soon brought him back to his usual genial and companionable self. For the girls, the officers turned out of their cabins and we slept two to a single, one in the bunk, the other on a mattress on the floor. The arrangements made for us were thoughtful and thorough, including chamber-pots in each cabin, procured from a Plymouth hospital, and canvas chairs on deck clearly marked 'Corporation of Plymouth'. We shared the wardroom with the ship's officers, and here we spent our days, playing cards and charades, drinking and eating, reading and talking.

The getting 'under way' at Alexandria was notable to anyone like me who had never before travelled in a warship. As the engines started there came a thrilling sensation of power from the guts of the ship and then quietly and smoothly she gathered speed and sped out of harbour into the rough green seas of the Mediterranean. For four days, till we reached Gibraltar, the waters were turbulent, covering our bows and the two escorting destroyers with sheets of green and white spray. No one was seasick, none of us had anything to do but enjoy ourselves, and sometimes climb up high to the bridge and watch the heaving world below us. Except Betty Green; she sat on the pitching deck, shorthand notebook on her knee, slim legs in silk stockings crossed, taking General Ismay's dictation. Then, in the ward-room, she typed as fast as if she were at her desk in Whitehall, oblivious to the two dozen people talking, laughing and moving around her.

After supper each evening Jean Crawford, Ian Fleming and I joined General Ismay in his cabin and played bridge, an uneven four because they were all good at the game and I was not. I did my best, mostly by protesting the advantages of my having played this or that card, but could never hide the truth from the General; he was a devastating player with an unimpeachable memory.

Jean Crawford I had first met on the *Queen Mary* going to New York for the Washington Conference; she was a temporary Civil Servant like me. A tall girl, with fair hair and a good brain, she took a detached but amused view of her position as a junior stenographer in the First Sea Lord's office. She was one of those who never pushed herself forward, but who was socially easy and appreciative, and on board the *London* it was she who particularly made us laugh with her impersonations of the child movie-star Shirley Temple.

We reached Gibraltar on 13 December. There was a message inviting me to lunch at Government House where, it said, I would find Third Officer Felicity Bright, WRNS. The unit of Wren cipher officers was an important part of life on 'the Rock', and Felicity a well-known and liked member of it. She was often invited to Government House by the Governor, General F. N. Mason-Macfarlane, sometimes especially to see General Wavell or Admiral Somerville as they passed through on their way to Asia with letters from me to her.

General Ismay was also invited, so together we went and, in the absence in England of Mason-Macfarlane, were fed by Major-General Hyland, the Acting Governor. Felicity looked fine and, as always, was laughing, gay and responsive. I detected some changes: she was more critical of people; not so gullible, nor would she let herself become as emotionally involved as Pamela. The war had not touched her as it had Pamela, but then her work was so different. Except for the 'watch' duties in the cipher office, she and the other Wren officers were free to have fun, of which there was no lack in a garrison town and fleet base like Gibraltar. As the youngest, she was closest to my mother; with Pamela there was a bond which stretched back through her life to the days in Spain when they had done everything together, and together been called 'the babies'. During the five days the *London* was in port we met constantly and talked of the family and of ourselves. I felt as though I had drawn a sisterly thread round the Mediterranean.

The five days' delay was due to our having to wait to share our escort with the battleship *King George V*. For many it was tedious, especially so because Christmas was near and they were anxious to be home. Not for Ian Fleming, however; true to his philosophy, he said he found it extremely pleasant to be forced to read and to eat bacon and eggs.

On Saturday, 18 December, *King George V* gathered us and two escorting destroyers behind her, like some great hen, and led us home, dipping her bows into the rough winter sea and bringing them up with all the strength of her huge frame. In the early morning of the 23rd we said a sad goodbye to the good ship *London* and her company, on the 24th we unpacked our bags in London and tied up the gifts we had brought with us, and by lunchtime on Christmas Day I was opening mine in Freshford with my mother, my sister Betty and her children John and Lucinda, Nancy, Michael and their daughter Prunella. Godfrey was in East Africa, but about Pamela and Felicity I had plenty to tell.

Chapter 9

Decision to embark (1944)

For the Allies, January 1944 was the start of the vital period towards which their discussions and decisions of the past two years had been directed. To the Germans, the public announcement of commanders for operations to the south and to the north of their borders could only mean that the final solution had begun.

General Eisenhower arrived in London as Supreme Allied Commander of Expeditionary Forces in the United Kingdom. Air Chief Marshal Sir Arthur Tedder was his Deputy, General Sir Bernard Montgomery, Commander-in-Chief of the British Group of Armies, General Omar Bradley of the US Group of Armies; as Allied Naval Commander-in-Chief, Admiral Sir Bertram Ramsay; Air Chief Marshal Sir Trafford Leigh-Mallory was Allied Air Officer Commanding-in-Chief and General Carl Spaatz in command of the US Strategic Bombing Force against Germany.

In the Mediterranean area General Sir Maitland Wilson became Supreme Allied Commander, General Sir Harold Alexander the Commander-in-Chief Allied Armies in Italy; as Deputy to the Supreme Commander commanding US Forces, General Jacob L. Devers, and Commander of the Allied Air Forces, General Ira C. Eaker. General Sir Bernard Paget became Commander-in-Chief Middle East; with his departure to Cairo, and Admiral Ramsay's involvement in *Overlord*, I lost my two most constant visitors to the Special Information Centre.

In Italy, on 4 January, the Fifth Army attacked east of Cassino, and on the 22nd the amphibious landing at Anzio got off to a sticky start. From then until May the fighting on all fronts was bitter, German resistance strong. The long months ended when the Fifth Army marched into Rome on 4 June.

For Poland it was a period of doom. The Russians wished to push back the frontier, and in January proposed that on the east it should be the 1919 Peace Conference 'Curzon Line'. The exiled Polish

Government in London asked for US and UK mediation, but the Russians were quick to say that this was as good as a rejection of their proposals and declined to accept it. The military axe was poised in July when Moscow broadcasts assured the hard-pressed inhabitants of Warsaw that the Red Army was on its way to deliver them. On 1 August the Polish underground forces rose and for two months fought a battle of hell against their German oppressors. The Red Army came to a halt, the Red air forces ceased activity. From the Mediterranean area the Allied air forces did their best, but the targets were far in distance, it was difficult to judge between ally and foe, and Marshal Stalin refused permission for our bombers to land for any purpose east of Warsaw. By 2 October all fighting had ended; the Russians moved on. Three months later they entered Warsaw. The axe had fallen.

In London, on 14 January, the future Allied occupation zones in Germany and Austria began their sickly and unhappy life when the European Advisory Council met formally for the first time. Composed of the US and Russian Ambassadors to the UK, Mr John Winant and Mr Gusev, and Mr William Strang, Under-Secretary of State, Foreign Office, it had been set up at the Foreign Ministers' Conference which took place in Moscow prior to the Cairo-Teheran meetings to consider problems attending on Germany's surrender and relative to the postwar period. One of its main drawbacks as parent of the future control of the conquered territories was that its ancestors were too busy waging war to pay enough attention to its offspring.

Except for the 'knife in the back' pause outside Warsaw, the Russian armies advanced everywhere. They raised in January the long and courageous siege of Leningrad, and in the spring recaptured Odessa and the Crimea.

The only 'advance' the Germans could boast at this time was their annexation of Hungary.

> This war [wrote General Wavell] is being fought now mainly by tired, bored and rather disillusioned people. If we are stale now, where are we going to get the fresh impetus of vitality and faith that the peace will require? Will your generation have it, Joan, and be prepared to take over from the older one, and will the older ones be prepared to withdraw gracefully and not interfere?

As Viceroy, General Wavell was finding it

> the hardest work I have ever done, and I am not naturally a worker, as you know. When I am not on tour I have to spend eight hours a day or more in the office, and the tours are almost more strenuous than the office. I have to meet so many dull people and do so many ten-minute talks (it usually takes me ten minutes to start talking at all to anyone now), and it is irksome to be always on the red carpet and my best behaviour (such as it is). Some of it is interesting but very much of it is dull, and a great deal is discouraging. I am afraid I am making myself a thorough nuisance to HMG over food imports, but I think I am saving them from serious errors and mean to go on.

As friend, guest and one-time fellow Commander-in-Chief, General Wavell had lost Admiral Somerville. When the decision was taken in Cairo that the British would join in General MacArthur's operations in the Pacific, the Eastern Fleet had been reduced and units of it sent East. Admiral Somerville was appointed to Washington as Naval member of the British Joint Staff Mission. 'I must confess', he wrote, 'I rather expected to be relieved because by now I am rather out of date, and if the main fleet is to operate in the Pacific I shall be too old and senior to go with it.' The man of the sea, the Admiral – experienced, dedicated and beloved – took his sense of fun, his jokes and his wisdom to the corridors of bureaucracy. He was not happy at first, but became much more so when he got himself a boat and kept contact with his love, the water, by rowing on the Potomac. 'I had a grand pull on Sunday afternoon', he said in a letter, 'about three miles, and resultant blisters on me "'ocks and me ass and everything that is mine."'

In South-East Asia land operations were going well. Between March and May the British Fourteenth Army entered Upper Burma and crossed the Chindwin river at several points, the Imphal Plain fell to the Allies, and US and Chinese forces captured Myitkyina airfield. In March Major-General Orde Wingate was killed in an air crash in Burma.

For us in the Special Information Centre the five-month period to D-Day was no more busy than any other, but it had about it an excitement and anticipation. The files D/FRANCE/1, 'Operation *Overlord* plans', /2, 'Availability of Landing-craft', and others in the same series grew fatter, while E/NORTH AFRICA/1, 'Operation *Torch*', and F/LIBYA/1, 'Operations in Western Desert', were approaching finality. Urgent anticipation made us do a big tidy-up of all the files and we tied tape round quite a few which had died a natural death. One day I went through the folders of the *Chieftel* and *Sictel* telegrams to see if there were any gaps which we could fill in for the commanders-in-chief. I took the *Chieftels* in a briefcase with me to the local post office, because afterwards I was going on to Lowndes Square with them to see General Ismay who was at home with a cold in the head. I put it down at my feet while I stamped some letters, and then left. Standing at the bus stop, a dead feeling came into the pit of my stomach; I had left the briefcase on the floor beside the counter in the post office. Feeling sick, I went back; it was no longer there. In a whisper, I managed to ask the girl who had served me if by any chance she had seen a black briefcase. I could believe neither eyes nor ears when she said casually: 'Yes, here it is,' and handed it to me. If she had done neither I had already decided to walk away from Whitehall and never come back.

I had two other bad experiences. The first was in May 1941. I was just running down the passage from my office, late for an appointment at Elizabeth Arden's to have my face – not lifted – massaged, when General Ismay came past. He looked very grave, stopped me and said:

'We have just had some ghastly news; the battleship *Hood* has been sunk, we think with few survivors.' I went on my way. As I settled back in the chair, I said to Bunty Awdry, an old friend of mine who was about to clean my face:

'Bunty, how's your brother?' I knew he was in the Navy and much loved by her.

'Oh,' she replied, 'so far as I know he's all right; he's still in the *Hood*, you know.' I sank back unable to speak, all pleasure gone. I could not tell her what I knew, but I knew at that moment that her brother was dead.

The other was on a Saturday evening, 7 November 1942. I had spent the day with some dear friends of mine in Surrey, whose house was always open to me for sleep whenever I wanted it, and as I left, my vanity – for the first and last time in this context – got the better of me. I said:

'I think when you turn on your radio tomorrow morning you will hear good news.' I was uneasy and felt guilty until I knew for certain that Operation *Torch* had taken place as scheduled in North Africa on Sunday morning.

Secrets! What burdens they put on us! All the girls in the War Cabinet Offices who worked for Ismay, Hollis, Jacob, Bridges, who filed or typed the minutes of Cabinet, Defence, Chiefs of Staff, Planning or Intelligence Committees, knew them. Many of us knew the date of D-Day from the hour Operation *Overlord* was first mentioned. Yet from not one girl during the whole war was a secret leaked. This speaks very highly for the discretion of a great many.

There were various events in my family and office life. Betty and Nancy produced a son and a daughter in January, Godfrey and Pamela came home, and Felicity went with her cipher unit from Gibraltar to Australia. Pamela had some leave and then, except for occasional visits home and to London, disappeared into the huge crowd of military units preparing for D-Day. Maurice Knott left us and went back to sea, his place with General Ismay being taken by Lieutenant-Commander Ian McEwan, Royal Naval Reserve. We called him 'Junior' and soon appreciated his conscientiousness in work, his good manners, black hair and dark blue eyes. The first conference romance to end happily was the wedding in January of Mr Leslie Rowan, one of Mr Churchill's Private Secretaries, and Miss Judy Love, who had been a Wren cipher officer at the Quebec Conference in 1943.

I have a theory that nice people usually have nice personal staffs, and in this instance I can extend it to include a statement that great Prime Ministers can also have a nice Private Office. Mr Churchill's was just this; John Martin, Leslie Rowan, Anthony Bevir, John Peck, Jock Colville, were his Private Secretaries at 10 Downing Street, each one of them authoritative, approachable and loyal. John Martin and Leslie Rowan were the most constantly beside him, and had with him a mutually appreciated relationship of trust and liking. With General Ismay, Hollis, who had recently been promoted General, and Colonel Jacob, they were on excellent terms and, by keeping the links with their 'Master' in good running order, knew exactly his mood and the moment it could be used for the best results.

London was full of visitors, not the tourist kind but those who had reason to be there, who came because, at this period, London was the centre of Europe. To bid them welcome, the Germans began air raids again, spasmodic but none the less dangerous.

Anxiously, Allied intelligence watched for signs that Hitler was withdrawing troops from his other battle-fronts to reinforce north-west Europe, but he did not. It seemed incredible. As the build-up mounted to huge proportions and turned the south of England into an armed camp, it was impossible to hide the fact that an invasion would take place. Storage of equipment, as it arrived from America and British factories, became increasingly difficult; when underground caves and quarries were full, use was made of hutments alongside many miles of country road, methodically stacked, easily identifiable, sparsely guarded – but never rifled or sabotaged.

Overhead, Allied bombers roared over to attack vital communication and other targets in France, the Low Countries and western Germany.

What it was possible to do was to try and deceive the Germans as to how, when and where the invasion would come. Civilian traffic between the UK and Eire was prohibited, thus isolating the Axis missions in Dublin. Foreign missions in London were stopped from ciphering their messages and their diplomatic pouches deliberately held up. In March, from the Wash in East Anglia to Land's End, Cornwall, the coast inland for ten miles became a forbidden area.

During the previous year the 'deceiving the enemy' staffs had put about false information that, although landings could be made on open beaches, a bridgehead could not be established without the use of a fully equipped harbour, and that the Pas de Calais area was the most likely one to fulfil this need. To reinforce the story during the weeks preceding D-Day a sham army said to consist of the Canadian First and the American Third was assembled in south-east England, General Patton its announced commander, ships and aircraft were built in dummy and many conflicting messages used in radio communications.

False cover for D-Day itself was assumed by a lieutenant in the Army Education Corps, who looked like General Montgomery and was an actor by profession. When the day was imminent, his departure for Algiers, via Gibraltar, might lead the Germans to think that, as he was an announced commander of invasion forces, nothing could take place until his return. He flew off, in uniform and beret, his mannerisms and movements copied exactly from a close study of his model, and, with his 'staff', landed at Gibraltar. He was officially received and driven to Government House in the Governor's car, flag flying, and was gratified by shouts from British soldiers in the streets: 'Good old Monty!' A known double agent had been encouraged to be at the door when the car drew up and deposited its distinguished passenger. He was – and duly reported whom he had seen to Madrid; from Madrid the news travelled fast to Berlin. Later in the day, Air Vice-Marshal William Elliot, now Air Officer Commanding, Gibraltar, saw him off, with a punctilious salute, and stood watching as the four-engined aircraft lifted off and headed for Algiers.

The true *Overlord* plan had been changed to allow for an increase in the initial assault forces. General Montgomery was to be in command of these until General Eisenhower established his headquarters in France, and he wished for more strength. As usual, this meant more landing-craft. General Eisenhower endorsed, and the Combined Chiefs of Staff agreed, that the additional forces should be provided, that therefore the invasion date should be postponed until June, the south of France operation reduced in size, and the extra warships in support should come from the US Navy.

The true solution of the fully equipped harbour problem was embodied in an ingenious and inspired idea which Mr Churchill had encouraged into reality since 1942; code-named *Mulberry*, it was an artificial floating harbour. In the event these harbours worked perfectly and were the means by which thousands of tons of stores were landed daily on the invasion beaches.

The true D-Day and H-Hour of *Overlord* had to be chosen with careful regard to moon phase and attack plan. The airborne forces which were to go in first needed darkness but enough moonlight to recognise their dropping zones; therefore the moon must be late-rising. There had to be enough interval after dawn for beaches to be identified by the seagoing forces and targets by the bombarding warships; but the interval must not be such that the enemy could recover from surprise and be ready for the infantry landings. The tide had to be low enough to reveal underwater obstacles, but not so low as to make it a long advance across the beaches. To fulfil these requirements, H-Hour must be three hours before high water; and for D-Day there was a choice of three days in June – the 5th, 6th or 7th. The 5th was decided on.

At lunchtime on Friday, 2 June, General Ismay left by train for Southampton accompanying Mr Churchill, who wished to be near to General Eisenhower's advance headquarters during the restless stress of the crucial days. On Saturday, 3 June, I was invited to the Supreme Headquarters, Allied Expeditionary Force (SHAEF), where

General Freddie E. Morgan, who had been its original chief planner, showed me the War Room, set for the big day, with the invasion timetable hanging large and clear on the wall. I had tea with him, and he said the *Overlord* commanders were 'blowing smoke at each other, and Bedell's stomach hurts'. On Sunday, 4 June, with Frank McCarthy I spent the day in the country with our mutual friends, and when I got back to the office that evening I heard that the invasion had been postponed for twenty-four hours because of bad weather, low cloud and poor visibility.

There was a note from General Ismay which revealed the agony of mind there must have been in those responsible for the decision – above all in General Eisenhower:

> This is the longest railway journey I've ever undertaken. It is 2 a.m. and I am just going to bed but am being called at 4.30 a.m. to take a very immediate and vital telephone call. My chances of getting back on Sunday or even Monday are very, very faint, as we've just had a sledge-hammer blow. It's hell here – impossible to get a moment to oneself, and ONE telephone, very inefficiently staffed, in a room four feet by three feet occupied by three people. Apart from the difficulties of working, the personal discomforts are considerable. No bath, except for a very poor shower – damned stuffy; and no privacy. 'Master' is 'on the ball' all the time.
>
> Today has been bloody. We said goodbye to a lot of good birds, embarked. Three of them at different times said 'I wish you were coming with us. We'll smuggle you in if you'll stowaway for a few hours.' I feel so gallant, staying behind! but that's just silliness.
>
> Tonight is the worst of the war from the 'decision' point of view.

> I was woken for work at 4.45 a.m., 5.15 a.m. and 6 a.m. The worst – or almost the worst – has happened. Anyway we're in the hell of a mess. But we'll get out all serene if we keep our heads and our tempers. I'm doing my utmost to get 'Master' to get back to London tonight. We are hopelessly out of touch here; and there are vital decisions to take which can only be properly taken if we get around a table and assemble all the relevant facts and arguments.
>
> How I've hated the last forty-eight hours.

The Prime Minister did return to London that Sunday night, and next morning the worst of General Ismay's fears – further postponement – was not realised. In probably the most lonely decision of his life General Eisenhower gave the 'go-ahead' for Tuesday, 6 June, when, the meteorologists said, there should be a short period of reasonable weather.

Monday, the 5th, was a long day for us all as it passed slowly by, in a pretence of work and burdened thought. That night in the dark hours there were few who did not hear the deep throbbing overhead which, for those of us who knew, meant that the airborne forces were on their way. At 6 a.m. for two hours the throbbing changed to a thunder, which shook the tall building in Lowndes Square, and told the world that the bombers were going in to support the invasion of occupied Europe. It was on; a thousand troop-carriers and gliders were landing behind the German defences in Normandy, and our Armies, supported by strong naval and air forces, were pouring out from their landing-craft and advancing up beaches of northern France between Cherbourg and Le Havre.

CHAPTER 10

Quartermaster at Quebec (1944)

COLONEL FRANK MCCARTHY HAD BEEN in England for D-Day. He had come to look for a house where the American Chiefs of Staff could stay when they arrived on 9 June to spend some days before going over to France to see General Eisenhower. He found one which he thought would be far enough from London to escape the intermittent 'nuisance' air raids. He brought me a box of chocolates from General Marshall, with a note. I was amused to read that ' . . . except at Quebec and Jerusalem you and I seem to move in widely separated orbits'. As, on 14 June, he and the other American Chiefs of Staff, with their British colleagues, were due to dine with the King at Buckingham Palace, I could not help but feel that he was right!

A new form of bombardment from the air began on 13 June, when the first of Germany's two 'secret weapons' the V.1 or flying bomb landed in the south of England. Frank McCarthy was not amused – though General Marshall was – when it blew in the windows of his 'safe' country house.

Lady Ismay and I shared our first experience of these uncanny, unmanned destroyers when two nights later several fell in the central London area. General Ismay had gone to France with the Prime Minister, Field Marshal Brooke and the American Chiefs of Staff. When he returned we described to him how beastly we had found these new weapons to be. He laughed:

'Nothing to them,' he said. That night we were almost glad that an increased number came over and that he would see for himself that we were not exaggerating their unpleasant nature.

'Just another lame duck making for its nest,' was all he said as we stood at the window and watched one cross the sky. Lady Ismay and I smiled at each other next day when he decided she had better go back to Gloucestershire and that we should sleep in the underground bedrooms at the War Cabinet Offices. The V.1 raids continued for over two months, on one occasion a total of two hundred falling on London in twenty-four hours.

On 26 July Mr Churchill announced that 2,754 had been launched to date and had caused 2,752 casualties – very nearly one for one.

There had been intensive bombing of the launching-sites before D-Day, their identification and location having become known through the sharp eyes of the Air Ministry examiners of air reconnaissance photographs, and this had reduced the weight of the attacks which the Germans had planned. Even so, their frequency, and the casualties which resulted, caused fear and distress in the areas where they fell, and there was some concern about the drop in morale among the men fighting in northern France who were anxious for the safety of their families. There was no public demand, however, that the invasion army and air forces should be diverted to attack the launching sites.

The V.1s were frightening, and they came at a time when we who lived and worked in the south of England were unprepared for further dangerous interruptions to our daily life. I can say, for myself, that I was always listening; in the street I wished the traffic would stop, among my friends that they would not talk, because there might be one approaching. When I did hear the jumping, throbbing, mechanical noise echo through the sky my heart missed a beat. Then its direction and position must be judged; if it sounded as if it was coming directly overhead, I waited, alert, to see if it passed over, or, if the engine cut out, ready to plunge for an inside wall or crouch under a desk or table away from the windows. A sickening moment of suspense, then 'CRRRRMP' and silence again.

One morning I was with 'Junior' McEwan and Betty Green in General Ismay's outer office. We heard a V.1 which sounded close, so we moved quickly to the inner access passage to stand upright and tense against the wall. It had just cut out when General Ismay came out of his room, saw us and said:

'What on earth are you all doing, standing there? *I* can't hear anything.'

'Of course you can't,' we replied, 'it's just cut out.' He moved swiftly and joined us.

We felt helpless because these 'lame ducks' were not affected by fog, or moon, or light, or darkness, and if they were shot down they could do a lot of damage where they fell. They were harmless when noisy, deadly when quiet. 'Isn't it the skunk', wrote General Wavell, 'which covers defeat and retreat by the emission of a cloud of stink?'

By the end of August, thanks to increasing accuracy on the part of the anti-aircraft defences, only fifteen per cent were getting through to London, and on 7 September the Government announced the danger as being over.

The very next day the first V.2 – the long-range rocket – fell on London. Attacks by these weapons went on for seven months until the Allies captured The Hague where most of their launching-sites were situated. The V.2 had no sound, no warning; it was like the hand of Fate; there was nothing anyone could do about it.

In August Mr Churchill took a step towards preserving Greece from the Communists. It had long been his concern that this was one country which should not fall to them. He decided that the British force which had been earmarked some time before should be put at instant readiness to move in when the Germans moved out. In October they did, and the British went into Athens, where there followed bitter fighting between them and the Greek Communist-controlled resistance groups. This intervention was looked upon with distaste by many people in the United Kingdom and United States, particularly by the American State Department and some sections of the press. Mr Churchill and Mr Eden went to Athens at Christmas 1944 and brought the contending parties round the same table, with representatives of America, Russia and France 'sitting-in'. A truce was called and a non-Communist Greek Government formed. Mr Churchill's foresight, and his courage in assuming responsibility, ensured that Greece did not become a Russian satellite nor Turkey a country isolated from Western Europe.

The other undertaking, the effects of which had caused Mr Churchill grave concern and against which he had fought so hard, began on 15 August. The landings in the south of France, weakened and delayed by the need to strengthen the *Overlord* assault, could no longer be regarded as being in support of the main battle. They proceeded peacefully, almost seemed an anticlimax, though on the credit side they allowed four French Army divisions under General Juin to take part in the liberation of their homeland. On 23 August Paris was freed by the French Resistance Army and two days later a French armoured division, led by General Leclerc, entered the city.

Mr Churchill watched the south of France landings and then returned to Italy where he stayed near General Alexander's headquarters and remained close to the Eighth Army operations in the Adriatic sector. President Roosevelt was in the Pacific area discussing a Philippines invasion with his commanders. Both returned in time to go to Quebec, where they had agreed to meet again at the Château Frontenac to agree on future strategy in north-west Europe and the Mediterranean and to concert plans for the overthrow of Japan. The President urged that the numbers for the Conference, which was due to start on 11 September, should be kept down to the size of the Teheran delegations. The British said that the fact that they would be absent from their headquarters for three weeks, whereas the Americans need only be away for one week and were in any case near enough to Washington to fill in when they needed to, made it imperative for them to have the usual full-size delegation. The telegrams surged to and fro across the Atlantic.

For this Conference I was to be in charge of the British administrative arrangements. Leaving the size to be settled between the contending parties, I went a week in advance, Mr Walters from Sir Edward Bridges' civilian side of the Office and the provisional lists coming with me. We flew from Shannon in Ireland in a flying boat. It was large and comfortable, and looked like a fat, white duck sitting on the water waiting to take off. I was given the 'honeymoon suite' in the tail, a big cabin with a full-sized bed. It showed how conditioned we had become to austerity that I had failed to unfold the blankets lying on top of it. I thought that because of textile shortages and economy they were only supposed to be three foot wide. After a freezing night, which led to a heavy cold in the head, I realised in the morning when they had become unfolded, that I had made a silly mistake.

From Baltimore we went straight on to Montreal where we were met by Dr Coleman, who, as at the First Quebec Conference, was in charge of the Canadian Co-ordination Committee. I felt rotten and could not smell the flowers which filled my hotel room. The next day was spent making up the train accommodation for the journey from Halifax to Quebec; for the third – and last – time the *Queen Mary* was carrying the delegation across the Atlantic. Dr Coleman drove us to Quebec where, to my surprise, we were made warmly welcome by Mr Neale, the manager, and the staff of the hotel; I had thought they might resent the taking over of the Château Frontenac at the height of the summer tourist season. They made it quite clear by their smiles that they did not.

Where the allocations of rooms, compilation of lists and trampings of corridors were concerned, being in charge was little different from being assistant to Commander Knott. The names on the lists, even when different, represented the same departments; the changes in the names on lists, as they were telegraphed in from London, were just other names, which meant more beds to find or less beds to worry about. The build-up of the British Delegation Telephone Directory, when the bedroom and office accommodation had been sorted out, had in it the same seeds of irritation because of the constant insertions and deletions. At their two or three desks not far from mine, the American administrative staff were suffering the same headaches. The big difference was in the fact that I was 'boss', that everyone asked me for my advice or approval before they did anything, and that the colonels and majors on the American side kept me supplied with bunches of flowers and even, after an amicable wrangle, let me have three good rooms which they had had their eye on for their own delegation.

Major Tony Bishop and two stenographers came up from our Joint Staff Mission in Washington to help Mr Walters and me. By mid-week we were all flat out from the moment we had finished our pleasant breakfast – with orange-juice – in the large, empty dining-room overlooking the old town of Quebec until we hit our beds at one in the morning. The size of both the delegations had by now reached the usual proportions – roughly two hundred and fifty people on each. Even though we knew the hotel and the hotel employees knew us and our requirements; even though Dr Coleman and his two excellent assistants, Mr Glenn McPherson and Mr Delaute, and the representatives from the Canadian Mounted Police and the Canadian railroad, had been at the First Quebec Conference and knew the form; even so, we were all stretched until the last moment. The evening before the *Queen Mary* was due and Mr Walters going to Halifax to meet her, we were finishing off the room and office lists, Dr Coleman punching the holes in the paper, Mr McPherson pushing through the tags to hold them together, and the rest of us assembling, sorting and making them up. I was determined that each person, as he set foot on Canadian soil, would be handed a card bearing his office and room number, his official passes and telephone directory attached to it. I thought that, by giving him his room number on a separate card, he could not judge whether or not he was sharing a room.

Mr Walters left, carrying two hundred or more of the individual 'tour guides'. In the peace of the interim wait Tony Bishop and I spent three and a half hours walking round the vast hotel looking at each bedroom to see whether our allocations fitted in with the size of the room and the rank of the occupant, whether there were twin beds or double beds in rooms destined to be shared. We found two which we had to change: the first, into which we had put a brigadier alone, was an inside box with no basin or cupboard; the other, which we had given to two Royal Marine orderlies, turned out to be one of the finest and most luxurious rooms on the upper floor of the hotel.

Dr Coleman took me and Colonel Chaffee of the American administration to pay a courtesy call on the Prime Minister and the Governor of Quebec Province. Walking into the Governor's office was like walking into an eighteenth-century French library; it was quiet, it was elegant, and the only pen on the desk was a long white quill.

The weather was glorious with sunshine and blue skies, a good augury for the Second Quebec Conference. The British trains came in on Monday, and from them two of my helpers – Major Tom Buckley of the Royal Marines with his group of guards and orderlies, who had been in charge of the delegation on board the *Queen Mary*; and Winnie Spearing, one of my three in the Special Information Centre. I was so glad to see her; we knew each other's methods of work and she was well used to my speedy and elastic ways, my, at times, maddening attention to detail. Of the three in my office, she was probably the one who understood best my manner of working; Laura Cooper was quick and intelligent, could be moody, but never minded, in fact enjoyed, having suddenly to work all through a night. She liked excitement and unusual happenings and adapted herself to them with verve and enthusiasm. Joan Umney-Gray, of the three, was the most serious, the most gentle and the most feminine. She was a perfect type of private secretary, tidy in her thoughts and in her work, and she enjoyed the times she was taken away from files and used for regular clerk-stenographer work. Laura and I loved the files in the Special Information Centre; each one was an individual to us. Winnie and Joan liked them but would not miss them when war ended and they were packed away for the future. Towards each other we were loyal, understanding and affectionate.

Tom Buckley said that the journey across had been uneventful and pleasant, but there had been trouble on the special train from London because naval commanders had had third-class accommodation and army lieutenant-colonels had been in first-class. There had also been complaints because it had seemed high-handed of the Administrative Office to lay down a scale of tipping for all ranks on board the ship. Dear, dear, I thought, I wonder what that brigadier would have said when he saw his original room in the Château Frontenac.

General Ismay was not happy when he arrived. Mr Churchill had not been at all well and there had been serious disagreements between him and his three Chiefs of Staff, which had centred round his obsession with the situation in north Italy and south-east Europe and his disinterest in British naval participation with the Americans in the Pacific.

A tremendous reception at Halifax had added to the Prime Minister's fatigue, though he had not shown any sign of it. As soon as the *Queen Mary* had come into harbour, she had been greeted by ships dressed overall, sirens in full voice, fire-boats playing their hoses, and, on the quay, hundreds of red-coated Canadian Mounties and dense crowds all around, on roof tops, everywhere they could find a vantage point. When he had come ashore, Mr Churchill had walked straight up to the crowd, who were being kept back from the two special trains, and had given the 'V' sign. He had then called them around his observation car at the back of the train, and after a short speech, had led community singing, beating time with his cigar as he sat on the steps of his coach. As the train left, the crowd spontaneously broke into the National Anthem; it had been an impressive and moving moment as the train drew away from the sound of 'God Save the King'. As before, along the whole route to Quebec there were groups waving, crowds at the different stations and the many motor-cars which had been driven from outlying parts of the country to be there when Winston passed by.

Lord Moran had taken the precaution of bringing a specialist in antibiotics, Brigadier Whitby, and a nurse. Such was Mr Churchill's resilience, however, that after a short period of private anxiety among those close to him, he recovered from the threatened pneumonia and once more confounded his doctors.

But not before there had been a crisis in the British inner circles. The Chiefs of Staff told General Ismay that if, as it seemed to them, the Prime Minister had lost confidence in them as a committee, they would proffer their resignations. General Ismay replied that this was not at all a good idea, that at this stage of the war it would destroy public confidence and would be a fatal step. A better way, he said, was for him to resign; he was not a public figure, but the effect on the Prime Minister might help to improve the strained relationships. He sent in his letter of resignation. It gave him a lot of distress to do so and his action was typical of his unselfish and honourable sense of duty. Mr Churchill was horrified and left him in no doubt as to his feelings, telling him in so many words 'not to write such rubbish again'. The clouds cleared away, the sun shone again in a blue sky and by the end of the week the atmosphere was friendly within and between the two delegations.

At the first Plenary Meeting on Wednesday, General Ismay told me he had been shocked by President Roosevelt's appearance, that he seemed to have 'shrunk in size', and that the beloved Field Marshal Dill had looked frail, 'almost at the end of his tether'.

I was invited by John Martin to dine at the Citadel, where President and Mrs Roosevelt, Mr and Mrs Churchill and Mary were staying, and then to see the film *Woodrow Wilson* which the President had brought from Washington. There was rather an awkward pause while Mr Roosevelt, sitting in the front row with an empty chair beside him, waited for Mr Churchill. Earlier in the evening, following a time-honoured custom, the President had gone into the drawing-room to mix the martini cocktails and had also waited for the Prime Minister. He had not appeared there or at the film; instead, he had asked General Marshall to come and see him and they were both poring over maps of the Continent and discussing the operations which were going on there. Jolly good for him, I thought, pays back Roosevelt for playing that 'two's company, three's none' game at Teheran.

On Sunday the Churchills left with the Roosevelts to stay at Hyde Park, and the delegations began to disperse. I saw General Marshall for tea one afternoon; he was worried and unhappy about the state of health of his friend Field Marshal Dill. Two months later Dill died.

The last two days were filled with the usual rush of departure and, this time, farewell to our Canadian hosts. The Prime Minister and his party were returning to England in the *Queen Mary* which would sail from New York on Wednesday, 20 September, with her usual load of troops. A special train would fetch those members of the delegation who were returning by sea and take them from Quebec to New York. Some decided to make their way independently, among them General Ismay, 'Junior' McEwan and I. With the kindness and generosity which is part of the American character, Mr Lew Douglas had invited us to be his guests for two nights at the Barclay Hotel. He had not been present at Quebec and was glad to be able to talk with General Ismay; they were friends who understood and trusted each other. We went with him and his witty and beautiful wife Peggy to see the musical *Oklahoma*, and they took us down to the dock late at night to join the stream of GIs as they climbed aboard the huge ship which would take them to battle in Europe.

The Second Quebec Conference established Britain's right to share in the war against Japan, an enemy which held captive some 160,000 British prisoners and internees. It also yielded some ground to Alexander's Italian campaign. If the Germans evacuated from Italy the Allies should be free to make an amphibious attack across the Adriatic to seize the Istrian peninsula and aim for Vienna. If this plan became feasible, landing-craft due to go to South-East Asia should remain in the Mediterranean. It emerged during the meetings that the Americans were willing to accept this option. It was therefore agreed that no major units would be withdrawn from Italy until the outcome of Alexander's offensive north of Rome was known and that the landing-craft would remain in the Mediterranean until 15 October when a decision must be reached as to whether they should be used for the Adriatic or for an assault on Rangoon.

The decision was made. On 10 October the Prime Minister reported to the President that because of heavy pressure in northern Europe the British forces needed for the amphibious attack on Rangoon must remain in Europe. He asked that two or three American divisions should be sent to the Fifth Army in Italy to strengthen Alexander's forward advance. But Roosevelt replied that by committing American divisions to the 'indecisive winter campaign' in Italy operations in northern Europe would suffer and it was here that fresh forces were badly needed.

By mid-November the armies in Italy had cleared the road to Florence and from then on no major offensives were possible until the spring.

CHAPTER 11

Spoils of war (1944)

WITHIN A WEEK OF OUR RETURN I was told to prepare for a delegation of forty people to accompany Mr Churchill to Moscow. He wished to discuss with the Russians the future of Poland and their intentions in the war against Japan. President Roosevelt was involved in a Presidential election in November and could not come; he would be represented by his Ambassador, Mr Averell Harriman, and in military matters by Major-General 'Russ' Deane. The British party would include Mr Anthony Eden, the Foreign Secretary, Field Marshal Sir Alan Brooke – promoted since 1 January – General Ismay and Colonel Jacob.

On Thursday night, 5 October, in two Liberator aircraft, twenty of us – clerical staff, cipherers – took off and for the first time since Dunkirk flew free over France. In eight hours we were looking down on sunny Malta and in another five we were swarming across the tarmac at Heliopolis, dirty, tired and dishevelled in our winter clothes.

The Commander of the Air Force station, Air Commodore Whitney Straight, looked morose when he saw us, more so when we told him one of the girls was unwell and would have to remain in Cairo.

'No one to leave the airfield!' he ordered.

'I must,' I said, 'I have business to do.' He was about to repeat the order when through the glass entrance doors behind him I saw a car slide to a standstill. General Paget, Commander-in-Chief Middle East, had not forgotten me. A salute, a click of the heels, and his military aide swept me out of the building. I felt mean leaving the rest of my party behind, but the small triumph gave sweet support to my civilian status. Away from the office and responsible for an aspect of its work, I was subject to no authority other than that of good manners and mutual respect, and I was sometimes conscious of a hearty dislike in the male breast for my type of woman. But in the bright eye of friendship General Paget made no distinction between the ranks of those above and those below; he had no patience for bureaucracy but he was just a little bit nicer to a junior than he was to a senior bureaucrat.

Over tea in a silver teapot, served with dexterous dignity by tall young orderlies, we went through the lists and discussed arrangements for meeting and accommodating Field Marshal Brooke and his military staff. By now blown out like a balloon with self-importance, I was escorted by my host to the door, handed into his car by his aide and driven off at arrogant speed to the office of Lord Moyne, the Minister of State. Lord Moyne was vague about Mr Eden's impending visit and had lost the telegram informing him of it. We hunted for it, he on the floor and I under the cushions on the chairs. I had just arranged with him who would stay and who dine when a signal came in from the Foreign Office repeating what I had just told him of the arrivals. I felt quite put out; my instructions had been to go secretly to Cairo and tell all. Why else would I have flouted Air Commodore Straight?

A quarter of an hour later I was with Mr Terence Shone, Chargé d'Affaires at the British Embassy, who wanted to know the order of battle for the reception of the VIPs. I had a message from the Deputy Air Officer Commanding, Air Vice-Marshal Toomer, that he wished to see me; he had insufficient information about the make-up and the flight plan of the Prime Minister's party. I gave him the list of aircraft loads and arrival dates, for which he was most grateful. It was a perfect example of efficiency being muffled by security. We had an Air Transport Command officer, Wing-Commander Harpham, with us and I could not see why he could not have been detailed to look after the air side.

After dinner under the stars at L'Auberge on the Mena Road with two friends on General Paget's staff, I was back at Heliopolis ready for take-off at 11 p.m. We were to fly to Teheran for a two-hour re-fuelling stop and then go on to Moscow.

At dawn we were high over the last ridge of mountains before Teheran; fifteen thousand feet and no oxygen mask, fatigue and too many cigarettes, gave me some frightening moments of breathless suffocation.

We landed at Mehrabad, the Royal Air Force base outside the city. Two airmen advancing towards our aircraft stood rooted as a string of girls stepped out into the fresh colour of a mountain morning. From the huts other figures emerged, rubbed their eyes and stood staring. The two strings met; after a moment's silence the words tumbled out: 'How long are you here for?' 'Where do you come from?' 'Where are you going?'

'To Moscow,' we said, 'in about two hours.'

By mid-morning we were still exchanging social chat in the officers' mess. Wing-Commander Harpham hurried through one door and was about to go out of the other when I asked him what was going on.

'It seems to me,' he said, 'that we shall have to stay. There is no fuel here yet, there are no maps and we have to wait for Russian permission to fly on to Moscow.'

'Oh,' I said, wondering.

'We expected to get maps in Cairo but they hadn't got any.'

'Oh,' I said. 'OK, then, we must have baths and rooms to change in.'

'There is one bathroom and you can use our sleeping quarters.' The Commanding Officer of the airfield was a man of decision.

Our suitcases were unloaded and my companions disappeared. I clutched at a private straw. I'll wait, I thought, and then I'll ring up my old friend the Ambassador, Sir Reader Bullard and perhaps he'll invite me to have a bath at the Embassy.

As the girls came out, clean, in cool clothes, their faces powdered, the morale of the station soared and soon they were being dated up for the afternoon by as many officers as could think of an excuse for getting the time off.

We had a meeting – the Air Attaché who had come out from Teheran, Wing-Commander Harpham, the Commanding Officer and I. Russian permission was expected, but a more important problem lay in the fact that at the moment they had only found one map of the route. If no others could be found – a search was being made in various mission headquarters in Teheran – the two Liberators must fly 'in formation' the leading one using the map. I offered a very small pocket atlas of the world which I always carried with me. Luckily, just then, the searchers turned up with a few maps which had been torn from various mission walls in Teheran, and the meeting broke up. I kept my thoughts to myself; Wing-Commander Harpham was far too nice a person to be held responsible; I just wondered why Air Transport Command, so faithful on most occasions, had slipped up on this one.

Beds for the night had been arranged for at a local British Military Hospital. I was free to put my call through to the Embassy. Sir Reader sent his car for me, took one look at me and said:

'A bath awaits you.' So began the most perfect half-day of my war.

In the room in which Mr Churchill had slept nearly a year ago I found towels, soap, and a maid who took my travelling clothes and returned them later, cleaned and pressed.

In the dining-room the Ambassador showed me the silver plaque which marked the historic dinner-party. After lunch, he found a deck-chair, some cushions and a volume of H. G. Wells, put them and me in the sun in the garden and left us. It was warm, the garden one of the most beautiful in the world; instead of the russet and yellow which I remembered from before, the trees were still green and the roses blooming. I slept and then strolled in the streets. A glass of sherry, a good dinner and civilised talk brought it to an end. I could not find the right words to thank Sir Reader Bullard but I believe he understood that for me it had been a complete holiday.

At Mehrabad I found a dance in full swing. Having promised the matron that we would report at the hospital by eleven, I swept up the party and we piled noisily into cars. As we entered the silent hall, I counted heads, watched by a neat and disapproving night nurse; Wendy Wallace was missing; Betty Green said she thought she had gone into Teheran with an army officer. She turned up half an hour later and we tiptoed to our beds, which were clean, hard and white. Some of us had a room to ourselves, others doubled up, and we all had a wonderful night's sleep. My face was turned towards a huge window through which I could see a thousand stars.

We came back to reality next morning, had breakfast and, with two Russians sitting beside our pilots, were soon airborne and heading towards Stalingrad. We flew low over the gutted ruin, its walls standing stark, straight and dead: then on, skidding in and out of low grey clouds, over clearly seen tank traps, bomb craters, criss-cross trenches and war debris, twisting and turning at about six hundred feet through rotten weather. At 4 p.m. our pilot came through and told us we would be there in half an hour. He had scarcely reached his cockpit, leaving us wondering what the big city on our left could be, when suddenly we banked steeply and landed at Moscow.

Two officers from the British Military Mission and one from the Embassy met us with obvious pleasure. New faces were always welcome. At the Savoy Hotel there followed a trying hour with a stupid woman 'Intourist' administrator who would not leave it to me to decide on room allocations but kept asking details of each person's rank: 'Should she have a bathroom? What is her grade?'

We were a day late. Within twenty-four hours the main party would arrive and expect to slip comfortably into gear. I knew I would have to make changes in the room lists which the Embassy had prepared; they had put all officers in the National Hotel and the clerical staffs in the Savoy. General Ismay liked to be under the same roof as his stenographers; he had strong feelings on the subject, so I decided to put the military into the National and the Foreign Office people into the Savoy. It was unfortunate that I did not inspect both hotels; the National was infinitely the better one.

I called on Sir Archibald Clark Kerr, the Ambassador, who would be host to Mr Eden, and gave him the good news that we had brought him three cases of whisky. Wines, spirits and other entertaining needs were in short supply in war-torn Moscow; indirectly we repaid the hospitality we received because, during any Heads of State or Foreign Secretaries' meetings, the Russians filled the 'foreign diplomats' special shop' with national delicacies like caviar, vodka and champagne. The supplies abruptly stopped when the meetings ended.

Sir Archibald's study had books piled one on top of the other from floor to ceiling. He was an inveterate reader but could give me no satisfactory answer when I asked him what he did if he wanted a book from the bottom.

At 8.30 next morning a Mission truck came to the hotel and fetched us, our typewriters, cases of stationery and other working paraphernalia. Cleaners were sweeping the hall in the British Embassy. A startled and angry Counsellor, Mr Moore Crosthwaite, rushed out in his dressing-gown, waved his arms and cried:

'You are much too early; you can't possibly arrive before ten!' I sympathised with his feelings; we did look rather a crowd; but we had to get in. After some more expostulation, we reached a compromise: if we crept in along the wall to the right and took our things into the allotted offices, he would pretend we were not there.

Two hours later, with Captain Bolton, the Ambassador's private secretary, and Mr Yirshov, a good-looking young Russian interpreter and liaison officer, I drove for sixty minutes to Mr Molotov's summer villa on the outskirts of Moscow where Mr Churchill was to stay. I felt worried because I knew he would not at all like being so far away. However, it was too late to say anything. We rushed through the Russian Foreign Minister's luxurious villa with its many reception rooms and its bathrooms as big as bedrooms. Every detail had been taken care of, even to a new toothbrush, toothpaste and a bottle of eau-de-Cologne in each bathroom. Russian eau-de-Cologne has a musky perfume all its own; by the end of the war I could smell a Russian a mile away.

Mr Churchill arrived, suddenly and unexpectedly early; we held our thumbs and prayed. He came into the hall, followed by Mr Molotov, said 'Hello' to Marion Holmes, one of his stenographers who had flown out with us, and asked:

'Where is my red box?'

'Your luggage is not here yet,' said his private secretary John Martin, firmly.

'Never mind; I will have a bath, put on my vest and get into bed,' and the great man climbed the stairs.

Five minutes later a distracted Inspector Hughes, his detective, rushed down the stairs.

'The Prime Minister,' he said, 'doesn't know which is the hot tap and the bath is filling with cold water!' He had turned on a tap marked with sticking-plaster 'Hot', had not, because it ran cold at first, believed what it said, had turned it off, turned on the other, and lost confidence.

Back at the Embassy, I found General Ismay and, now a General, Jacob, smiling and content, who said Field Marshal Brooke and his staff were comfortably settled in at the National.

Thank goodness for that, I thought. Rumbles of dismay and discontent were coming in from the Foreign Office party at the Savoy and I was being told that they were saying: 'Joan Bright looks after her own people all right; she couldn't care less about us.' Empty of food but full of remorse, I worked late into the evening rearranging their accommodation from the Savoy to the National, with the help of a charming and understanding 'Intourist' lady administrator called Nina Alexandrovna; she was sympathetic, efficient and free from consciousness of rank.

At eight o'clock, still without food, Brian Boyle, Sir Alan Brooke's Military Assistant, took me to a large cocktail party at the British Military Mission.

'Now,' said this most conscientious of workers, 'I can't stay more than twenty minutes. "Brookie" is waiting for me at the hotel.'

'OK by me,' said I.

Three hours later, cross-eyed, I tackled a merry officer.

'Shouldn't we go?'

Laughing gaily, Brian said: 'Yes, perhaps we should.'

The cocktails we had drunk had seemed so harmless, had slipped down so easily. But vodka is an insidious drink – 'the only one which goes to the middle and then round the waist,' said Sir Archibald Clark Kerr. We felt witty, important and light-hearted; even Brian was unworried when we got back to the hotel and found everyone had gone to bed.

Walking with General Jacob to the Embassy next morning we crossed Red Square, its vast size edged on one side by the Kremlin walls which extended their Tartar design down its length and disappeared round a bend to the River Moskva. The golden balls on top of the many towers were camouflaged and Lenin's tomb shut and empty. Ahead of us St Basil's Cathedral looked as though it had huge turnips squatting down hard on its body. The people were drab, the men slightly more colourful in uniforms of green, blue or grey. Traffic was lunatic; cars, trams and buses shot about, tantalised to a frenzy, playing a devilish game with traffic lights which showed first red, then yellow then . . . not green but red again; revving engines subsided, pedestrians took heart and began to cross: the lights turned green and the pushing eager traffic scattered them like chickens. Sleek, black Zis cars carrying officials ignored the game, they just drove straight through; except when their gasoline reached water-level and they had to stop. On one government building painters were replacing the green camouflage with white paint picked out in yellow. Gay, I thought, and confident.

Throughout the ten days of the Conference the Foreign Office was extremely busy, political questions filling the agenda. There were only two military meetings, at which there was a general exchange of information in a pleasant and friendly atmosphere and a confirmation of Russia's intentions to fight Japan.

This meant that my time was filled with requests for culture and sightseeing, and efforts to meet them. With the Prime Minister near, General Ismay was never free, nor General Jacob, but for Field Marshal Sir Alan Brooke, Brian Boyle and two Brigadiers from the War Office, Calthorpe and Peake, the days were long and needed organising. With help from the Embassy Chancery and an obvious loosening of social red tape on the part of the Russians, who seemed intent on spreading a carpet of goodwill, it was possible to arrange for visits to hospitals, museums, concerts and opera. In the Park of Culture we saw rows of captured German war material; on the Lenin Heights we stood where Napoleon had stood, and looked down on the shabby, sad city. I put in demands for tickets for opera and ballet; if I asked for double I usually got the number I wanted. They were not normally easy to come by – the Embassy and Mission staffs seldom get seats – so I issued warm invitations to some of them – many were kind and hospitable to us – to attend a performance of *Swan Lake* scheduled for the next Sunday night.

On Wednesday Marshal Stalin dined at the British Embassy, a break in precedent which caused many a raised diplomatic eyebrow, and some of us were invited to a reception afterwards. He and Mr Churchill came in from the dining-room around mid-night and Marshal Stalin raised his glass 'to the assembled company'. With the Ambassador, he went round shaking hands – I was asked if I would like to, but I said no; somehow I did not want to. I had been talking to two Russians who spoke Spanish and surprised me by their readiness to discuss political differences between our two countries. If Marshal Stalin had spoken Spanish I would have been pleased to meet him and include him in the conversation.

Next night, at the Bolshoi Theatre, a music-loving Chief of the Imperial General Staff and a tone-deaf General Ismay settled into a box to see and hear a spectacular and rousing *Prince Igor*. Behind them sat the two brigadiers and General Jacob. I gave two stalls to Brooke's sergeant clerks. Within minutes they were back saying they had been refused entrance because of their rank; only officers or wounded enlisted men with medals for gallantry were allowed in those seats. We did a change-round; the brigadiers went to the stalls and the sergeant clerks into the box. General Ismay did his best but failed to keep awake. Next morning at breakfast Field Marshal Brooke said in a tone of wonder:

'"Pug" doesn't like music, does he?' I was loyal; I said,

'Oh, yes, he loves it; he was just terribly tired.'

Sir Alan Brooke was enjoying himself; he did not seem in the least put out to be sitting on the sidelines with no work to do, but threw himself with zest into anything that Moscow had to offer. The day started when we all sat together in the breakfast-room. As he ate toast with caviar and drank Russian tea laced with vodka, he teased and talked and laughed. After a morning or two of silent surprise we realised that instead of a formidable and distant figure we had with us a delightful, amusing and easy companion who treated us with equal and courteous attention, from the brigadiers down to me and the other girls. He was a handsome man, strongly built, with broad slightly bowed shoulders, black eyes and hair, not very tall. He thought and spoke with lightning speed, reaching conclusions which darted into words and caught the listener unprepared. The mental agility revealed his French upbringing and education, and the rapid speech his perfect command of the French language. An abrupt manner and ready impatience misled people who did not know him well; if they had they would have appreciated that both characteristics belonged to a quick and concentrated thinker; if they had they would have known that he was kindly to subordinates. Most contradictory of all to these characteristics was his love of bird-watching and fishing – two recreations demanding the greatest patience. Brooke sprang from a European culture, an uncompromising and outspoken man who did not know the meaning of the verb 'to flatter'; these qualities were not the most likely to smooth over the disagreements in the counsels of the Combined Chiefs of Staff, and he lacked the light touch and detachment of his friend and colleague, Sir Charles Portal, the Chief of the Air Staff.

To me, at this Conference, he became a friend. I saw him as a rock with sharp corners which hid a mature and deeply loving nature. He adored his own family and would have been happy to retire to his home, look after his garden and his bird books and be with the wife to whom he wrote his diary every night.

We had heard a lot all week about the Command Performance but it was not until Saturday that we knew for certain it would take place that night. Our hosts must have taken trouble over the seating arrangements, because the officers of the delegation were placed in pairs alongside Russians of equal rank – good planning by a perplexing people whom you expect to be ignorant and inefficient and are constantly surprised to find meticulous and experienced.

The Bolshoi Theatre was packed. Strolling about the big foyer during the interval, in the traditional manner of two rings moving in opposite directions, I looked at the passing faces and saw them, not as aliens but as persons in clean shirts, dark suits and black satin dresses doing their best to imitate what they considered the standards of the West. The exiled 'London' Polish Government representatives and the 'Lublin' Russian-sponsored Warsaw Government representatives were there, in separate groups; the future of the former was being fought for with scant success by Mr Churchill, Mr Harriman and Mr Eden; the latter looked tough and successful – as well they might for, within the next three months, they were recognised by the Russians as the Provisional Government of Poland.

Though during the first half of the programme many eyes had turned hopefully towards the presidential box, there was no Mr Churchill and no Marshal Stalin during the delicate first act of *Giselle*, danced by Lepeshinskaya. I looked back again, and saw in the dim light Mr Churchill take his seat. The lights went up and everyone saw him. There was thunderous and prolonged applause as he stood there alone; when he went through the curtains behind him and returned with Marshal Stalin the roof lifted. For many people in the audience it was the first time they had seen their leader.

Russian practice demanded that, during the interval, the VVIPs and the VIPs should have a sit-down dinner. Kathie Harriman, who was there, told me that at one of the many toasts to 'Marshal Stalin, the great leader', Molotov said *sotto voce*:

'We're tired of that one; think up another.'

By Sunday morning my list for the *Swan Lake* ballet that evening had reached sixty, and my tickets thirty. The Chancery messenger shrugged his shoulders hopelessly, but I was desperate. I sent him down to the theatre again, this time with a message that 'Field Marshal Sir Alan Brooke wanted to take a party and was a member of the Order of Suvarov'. By 5 p.m. I had fifty-four tickets, and the show was due to start at six. However, some people did not come, or got tickets from elsewhere, because somehow or other the worry and confusion ended by the time the curtain rose. Semyonova was dancing; in the intervals diplomatic experts resident in Moscow argued her merits against those of Ulanova and Lepeshinskaya.

Mr Averell Harriman and Kathie invited some of us to a party afterwards at Spaso House – the American Embassy – to which Semyonova came. She was disappointing in ordinary clothes, with no make-up; her body looked unyielding in its ill-fitting dress; but she was strikingly unselfconscious, without conceit or affectation, and perfectly at ease in a room full of foreigners.

Since we had crossed together in the *Queen Mary* from Halifax in 1943, I had seen Kathie Harriman when she came to London and had also met her father. They were welcome people in England where his quiet and sage advice was heeded at the top levels. He had great kindness, and an unassuming manner which concealed a very powerful, tough and dedicated advocate. A rich man, he wore his wealth carelessly but with the grace of good breeding and an awareness of its responsibilities. He was meticulous as to detail, patient in negotiation, hard-headed in argument and ruthless in pushing through any policy of his Government with which he was in agreement. He did not seem passionate in his attachment to other people but he was loyal and steadfast in friendship; between him and General Ismay there was mutual affection and regard, each respecting the other's ability to tackle and straighten out twists in the cord which joined their two countries. Because Kathie and I liked each other, he accepted me into his circle of friends.

The next day, Monday, suddenly, the Embassy received word that the Russians wished members of the delegation to visit the Kremlin. Such an invitation had never been extended to either the diplomatic or the military mission; in the confusion, we were able to take some of their members with us. We went up the steep stairs to the low, small, richly-painted rooms of Ivan the Terrible, then down to the big reception rooms of the palace of the Tsars, ornately elegant with crystal and gilt, and ended in the huge chamber reserved for meetings of the Supreme Soviet; this was filled with ordinary wooden school desks which looked oddly out of place in their white and gold surroundings. On the way out of the red-walled city in miniature, our guides pointed to the door and windows of Stalin's apartment.

The open cordiality which the Russians had shown us since the start of the Conference led me to remark to Moore Crosthwaite that I would not be surprised if they sent us away with some pretty nice presents.

'I would,' he said. 'They've done you jolly well as it is; you needn't expect anything more.'

As Thursday, the day of departure, drew near, there were few of us who did not feel sad. We had been warmly welcomed and entertained, and we knew that, when we had gone, life in Moscow would resume its normal pattern – enclosed, secretive and elusive. There were two people I was especially sorry to say goodbye to: dark, calm, beautiful Nina Alexandrovna, whom I had talked with many times at her 'Intourist' desk in the National Hotel; it was doubtful I would ever see her again. And Major Arthur Cox from the Military Mission, an untroubled, helpful Reserve officer who understood and loved the Russians, spoke their language and sang their songs. He had been indefatigable in looking after the junior members of the delegation, contributing enormously to our enjoyment and to the ease with which we had slipped into our new life. One of his qualities was the ability to sum up a situation and take action without waiting for sanction – a gift to warm the heart of any conference administrative officer.

At ten o'clock on the morning of 19 October we were back at the airfield, waiting for a surprise farewell appearance from Marshal Stalin. He had made a sudden decision to be there at take-off; as he rarely went to bed before 4 a.m. or rose before 1 p.m. it must have been quite an effort. He was smiling and joking as he climbed in to look over the Prime Minister's aircraft. I thought what a lark it would be if we closed the doors and took this plum home to England.

Just before Marshal Stalin arrived, a truck loaded with crates covered in khaki canvas had been driven onto the tarmac. Some Russian officials approached it and, pointing to its contents, made it clear that these must go with us. They were quickly transferred into the two Liberators and a list written in Russian pushed into my hand.

'You see?' I said to Moore Crosthwaite. 'What did I tell you? Presents for us!'

The flight to Cairo included a stop in the Crimea where the Red Navy had invited the Prime Minister and officers of the delegation to an official lunch. We – the clerical staffs and 'Junior' McEwan – landed at Sarabuz airfield just as the top layer was being collected into motor cars and jeeps. I rushed up to the one containing Brian Boyle and Brigadier Peake.

'What do you suppose we are going to do?' I asked.

'Goodness knows!' they said airily. 'We are being given lunch at Simferopol.' I looked around; not a soul left except for our small group. A Russian admiral approached; eying him steadily, I said in English: 'What are you going to do with us?' He smiled kindly. A Royal Air Force interpreter joined us and told me we were expected to go and have a sleep.

'Bed!' I looked at him in amazement. 'On our one and only afternoon in the Crimea!'

I joined the others in a waiting-room in one of the huts, and we sat rather dispirited and near tears. Ten minutes later the door opened and the Admiral's black eyes made signs that we should follow him. We did – into a room where on a trestle table stood bottle upon bottle of wine, vodka, champagne, and plate upon plate of chicken, salmon and caviar. Most of us warily began with wine, but Sheila Minto, one of Churchill's staff, chose vodka and stuck to it for the rest of what was to be a long afternoon. One or two officers appeared, led by a diminutive colonel-general covered with broad ribbons from which hung stars of Lenin, of Russia, of Suvarov, of Stalingrad. We settled down to the food and the drink, gesturing, nodding and smiling, the lack of a common tongue being filled by toast after toast. At 5 p.m. the Admiral said he would like all the girls to follow him. We did, nervously signalling to the Air Force interpreter to come too, but the Admiral waved him away. We were taken into a dining-room, lit by candles, placed at a narrow table and given lunch. The Crimean wine I had been drinking became increasingly sickly and heavy. Sheila was thriving on her eighth vodka, showing no effects except in her eyes, which were bright and lively. I changed to vodka.

Presently the Colonel-General came in arguing with the interpreter. He spoke to the Admiral. The Admiral looked at me and replied. The Colonel-General got more insistent. The interpreter spoke.

'I want this type to come out and look at the flare-path for tonight's take-off, but he won't unless he can bring Miss Green with him.' Making him promise that he would never leave her side, we let her go. Half an hour later they were back, the Colonel-General looking sulky.

By now we felt stuffed and loaded and in need of exercise. '*Tanz!*' we said. '*Tanz! Tanz!*' Chattering volubly, they took us in jeeps to an enormous hall with a cement floor, full of potholes and shell-craters.

To the loud and discordant music of a military band, scores of handsome Red Navy officers and men were whirling around with girls in uniform. Our arrival caused quite a sensation and in no time at all we were among them, our feet lifted in sublime rhythm off the ground. When I danced with the Colonel-General – Bartonovsky was his name – Wendy Wallace said it looked as though I was stuck in a hole in the ground with him revolving round me like a top.

Feeling much better, we returned to the airfield just before the Prime Minister. I was carrying a bunch of flowers which the Admiral had given me. I was matched by Elizabeth Layton, the stenographer Mr Churchill had taken to lunch in case he wanted to dictate; when he had toasted 'the one lady with us and the many we brought along', one of the Russian hosts had seized a bunch of flowers from a vase on the table and dumped it on to her knees.

We left at 2 a.m. and spent the next day and night in Cairo at the Mena House Hotel. It was pleasant to be able to bathe in the pool and catch up on sleep; and pleasant also to go next day to Naples instead of straight home. Mr Churchill's plans were subject to changes and there being so few of us meant we could enjoy them too.

Our arrival at short notice was dealt with efficiently by the Supreme Commander General Wilson's staff; we were not only housed comfortably at Caserta but invited to a party at the officers' mess. Known as 'The Kennels', it was filled with American and British officers – both male and female – who regarded us with a mixture of curiosity and envy. It was nice to see the tall, familiar figure of General Beaumont-Nesbitt who was now Allied Liaison Officer to all foreign contingents under British and American command.

The weather ahead was bad, so it was decided next morning to send what Wavell called the CUBs (Completely Unimportant Blokes) ahead as guinea-pigs; if conditions were such that it meant Churchill's aircraft would have to fly higher than the eight thousand feet which medical opinion considered the highest he could go with his bronchial condition we would signal back 'don't come'. We flew low, uncomfortably near to the sea, but by the time we reached southern France the weather had cleared sufficiently for the report to be favourable. The Prime Minister's flight passed us over France, its fighter escort zooming round us in salutation. We landed straight at Northolt, making no turn, and had such a good run-in that his aircraft, which had just landed, had to stand by until we were down.

The Customs officer advanced and asked me the usual question as to what we had to declare.

I handed him the Russian list.

'As far as I can make out,' I said, 'we have two hundred bottles of Crimean champagne, thirty bottles of vodka and six tins of caviar. It's not our fault we've got it; it is a gift from our Russian allies to the Prime Minister and Foreign Secretary which they couldn't refuse.'

He gasped, and let us go.

A room was made ready in the War Cabinet Offices and into it went the khaki crates. Commander Thompson for the Prime Minister, Mr Millard for the Foreign Secretary, Colonel Boyle for the Chief of the Imperial General Staff, met me there and we made a careful distribution. A tin of caviar each to the four principals, and two tins to be divided into fair shares among the officers and private secretaries; so many bottles of vodka to each Private Office as would cover the principals and their staffs; by giving twenty bottles of champagne each to Mr Churchill and Eden and twelve each to Brooke and Ismay, we were able to be generous to all ranks with the remaining one hundred and thirty-six.

Typically, General Ismay gave each of us some caviar from his tin, and this, with some champagne, I took home and shared with my mother and some friends before lunch on Sunday. I went to see my sister Nancy in Bristol and Mr Shaw near Bath, and to each I gave a bottle of champagne. I compared notes with others when I got back to the office and they all agreed with me that they had had a lovely time treating their friends and relations and basking in their pleasure and gratitude.

On Saturday, 4 November, I was sitting quietly at my desk when the telephone rang.

'Do you recall,' said Wing-Commander Harpham, 'at Moscow Airport . . . some canvas cases . . .?'

My blood ran cold. 'Of course,' I said on the defensive.

'I'd be grateful to know where they are,' the voice went on relentlessly. 'I've just had the Russian Military Mission on the telephone asking me about them. They've had word from Moscow that the food and drink for their Red Army Day party on the 7th was brought over by us.'

I stalled, not daring to tell him; especially as he had not received any part of them.

'I'll see what I can do, Harpie,' I said, 'but I think the Prime Minister and Foreign Secretary . . .'

Without hope, I rang Thompson, Millard and Boyle. It was no surprise to hear their replies.

'Not a hope from the Prime Minister.'

'The Field Marshal gave a party for the Army Council and the rest he took home.'

'The Foreign Secretary? Well, I don't know, but I feel pretty sure that there is nothing left. I've still got a bottle of champagne if that's any good.'

I went to General Ismay, who heard my story with stunned dismay.

'This is a matter for the Foreign Secretary,' he said and picked up the telephone.

Mr Eden asked the Russian Ambassador to come and see him and with profuse apologies handed him a personal letter, six dozen bottles of Scotch whisky and a thousand cigarettes. Mystified but gratified, Mr Gusev went home.

My telephone rang and again it was the urgent voice of Wing-Commander Harpham.

'It's too late now, of course; the Red Army Day party's over; but the Mission are still asking me . . .

'It's all right, Harpie, don't worry. Mr Eden has seen the Russian Ambassador. . . .

'But it's got nothing to do with them!' cried Harpham, 'the Russian *Military Mission* are the ones who . . .'

Life is unfair. On 14 November General Ismay received a letter from Colonel Sir Eric Crankshaw, the head of Government Hospitality, informing him that the whisky and cigarettes for the Russian Embassy had been purchased at a cost of £116. 7s. and that 'as this transaction does not fall within the scope of Government Hospitality, I have referred it to the Treasury who will, I understand, defray the cost from the sum allocated to the British Military Mission to Moscow.'

CHAPTER 12

Basking on the Russian Riviera (1945)

ON NEW YEAR'S DAY, 1945, it could be fairly stated that most of the Allies' war aims were being successfully achieved. The Japanese Navy had suffered defeat at the great Battle of Leyte Gulf in October 1944; General MacArthur was beginning the invasion of the Philippines which would end victoriously in March. In Burma, the land route to China had been reopened, and by May British forces would be in occupation of Rangoon. A strong German counter-attack in the Ardennes had been repulsed, and General Eisenhower's armies were closing in on Germany from the west as the Russians moved relentlessly forward in the east. On land and from the air the Germans were pinned down in a last battle for survival. They were fighting for a lost cause, led by a demented Hitler, and it would not be long before the filth of the régime they had supported would shock the world.

For the winning three the time had come to set their sights on the picture they wished to produce of the future peace. Unfortunately there were three cameras held by three powers with three different viewfinders. If the postwar picture was to be in focus it was urgent that Roosevelt, Mr Churchill and Marshal Stalin should meet again. Confident that they would come to him, Marshal Stalin said he could not go further than the Crimea; it was therefore agreed that the meeting should take place at Yalta on the Black Sea, the delegations to arrive on 3 February.

General Ismay opened the administrative batting with a meeting on 8 January, from which flowed a stream of orders.

Would 10 Downing Street draft a telegram from the Prime Minister to Marshal Stalin telling him that, like the Americans, we proposed to handle our own communications from a ship which we would equip and sail through the Dardanelles? Would the Foreign Office agree with the State Department a message to be sent to the Turkish Government asking that these ships should pass without hindrance or inspection? What ship could the Ministry of War Transport make available? How much gasoline and oil would be needed and in what containers? The Admiralty must chart the route and find a posse of 'two Royal Marine officers and sixty other ranks' for guard duties. The War Office should earmark 'twenty cars and drivers', and, for the camouflaged passage through neutral Turkish waters, provide 'a hundred sets of warm civilian clothing for men and seventy-six sets for women', and – Oh, yes – a generous supply of DDT. Would the Air Ministry, through their Moscow Mission, find out the Russian choice of airfield and during the Conference arrange a daily Mosquito air courier service between London and the Crimea? The War Cabinet Offices, besides getting on with their usual administrative work, must find interpreters and make enquiries as to whether passports and visas would be needed.

By now, so efficient was the machine that, within days, it was possible to issue accurate instructions to the seven hundred and fifty probable travellers. Of these, perhaps two hundred would be delegation proper, and the rest naval communication personnel (forty of them from the Wrens), Royal Marine orderlies, army drivers and mechanics, a medical team, and some three hundred officers and other ranks from Air Transport Command.

S.S. *Franconia*, a 20,000 ton liner of the Cunard Line, was chosen as the headquarters ship, wherein, for the last time, our friends began to weave their web of thoughtful comfort and impeccable service.

Travel arrangements were further complicated by the fact that a preliminary Combined Chiefs of Staff meeting would take place at Malta on 29 January, followed a day or two later by the arrival of President and Prime Minister, the one sailing and the other flying in. This halfway stop made it a lovely jigsaw; some would go by sea to Malta and fly on from there; some would fly to Malta and sail to Yalta; others would fly direct to Yalta, or to Malta and then on to Yalta. Tongues and typewriters twisted and turned round the Ms and the Ys.

I should think, I thought, as I typed a list of what the War Office thought would be proper disguise for the travellers through Turkish waters, that the Turks will think we're nuts.

> for men: fur cap, woollen helmet, waterproof hood, felt boots, leather jerkin (with no sleeves for wear outside overcoat), kapok coat

(padded, waterproof, windproof but no hood), duffel coat, gloves, thick woollen stockings, thick woollen socks, rubber knee-boots.

for women: the same but with the addition of fur smocks, fur-lined gloves, brown leather boots, khaki slacks and woollen pants.

In the event none of these were worn; the ship was warm and the Turks uninterested.

Telegrams flew about. One from the British Military Mission in Moscow informed us that Saki airfield had been chosen because it had two long concrete runways, and that 'the Russians said it was preferable at this time of year not to run off the runway'. As to gasoline, twenty thousand gallons a day should meet the British requirements, but, please, the fewer personnel the better; the Russians were capable of servicing all the aircraft, and the Americans, who had enough maintenance personnel at their Poltava base, could supply the airfield motor transport if the Russians had dependable drivers and mechanics. It would be as well to ship as many tents, camp-beds, blankets, as possible, and there should be enough food on board *Franconia* to supplement Russian rations if necessary. The telegram ended with the suggestion that 'plenty of flea powder and toilet paper be issued to all ranks'. The reply went back that sixty-five officers and a hundred and twenty-six airmen would fly in on 23 January, two officers and a hundred and thirteen airmen were coming by sea, that we were sending one medical officer, three orderlies, and 'a small pack-up'. (Was this, I asked myself, a first-aid kit?)

On 25 January I left England, the long lists in my handbag weighing heavily against the latest message from Moscow that 'the People's Commissariat of Foreign Affairs were much perturbed at the extent of overcrowding there would be'. There had been some discussion as to whether I should take anyone with me, but I had thought not; for one thing the Embassy in Moscow were said to be making all the preliminary arrangements and for another, remembering how much store the Russians set by rank, I thought it better to be a civilian female, unaccompanied, than to have with me a major or a captain.

It was cold; snow lay over France and visibility was so bad that, though we flew over Paris at the usual 8,000–10,000 feet, we saw nothing of it, nor in fact did we see anything until the lights of Malta winked up at us around ten o'clock that night. I was met by the

Governor's aide and taken to Government House, where Sir Edmund and Lady Schreiber were my hosts. Before a good night's sleep I saw moonlight on an ancient garden wall and tree outside my bedroom window.

Next day I looked at the arrangements made by Group-Captain Earle, who had gone out from our office, and the local Army Headquarters in Malta for the reception and comfort of the Combined Chiefs of Staff. The *Franconia* had arrived, and a number of our old Cunard friends – Mr Smith, the chief steward, Mr Pearce, the chef, Mr Baker, the Prime Minister's steward – met us on board, their faces wreathed in smiles, the harbour behind us looking peaceful in the sunshine. Back to lunch with the Governor and Admiral Sir John Cunningham, Commander-in-Chief Mediterranean, who told me privately that he was doubtful whether 'the military' were capable of ever making successful arrangements for anything. The afternoon was spent walking round with Earle, seeing the Castillo and Montgomery House, where offices had been earmarked for the Americans; the YWCA hostel, where three of the Cabinet Office girls were already off the ship and waiting for work; the Savoy Hotel, empty of furniture but with a lovely view; the Royal Artillery mess at Tigne, quarters for the American Chiefs of Staff, spacious but sparsely furnished; back to Government House to plan dinner-parties for the visitors; and so, with weary feet, to bed.

Two refinements, added to our arrangements by experience, were that more coffee than tea should be flown out from England for our American guests and, where accommodation was concerned, it must be remembered that their warrant officer ranked somewhere near that of our second lieutenant.

At 5.30 on the morning of the 27th I was airborne in a Skymaster full of Americans, among them Captain Herbert H. Smellie, whose name was as known in Washington as the President's because it appeared on every Government pass. He showed me those for the Yalta Conference, which were made of a special cellophane which no one could forge because a glance through an X-ray machine would prove it. I wondered privately whether he had brought the machine. He was also proud of a pocket handbook for visitors to Russia which he planned to distribute to members of his delegation.

As we flew over the isles of Greece – as romantic as their names – I sat up with the pilot. From the wonderful sunrise that morning in

Malta until we passed over the Bosporus and Istanbul, there was nothing but harmony. When we were about over Lesbos and Lemnos, we were all asked to watch for enemy aircraft, which we did most anxiously, but all we saw, far below, were some British fighter patrols.

'One half hour to go,' said Captain MacOdrum.

We looked down and around and were rewarded by a glimpse of Sevastopol, black, forbidding and snow-covered on the edge of the sea. At 1.30 p.m. precisely the Skymaster's wheels touched down and crunched through mud and slush. We climbed out and trudged across to a huddle of buildings, over which hung a listless flag, watched by a standing group of Russian guards. I thought someone would be there to meet me, but I was wrong. I saw half a dozen Royal Air Force men some way off and hoped they knew there was an Englishwoman at Saki; they did not move, so I presumed not. I climbed into the Americans' car and drove with them the two miles to the mess, a converted sanatorium. There I was glad to be greeted by Wing-Commander Harpham, who was adjutant and interpreter for Group-Captain Pickard, officer commanding the dreary airfield of mud, slush and wooden buildings. It was extremely cold. 'Harpie' took me into a dark and cheerless dormitory with eight beds in it and introduced me to a Russian Army girl called Sima. She was fascinated by me, and followed me everywhere, stroking my arm, touching me, staring at my clothes. When I changed and washed in a basin that evening she and another girl watched my every move; I had to point to the door and tell them in rude English to 'Go away!'

But first I sat at a trestle table in a small room with Pickard and Harpham and, half-heartedly drinking vodka, we discussed the situation which existed at the airfield. Because Pickard was only a group-captain, the Russians paid no attention to him; the Americans had wisely imported a selection of brass-hats which included admirals and brigadier-generals, and were being treated respectfully. Pickard had no car and had been unable to push ahead with his ground preparations. We decided to build me up into a powerful figure. 'Harpie' telephoned to General Ermshenko, who was in command for the Russians, and told him that the 'Administrative Officer to the British War Cabinet who held the rank of major-general had arrived and wished to pay her respects to him; the British Government expected General Ermshenko to do all in his power to help'. The

General said he would call later that evening. He never came, but a car did, next morning, which broke down in front of the mess; all we saw of it was the bottom of the driver and much of the engine lying on the ground beside him.

I dined in the 'Joint Anglo-American Senior Officers' Mess' – a bedroom in the sanatorium – and, inconsequentially afterwards, we went to a dancing and singing show which had been laid on by the Russians for the entertainment of our personnel. It was very good indeed and I decided it was no use worrying any more about anything. All I had heard confirmed what we had already guessed in London and in Washington, that the Crimea as a meeting-place was far from ideal; and now it was also obvious that it was going to be difficult to get information about either its drawbacks or its amenities. How far, for instance, was it from Saki airfield to Sevastopol, where the *Franconia* was due in two days' time? How far from Saki or from Sevastopol to Yalta? No one seemed to know, and the Russians were being most unco-operative to us; it was not only because we lacked gold braid, we also lacked 'sweeteners'. The Americans were handing round cigarettes, chewing-gum, chocolates and sweets; we had nothing. The *Franconia* had plenty but she was steaming along somewhere and we did not even know if the Turks had let her through the Dardanelles. The Americans were altogether better organised than we were; their headquarters ship, the *Catoctin*, and four naval auxiliaries were lying snug in Sevastopol harbour, their communications system in working order. It was each for himself and let the best man win, and not a bit of good our asking help from them or they from us. Privately I was upset and disappointed that no one from our Embassy or Mission in Moscow had come to meet me or even sent a message.

I dragged my thoughts away from the snagging problems and concentrated once more on the smiling, kicking dancers on the stage.

A light shone suddenly into the darkened hall as a door opened and framed two welcome figures – Major Arthur Cox and a fellow Russian-speaker, Captain Hugh Lunghi. I scrambled from my seat and fell upon them, all hard feelings against their Military Mission gone. I knew that Arthur Cox was a man of action and ingenuity; it did not take more than one drink and one laugh to recognise the same qualities in Hugh Lunghi. At last we had two men who spoke Russian fluently and knew how not to let Russian grass grow under their feet. I fell into my hard bed at midnight with the feeling that we had reached the first step of the ladder. There were no blinds at the window, and Russian guards watched me as I undressed; I was too tired to care.

Two hours later I was woken up by a candle held close to my face as a Royal Air Force officer and a Russian stood peering down at me.

'This type,' said the officer, 'wants to know the date of your birth, your nationality, where you were born, your rank, your job.'

'Age 34, rank major-general, job Chief Administrator to the British War Cabinet, born Argentine – and go to hell.'

General Ermshenko had not paid his call in person: he was playing the favourite Russian game – list-making. At Saki this dementia had become so intense that Pickard was nearly out of his mind trying to satisfy the constant demands for every detail of the daily arrivals of men, stores and gear.

Sunday came, dirty and cold – so did breakfast. There was no telephone line to the British Naval Liaison Officer in Sevastopol and it was imperative to contact him and find out if he knew anything about the conference and the arrival of the *Franconia*. Arthur Cox went off to procure a car. General Ermshenko's was still lying gutted at the door. While he was gone, a long black Zis limousine slid to a standstill beside it, and from it stepped my old Moscow friend, Mr Yirshov. If familiarity with Russians had not bred suspicion, I would have kissed him. He had heard of my arrival and had left Alupka, the place near Yalta on the other side of the peninsula where the British delegation was to live, very early that morning. With him he had an army major of the Secret Police, the NKVD; the car was mine, the man was mine; I only had to give an order and it would be obeyed. At that moment, triumphant, Arthur honked up in an ancient car, which then broke down. We now had three at our disposal – two broken ones and Yirshov's. Leaving Yirshov to apply himself to the troubles of Pickard and Harpham, Arthur, Hugh, the Major and I climbed into the Zis and began the trek to Sevastopol. We had been unsuccessful in getting any food to take with us, but Hugh had some chocolate.

Never accept second-hand information! We had been told it would take us eight hours; it took us three. The road was rough and full of slush as our racy driver bumped us along. It was worrying to think of President Roosevelt, who had looked so sickly at Quebec, being driven over such surfaces – but that was just another headache among so many. For the present I must just absorb an impression of ruined Sevastopol, its former grace and beauty apparent through the delicate wrought iron balconies and gates lying forlorn and broken on the streets. Out of many thousand houses, only eight were standing – and one of these was the Villa Lee, home of the British Naval Liaison Officer. But which? We waited while Arthur and the Major went in to ask the Commissariat of Police. Our chauffeur crossed the road and stood looking at a gaping ruin. Hugh asked him whether he knew the house.

'Thirty years ago,' he replied, 'I had a stable there. I haven't been back since.'

We found the villa, a scruffy little three-roomed shack, warm, shabby and ill-furnished. There lived Commander Lee, Royal Navy, and his staff Lieutenant Martin, a young man fresh from England. They produced tins of self-heating cocoa and kidney soup – ingenious 'winter rations' I had never seen before. A wick stood out from the top of the tin which, when lit, embraced the contents and in a few minutes gave us a heart-warming drink. We told them what we knew of the *Franconia*'s schedule, and startled them with the numbers and ranks of the people who would be arriving so soon to share in the comforts of the Crimea. I believe the Commander felt as we did – that it would have been very nice if the 'Big Three' had decided to meet anywhere in the world except in this area; I wondered whether the ark of comfort now sailing towards his doorstep would match up to his memory of the life it represented, or whether the desolation which lay around him, for him, came nearer to the truth of life as it is.

Ignorance continued not to be bliss. There was no telephone communication with our delegation headquarters at Alupka so, once more, it was up to us to provide the link. At 5 p.m., still hungry, we left the Villa Lee and drove doggedly for four and a half hours while Arthur Cox kept up our spirits by singing Russian songs, of which he knew many, and sang them well. The road was winding, with quite a good surface, and, as long as daylight lasted, spectacular; it took us through Inkerman, with Balaclava on our right, round, up, and over a high pass – the Baidar Gap – and then down into an astonishing change of temperature. The air was balmy, sweet-smelling, no longer harsh.

At this moment of change it was right to think over the thirty-two hours since I had stepped from the warm and comfortable Skymaster.

Nine months ago the Russians won back the Crimea by fighting some of the bloodiest and most bitter battles of the war. Commander Lee said there was an area between Sevastopol and the Baider Gap where there were collected hundreds of German tanks, in them as many dead bodies, because there had not been time to clear them away. Saki, famous in peacetime for the curative properties of its mud, had no buildings – they had all been destroyed; the sanatorium where I stayed had been used formerly for mud-cure patients. The runways were covered with shell-holes and craters which the Russians had done their best to fill. The size of the ground staffs which the Americans and British had brought in for the airfield astonished and upset the Russians; the mud upset the nerves and tempers of the newly-arrived ground staffs.

Sevastopol had been a graceful city, constructed of a very fine local limestone; it had been stubbornly defended by the Red Navy and the result had been as we saw it. I remembered particularly one moment of that afternoon: two English officers and a girl stood with two Russians, looking silently at the stark ruins under the cold, hopeless sky; shuffling past us came a slippered, ill-clothed group of prisoners from Germany and the Balkans, each one pushing a small wheelbarrow holding a few pieces of stone debris; down the centre of the road an American drove a truck, filled with sailors, spruce and trim, from the *Catoctin*. For those few seconds, the awfulness of war came closer.

As far as distances were concerned, we reckoned that, from Saki to Sevastopol, it was seventy miles; from Sevastopol to Alupka, ninety; from Alupka to Yalta, twelve; and from Saki to Yalta, ninety. 'Imagine,' said Arthur Cox, 'running a conference with three focal points, one at each corner of Wales, linked by bad mountain roads covered with snow, ice and slush.'

It was too dark to see the form of the British delegation headquarters house – the Vorontzov Palace – but inside it was a dream. Inside the large hall there blazed two wood fires in two baronial fireplaces; on the floor were Persian rugs, on the walls and at the windows pictures and velvet hangings. Nicolaev Yirshov was there to greet us and introduce us to his senior colleague, Constantine Zinchenko, who would be attached to Mr Churchill. In contrast to Yirshov's dark hair and aquiline good looks, Zinchenko was fair, looked English and had been for four years at the Russian Embassy in London. We talked and laughed at a gay and satisfying meal.

I appropriated the Prime Minister's suite, which was on the ground floor to the left of the hall. I did not see more of the house that night but what I had seen was sumptuous; the linen at table had been speckless, the waiters to the manner born, the food something out of a fairy-tale – the whole a telling contrast to the poverty and misery we had seen that afternoon.

Next morning, Monday, after glasses of Russian tea, tangerines, some caviar and an omelette, we explored the palace inside and out. A pseudo-Scottish-castle-cum-Moorish-palace, it had been built in 1837 by a member of the Vorontzov family. Alongside Mr Churchill's bedroom, bathroom and office suite, which had a fine view of the Black Sea from its windows, there was a small drawing-room. Half of this would need to be converted into Captain Pim's Prime Ministerial Map Room. Then came an orangery – green with orange and lemon trees brought by the Russians from Georgia, and goldfish in a stone pool brought from who knows where. Beyond were two large reception rooms; one, I thought, for a VIP sitting-room and the other for their dining-room. Mr Churchill could eat in the other half of the small drawing-room. Upstairs from the main part of the house there were two suites of bedroom, bathroom and sitting-room, and two other bedrooms. That lot would do for the Foreign Secretary and his staff. In an annex, known as the Shuvalov, the only access to which lay through the two reception rooms, there were thirty small bedrooms, two small reception rooms and one bathroom which included the only lavatory, and one wash-room. I shook with inner laughter, which Yirshov must not see. No Russian who had experienced the hard side of life must know how tenderly our VIPs regarded conference comforts.

Outside the sun was shining. The Black Sea matched its name; it lay smooth and heavy, like a deep grey oily liquid. To reach the garden, we walked under a tall Persian-type arch, inset with mosaics and, carved into its inner sides, extracts from the Koran. From it there were broad steps going down towards the water, flanked by three pairs of finely sculptured lions looking proudly eastward. On each side there were gardened terraces, their flower-beds bright with zinnias and geraniums, blooming hypocritically in their buried pots. Near one wing of the building there was a copy of the Bakshiserai

Fountain, designed of cups which held and dripped water as it constantly fell upon them. A Tartar king had loved a Circassian lady, brought to him as booty from a war; when she died, he made such a fountain to hold his tears forever.

Yirshov told us that the Vorontzov Palace had been left intact by the Germans because they had decided it would make a good gift for the general commanding them. A year ago last Christmas, German officers had had a party there.

Around us lay another world: no more snow, slush, flat unyielding cold, but orange groves, vineyards, palms, olive trees, sloping down to a rocky coast, the high mountains behind keeping away the cold winds and making the whole area into a resort.

We returned to the hall of the palace just as Moore Crosthwaite, from the British Embassy in Moscow, came breathlessly in. He was staying at the Palace of Livadia, winter residence of Tsar Nicholas II, the US delegation headquarters at Yalta, with Kathie Harriman and a large advance party of Americans, and did not seem keen to come and live with us. In fact, he brought an invitation for me from Kathie suggesting I go and stay with them, but, needless to say, I refused; the little time I had – four days – would be needed right here.

Yirshov explained that when, instead of undamaged Odessa, Yalta had been chosen, his government had had two weeks to prepare it; we could see, couldn't we, what the German Army had done to the Crimea? How, of the few buildings left standing, the Vorontzov and Livadia Palaces, and some adjacent houses were least damaged because they had been used as headquarters by the enemy. He looked smug as he spoke – and had every right to. The result was a monument to Russian efficiency. In that short time, a thousand or more soldiers had restored roads, rebuilt and repainted houses, replaced broken windows and planted gardens. Hundreds of railway trucks had made the long slow journey from Moscow bringing furniture, carpets, bedding, pictures, food and the wherewithal to cook and eat it, drink, glasses, chefs, waiters, housemaids. Moscow hotels had been emptied of staff, tall, dear Nina Alexandrovna, whom I thought I would never see again, among them. Many of them had been aroused secretly during the night, told to pack their bags and leave their homes, with what misgivings it can be imagined. They were anxious for the Conference to end so that they could relieve the distress of their families.

The security arrangements which covered all the area were thorough. Besides its own guards, each house was completely ringed by sentries, who were doubled at night, with the addition of dog patrols. Around these rings another, and another round that. The water supply for Vorontzov which came from a natural spring was guarded for the whole of its length. Every ten yards of the roads between Sevastopol, Saki, Yalta and Alupka, there were men and women guards. Movements of transport were strictly governed by passes, and we were told by a suave Russian general there would be times when certain movements would be going on for which no pass whatsoever would let anyone through. By his sly smile, we knew he meant the exits and entrances of Marshal Stalin. The strict patrolling of the countryside had added reason when we realised that around us lay large numbers of live mines and booby traps, left by the war.

In the Vorontzov, as at Livadia, the modern Communists, our hosts, had turned the clock back to the days of the Tsars. Our walls were hung with pictures from Moscow art galleries, our fireplaces crackled with burning logs, our waiters were immaculate, our maids in black dresses with white aprons. They provided a barber and manicurist for men; nothing for women, but there was a hairdresser on board the *Franconia*, whose services we were able to offer to Kathie Harriman and to Mr Roosevelt's daughter, Mrs Boettiger, the only ladies with the US delegation.

The reconnaissance was over, and we had lunch before going down the road to look at the other houses. Nina Alexandrovna came in and said the Russian liaison officer for the British delegation had arrived. With Yirshov, Arthur and Hugh, I went into the hall and said how-do-you-do to General Karanadze, a Georgian, short and stocky with a completely bald head. He spoke no English, but by the end of the Conference he said he would learn, and at Potsdam, where I met him again, he had got a vocabulary of at least thirty words. Through the interpreters – there were four including Zinchenko – he told me that they had been patiently awaiting the British advance party. He looked surprised when I said I was it; but I think my reason for coming alone justified itself; not only could they not categorise me but it tickled their ever-present sense of humour to deal with a woman; from the first they gave me all possible help.

We walked down the road to look at the rest of the accommodation. My heart sank when I saw that all we had for our large delegation was two sanatoria of two houses each, used in peace-time as rest homes for overworked Civil Servants. Though they were clean, with new paint, their amenities were meagre, and I could not see my military and diplomatic charges exactly greeting with joy dormitories for six without bath – or, to be more explicit, with one bath to each house.

There were administrators at each house: Sanatorium A had what the Russians called two 'Corpus': Corpus 1, in charge of a pock-marked civilian in a cloth cap, Razin, and a uniformed Colonel Charapov with an Order of Lenin hanging on his breast, contained offices and a dining-room, whose *maître d'hôtel*, Mr Cibizov, was fat and cheerful; Corpus 2 had thirty-one beds in it. Sanatorium B had Corpus 1, under the care of a lady called Madame Sakhnina, slept fifty, and Corpus 2, with thirty-seven beds. This Corpus was in the care of two charming majors, Pokashkin and Chelidze, the one a husky man with a sweet smile, the other a tall Cossack, blue-chinned. No English spoken, but they were delighted with me and told Arthur Cox privately that they hoped they would see plenty of me. I was not so sure then, but by the end of our stay I loved them both dearly. One hundred and eighteen beds, but not all of them could be used by delegation staffs; there were Royal Marines, War Office drivers and people from the ship to be considered. With thirty beds for VIPs and Private Secretaries in the Vorontzov, we should just be able to manage a reasonable-sized community.

'Sufficient unto the day is the evil thereof' and, with Moore Crosthwaite, I climbed into a car and went to Livadia to have dinner with my American counterpart, Rear-Admiral C. E. Olsen of the US Military Mission in Moscow, Brigadier-General W. W. Bessell of the Joint War Plans Committee, Kathie Harriman and others. I was glad I went because I saw that my mathematical problem of six brigadiers into one room was elementary compared with theirs; they were sleeping eight generals to one room, sixteen full colonels to one and forty middle ranks to one. At the end of a long corridor, I stood looking at what seemed to me an impossible equation: my eye was on a door bearing a notice which read:

General Marshall
and
Admiral King

It could not be, they could not be sharing! I turned with pity towards the Admiral – but it was all right; they were in the Tsarina's suite, General Marshall in her bedroom and Admiral King in the boudoir, which had the garden entrance Rasputin had used.

The difference between Livadia and Vorontzov lay in the size of the rooms. The Americans' were very big and they were able to fit their whole delegation under one roof; but I thought, they will have the misfortune to receive the complaints and criticisms in one concentrated place, whereas mine at least will be spread apart and out of earshot.

I had not got far with my lists and allocations next day when, via the American link from *Catoctin* to Yalta, we received word that the *Franconia* would reach Sevastopol that afternoon. With Moore Crosthwaite, who had brought the message, Arthur Cox and Hugh Lunghi, I left immediately after breakfast. It would probably have been better if I had stayed behind and done my necessary work, but I wanted to think out and send a telegram to General Ismay in Malta, giving him some idea of our difficulties and felt, when I saw the members of the delegation on board, I would be able to judge the situation more clearly.

As we were driving over the Baidar Gap, we saw a ship steaming along offshore, flanked by minesweepers and destroyers. We were so stupid that it was twenty minutes before it hit us that this was, indeed, the *Franconia*. Down the mountain road, 'into the valley of Death' we rode – to meet the six hundred! At Sevastopol we found Pickard, Harpham and an interpreter, Boris Trapp, and repaired to a small room in the Customs House, where we waited for three hours, drinking from their stock of the miraculous self-heating cocoa and kidney soup tins, and playing dice. The delay was caused by a sudden deterioration in the weather; outside there was a blizzard where in the morning there had been rain; and the *Franconia* was having some sort of pilotage hold-up. We watched her come slowly in, her lights blazing, her cargo, her decks and her rigging covered with snow.

Looking like Antarctic explorers, we went aboard; I was wearing a sheepskin coat which Lady Ismay had lent to me and for which I was more than grateful. The welcome was warm and so was the ship, but outside there was chaos. There were forty-three army motor cars on the deck besides some Air Force trucks containing wireless equipment, and they were all frozen tight, immovable. Gangs of men were struggling to free them, but as dark day gave place to black night, they were forced to give up and leave the unloading until daylight. I looked at Captain Peter Dawnay, the Royal Naval officer in charge of signals, and we lifted our shoulders hopelessly.

'I want to send a message to General Ismay,' I said.

There was not a hope of our getting back to Alupka that night, so we stayed aboard and enjoyed a meal of steak and onions. Mr Baker gave me a cabin and when I entered it there on the bunk lay a new nightdress, a toothbrush, toothpaste, powder and cold cream. The Cunard service was unbeatable.

I composed and sent my telegram to General Ismay in Malta, where the Combined Chiefs of Staff Committee was grinding through its three days of overcrowded living. Overcrowded? I said to myself, and laughed. I told him all I knew and warned him that 'accommodation will stretch people's tempers to limit'.

The snow had stopped falling next morning and unloading was proceeding at a snail's pace. We decided that Captain Dawnay, Captain Pim with his boxes of maps, Commander Peter Pelly of the Admiralty, Hugh Lunghi and I would return to Alupka, leaving Arthur Cox to supervise the unloading and Moore Crosthwaite to smooth out the difficulties we were experiencing with the Russian naval authorities over security passes. We were just clear of Sevastopol when the car broke down. Arthur Cox, wise in the ways of Russian transport, had sent a jeep to follow us. After some worried words, Captain Dawnay decided his place was with his ship and we waved him off down the snowy road in the jeep. On his return he sent poor General Ismay another signal, telling him we were snowbound and that a relief car was being sent to fetch us. The effect on our friends in Malta, who were already shaken by my message, was electrifying, not to mention our colleagues in Whitehall, who read the repeats with feelings not unmixed with pleasure. We could not have achieved our ends in a more satisfactory manner: future complaints were stifled before birth.

In fact the car started the moment Captain Dawnay had disappeared round a bend in the road; if it had not boiled over at each rise, we would have had an easy drive.

A lot of time had been lost; Commander Pelly assumed temporary administrator officer rank and together we tackled the jobs that must be done, and done quickly. We went round the area and began in earnest to make up the lists. The American contingent came to dinner, but directly they had gone, we went on working till dawn. At 3 a.m. our morale was so low that we asked one of the internal guards to fetch us some vodka. Ten minutes later the *maître d'hôtel* Agasafianz, fully dressed in white tie and tails, brought in a silver tray with a bottle and two glasses. He must have got up from his bed to do it. A further example of the disciplined regard that was paid to our wants happened to me a few days later. In friendly conversation with Mr Agasafianz after lunch I said I had never eaten a '*Kotelette po Kievski*', the name the Russians give to a fried breast of chicken filled with hot butter. Within the hour, to my desk, there was served a tray with, on it, a dish holding two '*hotelettes*', a salad and a glass of wine. I could hardly get through it, it was so soon after lunch, but I had to; the butler stood and watched me with a proud smile on his face.

By 6 a.m. Peter Pelly and I decided to call it a night and went to bed. I asked to be called at eight, but they forgot and I was not in my bath until eleven. I was just stepping out of it when I was called to the telephone in the hall. As we were anxiously waiting for news that communications had been established between ship, airfield and palace, I hurried out in a dressing-gown, dripping wet underneath, my face covered with cold cream. I was talking – it was Peter Dawnay, very faint – when to my slow horror I saw a very senior Russian general, flanked by officers, advancing through the front door and stopping to stare. There was no escape.

'I must go,' I said to Dawnay, who sounded rather put out to be stopped in the middle of a sentence, and mustering my dignity and my dressing-gown around me, I stepped forward and introduced myself. He was Colonel-General Kruglov, Vice-Commissar of the NKVD Secret Police, the most powerful-looking man I had ever seen, with huge shoulders, face, hands and feet. He did not attempt to hide a smile of disbelief when I said I had spent the night doing conference work. In fact, he said, the British delegation were in the Russian bad books. He spread his enormous hands:

'From the Americans we have received many requests and have done our best to fulfil them; from the British nothing, nothing . . .' I told him there was little that we needed, that everything was perfect, and then gave him a long list of requirements.

In the afternoon, looking very cross indeed, General Karanadze arrived and had a long conversation with Yirshov. I watched uneasily; the General seemed strained. I took Yirshov aside.

'What is biting the General?' I asked.

'Oh, nothing,' he replied.

'Don't lie to me,' I said. 'He looks furious. You must be honest with me.'

'Well,' said Yirshov, 'the General is very upset by your list.' We had asked for tables, chairs, cupboards, basins, and for a double bed for the Prime Minister. The bed was coming, that was all right; but basins! He doubted very much whether he could find basins. He had been doing his best for us, but what could he do when we wanted so much and his orders were that everything had to be ready by Friday evening?

I got cross, told them that it was not fair, that they must play straight:

'Whatever I ask for, you nod and smile and say "*Da, da,* you shall have it – that's quite easy." In England we have done without many things for five years – we're used to it. So if you can't give us the things we ask for, say so. I suppose if I asked for an emerald from Lake Baikal you'd say "Yes".'

As Yirshov translated my words, General Karanadze's eyes softened, and he said he would like to go over the house with me again. Wearily I went, and we stood in each room of the palace while I rapidly watered down my demands. On the first floor, I had wanted to turn the Foreign Secretary's second sitting-room into an office and had asked for some tables; it was only after long and patient questioning that the General admitted that (a) the staircase was too narrow so all furniture for that floor had to go through the windows, which were now sealed up, and (b) he did not want to change the room into an office, it looked nice as it was. Nina Alexandrovna was with us, and she gave me one or two little smiles, so I kept my mouth shut and concentrated instead on begging that a window in each room should be made to open. We then went to the two reception rooms on the ground floor, which each contained a dining-room table. I said I would like to have the one which had the biggest table as a dining-room and conference room, leaving the other to be used as a sitting-room. At the end of an hour of polite but stubborn cross-talk, I learned that in Russia no one ever ate off a conference table. That was that. The table remained and the other third of the room would have to be the VIPs' 'rumpus room'.

Frantic with fatigue and irritation, I smiled at the little man and said goodbye; he looked happier – and we were the poorer by a good many tables and chairs.

When I had given the list of requests to General Kruglov, I had told him that Mr Churchill preferred a double to a single bed, as he was accustomed to do his work in it and spread his papers around. But, I said, do not go further for it than the Livadia Palace. There I had noticed that President Roosevelt and Mr Stettinius each had a double; give Mr Churchill's to Mr Stettinius and Mr Stettinius's to Mr Churchill; this would be most equal because it would give the 'Big Two' a large bed each. Kruglov made no comment, but when General Karanadze came in the afternoon he told me quite crossly that my suggestion would not do and that he had sent to Moscow for one. It arrived just before the Prime Minister, a close shave.

Agreeing, when General Karanadze had left, that men talked too much, Nina and I went upstairs and moved the furniture around, doing our best to give the Foreign Secretary an adequate office.

By Friday, telephonic and road communications between *Franconia* and Alupka were in order; the War Office drivers began a courier service which would run each way four times a day, with a standby at night. By the end of the Conference, they had shortened the journey time from four hours to two and a half; they were a first-class lot of men who worked long hours and were cheerful and willing. Major Tom Buckley, the tireless and thoughtful officer in charge of the Royal Marine contingent, sent us a detail of orderlies and guards for the Prime Minister. Commander Pelly was finishing off the room allocations, and I was in an alcove off the hall in the Vorontzov sorting out and sending to their offices and dormitories the clerical staffs as they arrived from the ship. The British Ambassador from Moscow, Sir Archibald Clark Kerr, with some of his people, came in; he told me not to look so harassed. Bangings and hammerings made it clear to everyone within earshot that Captain Pim was organising the walls of his Map Room. It was a hectic, interrupted and muddled day. So many people were involved in the Yalta meeting that it was an administrative officer's nightmare.

At 4 a.m. on Saturday morning I was called to the telephone. I heard a faint voice saying 'Accident to one of our aircraft. Here is the list of those killed' – then the names of twelve people, so many of them my friends. Nice, tall Inspector Batley, Mr Eden's detective, companion of so many conferences; Captain 'Barney' Charlesworth, personal friend and aide-de-camp on the staff of Field Marshal Brooke; Captain Finch, personal assistant to the Director of Plans in the War Office, who had been kind to me in the old MI(R) days and who had wanted so much to come on one of the conference trips, and this time had; Mr Peter Loxley, a promising young man in the Foreign Service. My immediate reaction, which came flooding in before I could stop to think, was one of relief; fewer beds would be needed and the accident had happened in the Mediterranean and not at Pickard's Saki airfield. Before I had replaced the receiver I was regretting such a horrible reaction.

Saturday was D-Day – Damned Day – the day the main delegation would arrive. The die was cast, and it was doubtful whether anyone would be pleased with our arrangements. In the Vorontzov Palace there was accommodation for Mr Churchill and his daughter Sarah, his private secretaries John Martin and Leslie Rowan, his aide Commander Thompson, his clerk Mr Kinna, his valet Sawyers, his two detectives and Lord Moran; for the Foreign Secretary and Sir Alexander Cadogan, with two private secretaries Mr Pierson Dixon and Mr Lawford; for Lord Leathers and Sir Ralph Metcalfe of War Transport; for Sir Edward Bridges, Lord Ismay, and the three Chiefs of Staff; for Major-General Laycock, Chief of Combined Operations, and Field Marshals Wilson and Alexander, Admiral Somerville and Sir Archibald Clark Kerr. In Corpus 1 of Sanatorium A were offices and the general dining-room; in Corpus 2 such diplomats as Mr Gladwyn Jebb and Moore Crosthwaite would share a dormitory with four others of equivalent rank. The beds were hard and narrow, close together, there was one bathroom; I knew they would be uncomfortable, I did not know if there were bed bugs. The Americans had brought a machine and de-loused their beds most thoroughly, offering to do the same for mine. It seemed rude to our hosts, so I refused. In fact, it made no difference; the Americans had bed bugs; so did we, but very few.

In Sanatorium B one Corpus was for women and junior officers, and the other for the Royal Marines, transport and other personnel. Here there was a bath-house in the garden, with a Russian girl standing by to scrub bathers of either sex; Commander Pelly drew up a roster of bath-times. They had more fun in that house than the aesthetes in Sanatorium A. I had put myself to sleep down there, sharing a room with my friends, Diana Lyttelton, a Waaf officer in the Prime Minister's Map Room, and Mary Grepe, a secretary in the Air Ministry, but Nicolaev Yirshov and Nina Alexandrovna thought otherwise. They looked knowing and smiling on Saturday morning when they asked me to have a word with them alone. Afraid of something untoward, I said rather crossly that I was too busy. I felt a pig, later, when I realised they had wished to tell me that Nina had moved out of her little bedroom in the Vorontzov to share with her assistant, Gala, so that I could have it. They were so pleased; often, when dealing with the Russians, it was like that; they did things which were touching and were delighted with what they did.

The VIPs were not due until teatime, so it was a nasty moment, at 1.30, to see a haze of colour at the front door which clarified itself into the figures of the three Chiefs of Staff and other senior officers. Battered by their journey over the mountains, they looked as dazed as I felt and needed no second bidding to go straight into lunch. There was no time to worry as to whether the magician chefs and waiters would collapse, just a prayer that the length of a Russian meal would keep the new arrivals quiet. A horrible thought that Mr Churchill might also come sooner than expected sent me into his bedroom. The double bed was in position and Gala was moving my things out, with two maids cleaning and polishing. It was too bad if the Chiefs of Staff thought it odd to see my clothes being bundled through their dining-room into the Shuvalov wing. They would have to get used to Yalta.

The Prime Minister arrived at four. I showed him his suite, feeling like a hotel housekeeper as I murmured,

'Your bathroom, your bedroom, your office.' He growled:

'But where is Sarah? I said she was to sleep in my quarters.' He had, in fact, reacted to my Malta telegram and sent us a message to this effect, but it had been impossible to arrange. The only place where she could have slept was in the hall outside his door watched by Royal Marine and Russian guards. He was in an ill temper, so aide Commander Thompson signalled me to clear off, and fetched Sarah to calm him down.

It was a dispiriting day, and my sense of humour had gone by its end. The end was a long way off, too; people kept on arriving in bunches throughout the rest of the evening until 2 a.m. As they drove up to the doors of the Vorontzov, hungry and tired after long delays at Saki because of transport shortage, we sent them off to their sanatoria. The Russians had made specious promises that we would have twenty, thirty cars at our disposal, but they only gave us three; how we would have managed without those we brought with us and the tireless work of our own drivers, I do not know.

The last, the 2 a.m. party, included Mr Gladwyn Jebb, and I took them down myself to Sanatorium A to see if I could find some food and drink for them. I lost my head and passed the house three times, the heavy silence of my companions weighing on me until, suddenly, Captain Richard Coleridge, a sailor with our Joint Staff Mission in Washington, burst out laughing. I was grateful to him and to the Russian servants who produced vodka and omelettes when we finally stopped at the right door. There were some embarrassing moments when I showed them their dormitories; twice I opened a door and pointed to a bed to find someone else in it. Mr Jebb's suitcase was missing.

'Tomorrow morning,' I said, 'I will find it.' I was wrong. As I was saying the words, a Liberator took off from Saki for Cairo, the missing case tucked beside one of the crew who thought it was his. It was returned eventually, but its absence did not add to the pleasures of Mr Jebb's dormitory life.

I rolled into my bed, conscious that we had not been ready and that my organisation had been too little, too late.

A cautious reconnaissance next day brought me some relief. The groups were settling in, almost enjoying themselves. Domestically, the service was impeccable, only the lack of sitting and bathing facilities difficult. The Prime Minister and Sarah shared his bathroom; the Foreign Secretary and four others had the two on the first floor; in the Shuvalov wing the one bathroom and wash-room had to serve twenty-four people. Efforts to keep a roster were frustrated by individual enterprise as each VIP tried to outdo the other by getting up earlier and earlier to catch the bath. Sir Archibald Clark Kerr was determined to stick to his custom of a hot bath at night and a cold one in the morning; the Chiefs of Staff sent their batmen to queue, and General Ismay's Corporal Cartmel did the same for his chief and for me. Sir Charles Portal had definite ideas as to etiquette; it was unco-operative, he said, if the bathroom door was locked when the only lavatory was beyond and through it. I saw him one morning jumping up to try to see through the fanlight who was in the bath, calling out the while. The door opened and a blushing Field Marshal

Wilson, clutching his dressing-gown round him, stumbled out and hurried wordlessly down the passage.

The accent of the Yalta meetings was on postwar affairs – the occupation of Germany, the frontiers of Poland, the conditions demanded by Russia in return for her entry into the war against Japan, a World Organisation for Peace. Upstairs, on the first floor, the Foreign Office staffs worked eight deep at one table in one room, with their eight stenographers banging eight typewriters in the passage outside. Mr Eden's lot was not a happy one. Apart from the cramped space, I had had to face him with the news that his windows were tightly sealed and that I had failed to get them opened; and I apologised for the fact that his only desk was a small, thin-legged French occasional table.

The large military staffs need not, in fact, have come. Except for the future of Russia's entry into war in the Far East, which scarcely came up for discussion, current military operations had been discussed in Combined Chiefs of Staff meetings in Malta. Plans for the final assault on Germany from the west had been argued: Eisenhower's embraced an advance over the whole length of the River Rhine and on a wide front into Germany; the British thought this was too cautious an approach and that it would be better to follow General Montgomery's proposal to concentrate forces for an attack on Berlin via the Ruhr. After frank and sometimes acrimonious argument the British gave way before the Americans' determined support for the Eisenhower strategy.

General Karanadze's conference table was rarely used; instead, round the large fireplace, each morning gathered the great. Field marshals, admirals, one Marshal of the Royal Air Force – Portal had been promoted – sat where they could. Field Marshal Wilson, a tall, broad figure, stood near the fire with a copy of *The Times* brought from London by the daily Mosquito aircraft service; the Ambassador from Moscow, with his back to the room, read his books on Chinese philosophy; Lord Moran parried provocative thrusts from Admiral Somerville, who called him 'the apothecary'; Lord Leathers and Sir Ralph Metcalfe talked about the use of ships and landing-craft in the Far East; and Field Marshal Alexander – promoted as Supreme Allied Commander in place of Wilson who had become Head of the Joint Staff Mission on the death of Field Marshal Dill – in field boots shining like mirrors, took his sketch-book and departed to paint in the garden.

At the far end of the Shuvalov wing the three Chiefs of Staff, a cordon of assistants round them, were sharing one office for the first time in their lives.

One night, in the half sitting-room next to his Map Room, Mr Churchill sat with Sarah and Mr Eden before a table covered in spotless white, delicious food being served by deferential waiters. He leaned back against the cushioned chair-back, and said:

'I don't know why they say this place is so inconvenient; I find it very comfortable indeed.'

From Vorontzov down to Sanatorium B, things settled; those not needed at Alupka went to *Franconia*, and those in Alupka eased themselves into the familiar routine of work and fellowship. We absorbed the beauty of the surroundings and watched the calm swell of the deep grey ocean lying below us. The Prime Minister telegraphed to Mr Attlee, his Deputy, at home in London:

> . . . This place has turned out very well so far, in spite of our gloomy warning and forebodings. It is a sheltered strip of austere Riviera with winding cornice roads, and the villas and palaces more or less undamaged of an extinct imperialism and nobility. In these we squat on furniture carried with extraordinary effort from Moscow and with plumbing and road-making done regardless of cost in a few days by our hosts, whose prodigality excels belief. All the Chiefs of Staff have taken a holiday today to see the battlefield of Balaclava. We are not stressing this in our contacts with our friends.

Colonel Frank McCarthy fetched me to go and lunch with General Marshall at Livadia. I was interested to see how they had settled down, and I could not help feeling that it all looked more workmanlike and efficient – perhaps because everyone was in uniform, or only men in civilian clothes, and there were no girls in bright colours. I tried to keep my own clothes on the dark side and tailored, looking uniformed, thinking that this gave me more authority. It was an odd quirk because nothing would have induced me to join a women's service.

Whether I was uniformed or in plain clothes, my host was the same charming, courteous, remote person. General Marshall asked me to describe my afternoon in the Embassy garden at Teheran; I had written to him after the Moscow Conference thinking it would amuse him; in his reply he had said: 'The fact that you found the garden at Teheran a charming and restful place in contrast to England made me realise how great our blessings are here in continental United States. I am sorry you cannot have a week on a Florida beach.' Now he wanted to know more because, he said, he liked the quiet things in life. At lunch I saw that there was no vodka, champagne or caviar. I asked General Marshall whether they had had any. He replied,

'Yes, sometimes', so I kept to myself the news that at our British headquarters we had a constant and liberal supply. I wondered whether the casual ad hoc way by which we ran our conference administration brought out more warmth from our Russian hosts; an unpredictable people themselves, they enjoyed unpredictability in others. Or perhaps it was that General Karanadze was more human and generous than whichever Russian it was who looked after the American delegation.

My meetings with General Marshall were events I always spoke of with pride when I got back to my own side, but I cannot say that they added anything in the way of new information about American military thought. Not that I looked for it; it was not my job to be more than social. I did pick up bits of background interest sometimes, from letters or conversations, which I could retail to General Ismay, but he was not a man who listened to tittle-tattle and only paid heed if what he heard had a direct and true bearing on events. The only gossip he liked to hear was a funny happening; where General Marshall was concerned, there could never be that sort of story; he was far too reserved and dignified a figure.

At the end of the week there was a big exodus as the military staffs packed their bags, climbed into aircraft at Saki and flew off to London, Washington and Italy. I had a nice and unexpected invitation from Field Marshal Alexander. He told General Ismay that he thought I looked as though I needed a holiday and would be glad if I could be allowed to stop over as his guest in Naples on my way home. Always generous with kindness, General Ismay said 'Of course', and it was agreed that I could take Diana Lyttelton with me.

On Saturday night the 'Big Three' dined at the Vorontzov. Once more we stood in the hall and watched the arrivals. President Roosevelt looked dreadfully ill and there were few of us who felt we would ever see him again; Marshal Stalin repeated the performance of taking off his own coat, and he and Mr Churchill had the same tussle together in hanging it up as they had had at Teheran. Zinchenko and Yirshov were stiff and solemn; it had been notable to Moore Crosthwaite, Arthur Cox, Hugh Lunghi, and me, that their manner towards us had altered from the moment Marshal Stalin had arrived at the Russian headquarters in the Yusupov Palace. Until then, they had been ready to enter into argument about many subjects, not least the differences between a democratic and communist state, had even accepted proffered books. But afterwards the books were returned without comment, and conversation was kept to essentials.

On Sunday it was all over; I lined up the Vorontzov staff in the hall and Mr Churchill shook hands and thanked each one in turn. Unfortunately there were no presents to give. At my request, what Mr Lawrence Burgis in London described as 'the whole of Dunhill's quota for the month' had been flown out to us: two silver cigarette-boxes, four cigarette lighters, a silver powder-compact, six silver propelling pencils and four leather powder-compacts. I had put them in a drawer in one of the offices. When I went to get them they had disappeared. It was very awkward. I could not ask the Russians; if I did, to save their face they would have probably accused, rightly or wrongly, some wretched domestic. So I said nothing – and they got nothing. I wondered whether any of their officials knew about the theft and were waiting to see what I would do.

The people who were sailing back in *Franconia* left that morning. The Prime Minister had intended to be among them, but he changed his mind and decided he should join Mr Eden on a visit to Athens, where order had been restored since the severe civil strife of the previous Christmas. General Ismay did not go with him, which pleased his fellow passengers; his company was always welcome.

Arthur Cox and I were the last to leave. We had lunch with Yirshov and Nina Alexandrovna, back to their natural social charm because Marshal Stalin was somewhere in the air on his way back to Moscow. Then we drove to each sanatorium to say goodbye. At Sanatorium B, Major Chelidze came out, beaming; would we wait, he said, Major Pokashkin was just coming – in fact there he was! He pointed. Down the hill on the other side of the road leapt and ran the tall Cossack with the blue chin, across the road and up to us, one arm held behind his back. With a bow and a kiss on my cheek he swept it at me and thrust a huge bunch of snowdrops into my hand. 'He went up the mountain specially to pick them for you,' said Major Chelidze.

We had a sad drive to Sevastopol, neither of us talking, each with our thoughts; Arthur, because he was returning to Moscow, the party over; I, because of the friends I had left behind and would most likely not see again. The lights and comfort of the ship did not beckon, rather repelled; through the cold curtain of language and security I had received warmth and affection, the beginnings of human communication.

It took three days to load up the *Franconia* again, during which we, the lucky passengers, went sightseeing – to Balaclava and to an intact Tartar Palace at Bakshiserai, where we saw the original fountain of tears and the harem where the King's beloved mistress had lived. We gave two parties for the Red Navy. We only meant to give one, but the large group of officers, men and women, who came aboard at the first invitation had obviously enjoyed themselves, because they turned up again, uninvited, the next night. One rather small Hero of the Soviet Union attached himself affectionately to General Ismay, leaning against his shoulder at dinner, 'and,' said the General, 'he smelt so high, he would have charmed a bird off a tree'.

The voyage up the Bosporus, past Istanbul, and through the Dardanelles was a luxury cruise. Some Turkish officials came out in a small motor-boat to have a look at us, but, as something had gone wrong with the ship's steering apparatus, all they saw was the *Franconia* revolving in circles. We waved, they waved, and then she straightened and on we went.

On the notice-board was pinned a signal from the British Naval Liaison Officer, or, to the Russians, *Pozharnaya Commanda Severnaya Starona*:

> Very many thanks for the hospitality and good times we had on board. We now resume our normal life as exiles. We will always remember *Franconia*. Good Luck and Bon Voyage.
>
> Lee

Chapter 13

Supreme hospitality (1945)

MARY GREPE, DIANA LYTTELTON AND I had been friends for the past three years. We felt sorry to wave goodbye to Mary in Malta and see her fair hair and blue eyes disappear into a car heading for the airport. It would have been too ideal if she could have come to Italy with us, impossibly ideal, so we cut all thoughts of the *Franconia* and the retreating air parties from our minds, and took firm steps in the direction of Government House. The Schreibers had asked me again to stay, and, of course, Diana. Feeling as though we were moving through a dream sequence, we went to our two bedrooms, looked at each other, laughed, and began talking. A sharp knock on the door and an urgent shout from an aide-de-camp caught us unready:

'His Excellency,' said the herald, 'is about to come down for drinks before dinner. For God's sake, hurry!' But of course! The Governor was the King's representative; etiquette demanded we get there before him! I envied Diana her Royal Air Force uniform; no clothes problems for her. Squeaking, we rushed downstairs, getting into the room just one minute before the royal entry. The Schreibers were so nice and easy, it seemed uncharacteristic; after the Yalta scrum it seemed unrealistic. The war receded, and we ate our meal.

A telegram arrived from Supreme Allied Headquarters saying that 'Miss Bright and party' would be met at Naples airport the following afternoon.

We were. For six days we received the full VIP treatment; two, three, young staff officers at our service; soldier servants who washed and ironed our shirts and laid out our night attire on beds which had been scrupulously turned down ready for our repose; generals and admirals gave us drinks and meals in palaces and villas; an official car took us to Rome and to Pompeii. The whole operation was controlled by the unseen hand of Field Marshal Sir Harold Alexander – until the last night when we were bidden to dine in his mess in the hunting lodge of the Palace of Caserta.

Diana was a tall girl, with red hair and dimples; she was an amusing talker, and her observations were spiced with a wit which gave them an original flavour. We enjoyed ourselves thoroughly, accepting all that Fortune saw fit to offer us. We found we had not quite got the 'feel' of life in a military outpost; we felt in some way like fish out of water – not deep water, but the kind that splashes down from Italian fountains of baroque design. Our pedestrian Whitehall life, with office hours and hurried canteen lunches, was not like the life lived in the courts of Caserta in Naples. The ladies and gentlemen – captains, lieutenants, Wrens, Waafs and Ats – knew each other so well that, to them, we were emissaries from a strange land. Yalta was a strange land, so they were probably right. Perhaps we had become too used to hobnobbing in foreign places with prime ministers and commanders-in-chief because when we dined with Field Marshal Alexander and his senior officers we felt completely at home and at ease.

There had to be a disaster to the one and only suitable dress I had to wear; it was pale yellow wool and a better alternative to the tired navy blue suit and dress which had carried me through Yalta. I had reckoned without the scrupulous soldier servants. I could not get it on, it had shrunk to the size of a thigh-length tunic. They had given it a good wash in soap and water.

Alexander was probably the most liked and respected British military commander of the period. Mr Churchill had great affection for him, felt comfortable with him, shared his interest in painting, and gave him his friendship. His conduct of the Italian campaign had been exemplary; for nineteen months, since the landing in September 1943, he had advanced up Italy an army of British, Americans, Poles, Jews, Brazilians, South Africans, New Zealanders, British-Indian Gurkhas and Italians; he had fought it against seasoned and numerically superior German forces. The conditions of Anglo-American strategy had removed men and equipment from his front; he had not shown rancour but had remained sturdy and silent, in control of himself and his troops. In fact, from January to May 1944, at Anzio and at Cassino, his contribution towards this strategy had gone far towards accomplishing the purpose contained in the planned south of France diversionary operation to *Overlord*: he held in battle some of Germany's best divisions. The options, for which Mr Churchill and the British Chiefs of Staff had fought so hard at Cairo and Teheran, should not have been closed by the American determination to proceed with the south of France operation, a determination backed by Marshal Stalin's will that they would do just this. When the Allies entered Rome on 4 June Kesselring's armies were in retreat; this would have been the time to choose the option which would have allowed Alexander to receive reinforcements, to push into the Po Valley, to swing right into the Ljubljana Gap and beyond. Such danger to the upper Danube would have forced the Germans to defend in strength, and it would have given the Allies a foothold in south-east Europe.

Mr Churchill felt deeply about the failure to support Alexander. When, in the House of Commons on 6 June, 1944, he rose to announce the Allied invasion of the Continent, he spoke first of the 'great and timely operations' which had resulted in the capture of Rome.

At the dinner-table in the Field Marshal's hunting lodge we none of us knew that in two months, on 1 May, he would have accepted the surrender of a million German men and that the war in Italy would be over. Instead he told me that marriage was the only happy state for man or woman, and that he thought I would be wise to adopt it. He gave me two handbags to take home to Lady Alexander and a packet of red Siena chalk to give to the artist Augustus John, because he had had none for the years of the war.

When I declared the two handbags to the Customs officer on landing at St Mawgan's in Cornwall next day, I said they were a gift to his wife from Field Marshal Sir Harold Alexander.

'I don't care who he is,' snapped this flower of English man-hood, 'he must pay duty on them just the same as anyone else.'

CHAPTER 14

Musical chairs (1945)

OF THE CONFERENCES AT WHICH I had been administratively responsible to the British delegation, the one at Yalta had seemed to me the worst organised. And yet it was this one which yielded me the most gratitude. Field Marshal Alexander's holiday in Italy had been one result of it; the other I learned of when I returned to the office. The British Chiefs of Staff had placed it on formal record that I deserved thanks for the work I had done there! If it had related to Anglo-Russian friendship I would have felt less guilty, and would have thought with affection about Nina Alexandrovna, General Karanadze, Nicolaev Yirshov, Major Chelidze and the snowdrop picker, Major Pokashkin. But to tie it to the arrangements so hastily and belatedly made caused me to feel quite unhappy inside; I knew only too well the sum of my failures.

I would have felt the undeserved kindnesses better earned if they had been concerned with the files in the Special Information Centre. Of all the jobs I did, these were nearest to my heart. I cared for them because I felt convinced they could contribute to the future histories and, with the help of Winnie, Laura and Joan, had aimed at making them as complete as possible. I would like, when the war ended and we closed up the section, to be able to say: 'Here is the history of the Second World War as it was fought and won on paper.'

Winnie, Laura and Joan had each been to a conference; Winnie to Quebec, Joan to Cairo and Laura to Yalta, the last two thanks to the thoughtfulness of General Hollis who had sent them as a temporary part of his own clerical staff. He was, like General Ismay, a supporter of women workers and made the four of us in our filing section feel we were tied in with his Secretariat. He did not encroach on the preserve in which General Ismay was my employer – the Commanders-in-Chief Information Room, the *Chieftel* and *Sictel* telegrams – but he never failed to back me up and support me where the files were concerned. If we lacked a highly restricted Churchill minute or Prime Minister–President telegram, he did not suspect me of idle curiosity but saw to it that we received a copy. His was a different personality from General Jacob's more serious one; he was worldly and, being so, his temperament suited General Ismay; they looked at people and situations in the same way and often found themselves in agreement about them. Hollis had a highly developed sense of humour and was the best mimic on the second floor of the War Cabinet Offices. His imitation of the Prime Minister asking him one Sunday, at a particularly pregnant period of the war, where the three Chiefs of Staff were, and Mr Churchill's reaction to General Hollis's reply 'They're fishing', was one that could be repeatedly heard and never tired of. There was another which related to a visit to Turkey by the Foreign Secretary. Mr Churchill, who loved codes, told Eden that they must agree beforehand on a set of code words connected with hardware merchandise in an ironmonger's store. He must be sure to use the code when he spoke to Mr Churchill on the telephone from Cairo as it would disguise the fact that he had been having secret talks with the Turks. The call came through and an anxious Mr Churchill asked *en clair*:

'Well?' Speaking slowly and carefully, Mr Eden replied:

'I went to the ironmonger's and there I bought . . .'

'*What?*', the line from England fused. '*What* are you talking about? I thought you had been to see the Turks!'

The three men – Ismay, Jacob and Hollis – worked together as a remarkable team, without jealousy or disloyalty towards each other. They were friends, they were liked by all with whom they had dealings – from the Prime Minister and Sir Edward Bridges down through all ranks and nationalities – and they were very hard workers.

There were many files we would not need again, which we could check through to see they were complete, tie up and put away. There were others which would remain in current use, we knew not for how long: the files about Germany, the whole Far East Section. There was one thin folder marked 'A Certain High Explosive' which had been in the steel cabinet unopened since 1942. It came alive in August when the first two atomic bombs ever used in war were dropped on Japan, to be followed not many days later by 'Victory in Japan Day'.

It was no surprise to those of us who had seen him at Quebec and Yalta when President Roosevelt died on 12 April. The messages between him and Mr Churchill would no longer pass, telegrams which, particularly during the earlier period of the war, had been sympathetic and sustaining.

A day later the Red Army entered Vienna, and on 25 April Russian and US forces met at the River Elbe. The war in Europe was nearly at an end.

It ended on Friday, 4 May, when we heard that Montgomery had reported to General Eisenhower's Supreme Headquarters the surrender of the enemy in Holland, north-west Germany and Denmark. At the Ismays' flat that evening we drank champagne; Félicien, the Belgian butler, raised his glass and in his own brand of broken English said:

'Cheneral, I sink we should trink to you ass well.' We did.

General Ismay had come from 10 Downing Street. Mrs Churchill was in Moscow on a visit connected with the Red Cross Aid to Russia Fund, of which she was Chairman, and the Prime Minister was alone. He had sent messages that he wished his Chiefs of Staff Committee to celebrate with him the first news of Germany's defeat and with his own hands had put out a tray of glasses and drink.

It was a sad example of human imperceptiveness that neither the Chief of the Imperial General Staff, nor the First Sea Lord, nor the Chief of the Air Staff saluted him in a toast. General Ismay, in his modesty, in their presence would never have done so. Mr Churchill drank to them, each one in turn. It is possible that they were shy, it is certain that they were British, it is probable that they reacted as a committee, a body without a heart, and that each waited for the other to take the initiative. Whatever the reason it was an opportunity missed that the Grand Old Man, who had been the architect of the victory they were marking, did not receive a tribute from his three closest military advisers.

In May the balance sheets of the war in Europe and in the Far East were presented. The British civilian casualties were 60,585 killed and 86,175 seriously injured by air attacks; to the end of February 1945, the total casualties of British Armed Forces of the Commonwealth and Empire were 1,128,315, of which 307,210 were dead. The American figures were in the round 800,000 casualties, of which 150,000 were dead. The US War Department announced that 400,000 men would stay in Europe for occupation duties, two million would be discharged, and six million would go to fight the Japanese.

In lend-lease, up to 31 March 1945, the United States had sent to Britain aid valued at $12,775 million, to Russia $8,409 million; and in return had received nearly $5,000 million worth of assistance from its allies up to the end of 1944.

As the church bells and sirens of 'Victory in Europe Day' faded into the past, we began to prepare for the last Big Three conference of the war. President Roosevelt was dead; Mr Churchill's days as Prime Minister were numbered; only Marshal Stalin seemed secure.

Mr Churchill sent a telegram to Mr Truman, now President of the United States of America:

> I am profoundly concerned about the European situation. I learn that half the American Air Force in Europe has already begun to move to the Pacific theatre. The newspapers are full of the great movements of the American armies out of Europe. Our armies also are, under previous arrangements, likely to undergo a marked reduction. The Canadian Army will certainly leave. The French are weak and difficult to deal with. Anyone can see that in a very short space of time our armed power on the Continent will have vanished, except for moderate forces to hold down Germany.
>
> Meanwhile what is to happen about Russia? I have always worked for friendship with Russia but, like you, I feel deep anxiety because of their misinterpretation of the Yalta decisions, their attitude towards Poland, their overwhelming influence in the Balkans, excepting Greece, the difficulties they make about Vienna, the combination of Russian power and the territories under their control or occupied, coupled with the Communist technique in so many other countries, and above all their power to maintain very large armies in the field for a long time . . . .
>
> An iron curtain is drawn down upon their front. We do not know what is going on behind. There seems little doubt that the whole of the regions east of the line Lubeck-Trieste-Corfu will soon be completely in their hands. To this must be added the further enormous area conquered by the American armies between Eisenach and the Elbe, which will, I suppose, in a few weeks be occupied, when the Americans retreat, by the Russian power. . . . And then the curtain will descend again to a very large extent, if not entirely. Thus a broad band of many hundreds of miles of Russian-occupied territory will isolate us from Poland. . . .
>
> Surely it is vital now to come to an understanding with Russia, or see where we are with her, before we weaken our armies mortally or

> retire to the zones of occupation. This can only be done by a personal meeting. I should be most grateful for your opinion and advice. . . .

Mr Truman's answer was to send Mr Joseph E. Davies, who had been US Ambassador in Moscow before the war, to tell Mr Churchill privately that it might be better if the President met Marshal Stalin first, alone. Mr Churchill's reaction was immediate; he was wholeheartedly against such an idea, and made it clear that he did not consider the problems were ones arising only from Britain's relations *vis-à-vis* Russia, but that they were for America *with* Britain to face together and try to solve.

The American suggestion was an echo from the first meetings with the Russians at Teheran and Yalta, where there had sounded, very faintly, the theme that 'two's company, three's none'.

Mr Churchill continued to plead for the Americans to agree that their forces should remain in the forward positions until the Big Three conference had taken place. But the answer was categorical: the agreements reached at Yalta over the zone boundaries must be honoured. The withdrawals began on 1 July.

It is doubtful whether a different decision would have changed anything. Presumably Marshal Stalin would have refused to meet the Prime Minister and President until the withdrawals had been carried out; and it is probable that the Russians were as suspicious of Western motives as the Western democracies were of theirs. It had taken them four bloody years to vanquish an enemy which had reached the gates of Moscow, and they had every intention of ensuring that such an invasion would not happen again. This was not the time for a confrontation between West and East in Europe; the opportunities for this had been lost in 1943 and 1944 round the conference table. Now there was another enemy to be beaten – Japan – and, in a wish for future benefit, the Russians had undertaken to be the allies of the United States and Britain to achieve this end.

It was decided that the Big Three would meet at Potsdam – cradle of German militarism and suburb of the Berlin graveyard – on 15 July. Each delegation would make its own arrangements and be responsible for its own enclave, the venue for the main meetings to be chosen by the Russians. The decision on the enclaves had also to be left to the Russians since they were already there, and the Americans and British were only just moving into their zones of occupation in Berlin. Marshal Stalin telegraphed that the delegations would be housed in the suburb of Babelsberg, south-east of Potsdam, that the place for joint sessions would be in the palace of the former German Crown Prince, the Cecilienhof, the airfield at Gatow, and that all further information and details about the buildings could be obtained from General Kruglov 'who is known to your people from Yalta'.

An administrative reconnaissance party flew from London on 30 June: Colonel Sir Eric Crankshaw of Government Hospitality, because on a terrain so recently a battle ground there would have to be a major import programme of food and other supplies not available there; Mrs Betty Gibbs representing the Foreign Office – at last they had their own officer who would put their interests first; Mr William Armstrong from Sir Edward Bridges's office, and I. Laura came too because I had decided I wanted Winnie to help me at the conference proper to which I knew Joan was also going. Our mission was to co-operate with a staff from the British Army of Occupation, which was in charge of Brigadier Wales and had the military title of 'No. 4 Lines of Communication'.

We met Brigadier Wales on the evening we arrived, and it took me precisely five minutes to realise that my days of haphazard personal control were over – or would be unless I fought hard to keep my end up. We were handed sheaves of paper, closely typed, their military jargon tripping us up and making it difficult to sort out exactly what the arrangements were going to be. We said we would take them back to our quarters, study them and meet Brigadier Wales's representatives for a tour of the area next day.

As we strolled along the pleasant, tree-lined street, past fine houses set back in gardens – incredibly, though so near to Berlin, undamaged – a squat and familiar figure came into sight – and into my arms! Dear, bald General Karanadze was there, beaming, making it cosy again. He said he was appointed, and also Nina Alexandrovna and Gala, to see that the British delegation had all they needed: we had no interpreter with us but the thirty words of English he had learned were enough to establish this fact.

We spent the next day plodding around the part allotted to us; it was next to the Americans'; the whole was a rich, residential area which the bombs had missed – they had fallen on Potsdam which lay in ruins two miles away and which smelled of death's decay in the warm summer sun. The houses were spacious, well furnished and in each, I noticed particularly, there stood a beautiful Steinway or Bechstein grand piano. A row of large houses had gardens at their rear which ended at a lake – the Griebnitz See; their size and disposal made it easy to choose which was the right one for the Prime Minister, for the Opposition Leader, the Foreign Office, the Chiefs of Staff and the civilian and military officials who would be coming and going during the course of the meetings. Altogether we had fifty houses, so there was no need to worry about dormitory sleeping or overcrowding. Nor were we short of staffs; Brigadier Wales's were already hard at work preparing each house, cleaning up the streets, setting up telephones and weeding the gardens. We would not be so much administrative as liaison and information officers. With details of each house and the Brigadier's sheaves of paper, we flew back to London the following day, leaving Colonel Crankshaw to look after himself; his was by far the more complicated responsibility, consisting as it did of arranging all the catering for the delegation and its many hangers-on, providing the cooks and planning an import programme.

On our way home the pilot took us low over the Ruhr so that we could see the black, smoking, gutted ruins. In contrast it was heartening to see that in France the roads were crawling with civilian transport, and country matters such as plantings and tidyings-up were proceeding. From above it looked peaceful and ordinary.

There was to be a General Election in England on 5 July, the result of which would not be known until the overseas votes had been collected. Until then Mr Churchill was in charge of a 'Caretaker' Government and would bring Mr Clement Attlee, the Opposition Leader of the Labour Party, with him to Potsdam so that both would be present at the meetings and cognisant of the proceedings. They would return to London to hear the nation's verdict on 26 July.

Not for me the changing fortunes of government, however, but the present necessity to fit familiar bodies into unfamiliar beds. To do this it was better to be on the receiving end. I left Winnie to chase the delegation lists, said goodbye to William Armstrong, who was going to be the 'rear headquarters', and went back to Babelsberg and Brigadier Wales on 7 July, taking with me Arthur Cox, who had been released by the Moscow Military Mission to work on administration.

We took over 43 Ringstrasse, on the main tree-lined street, and for the first time had a proper administrative headquarters. It was a nice house, with a garden behind overlooking the lake, a big dining-room where the juniors of the delegation would feed, bedrooms and – most valuable of all – enough rooms on the ground floor for our offices. We could spread out. Winnie and I would share, and she would be responsible for travel arrangements, keeping the telephone directory up to date and accommodation; Colonel Crankshaw, with his staff, Major Ker, VC, Captain Bird and Miss Smith, had enough rooms to pursue his onerous catering duties; the Finance Officer from the War Cabinet Offices, the Transport Officer and his staff, and a major loaned to us to look after the houses and their upkeep, would all have their offices under the one roof. We were in clover.

The grass was not so green where working relationships with Brigadier Wales's No. 4 Lines of Communication unit were concerned. I noticed a definite coolness when I arrived, a cold-shouldering and 'keep off our preserve' attitude. However, as far as I was concerned, this was not going to continue; I had had enough experience of conference administration to know that we must hold together amicably if we wanted good results. Colonel Crankshaw and I agreed together our course of action at the Brigadier's evening meeting on the first night; we would be deferential, agreeable but firm. We must have been all these things, because we could feel the atmosphere improving and, by the end of a long session, it became warmly friendly. We continued as we had begun; the daily meetings, interminable in their length, tried our patience and our sense of humour to the limit. Colonel Crankshaw, who had one arm and blue eyes, looked on humanity with humorous detachment; he had had many years' experience as head of the Government Hospitality Fund, the department responsible for all official entertaining. He was too much a man of the world not to laugh at the knotted and complicated arrangements which were being made by the representatives of the British Army of Occupation. But we kept our smiles hidden. It was not that the work being done by our army friends was laughable, it was not; it was very thorough and very efficient. It was just that it was the military, as opposed to the civilian, way of doing things; the yards of paper which were produced each day; the regulations, the orders and counter-orders; the chain of command, the saluting and the discipline; the dotting of every 'i' and the crossing of each 't'. Points raised at the meetings had serial numbers which continued on and reached the 500s by the time the preliminaries were over and the Conference began. For instance:

> 53. Laundry for V.I.P.s will be located in Delegation Area.

Next day:

> 87. (see serial 53). Miss Bright will be asked to state who should be permitted to use the special laundry facilities.

Eight days later:

> 253. (see serial 87). Ordnance has obtained agreement with Russians to use a German laundry for V.I.P.s. This laundry is able to accept laundry for all the troops of 4 L. of C. if materials (soap and coal) are provided.

There were others which caused me delight and changed my whole outlook on administrative instructions as a means of communication:

> 18. Furniture taken out of houses will be stacked reasonably and not thrown into heaps. Articles such as desks, tables, chairs, etc. which are likely to be required elsewhere, will be placed alongside roads and on pavements and sorted at the time of removal from houses.
>
> 59. Although a certain amount of bunting has been flown over, it is not considered likely to be required. Decoration of the Central Conference Hall is the responsibility of the Russians.
>
> 61. It has been reported that personnel on hygiene duties have been stopped on occasions by officers from carrying out their duties in the Delegation Area. Personnel will be instructed to ascertain the name of any officer who restricts their movements for these duties in future. Where possible, plimsolls will be worn by hygiene personnel when entering V.I.P. houses.
>
> 336. New shirts are available for issue to the Prime Minister's guard if required. The standard of dress of troops in Delegation Area must be improved immediately.
>
> 357. (see serial 336). Shirts will be provided only for personnel of Scots Guards who do Guard Duties.
>
> 29. Russian policy will be adhered to, i.e. civilian labour will NOT be fed by us.
>
> 48. (see serial 29). Delete the word 'NOT'.

The last Big Three Conference was a military operation which was mounted in an undamaged suburb, an oasis of material comfort in a desert of devastation. The Allied Control Commission in Germany was its commander, the Allied Armies of Occupation its staff; they provided security police, engineer resources, medical units, fire brigades, gasoline depots, workshops for transport, and much of the transport itself, the rest coming from England. They provided postal services, guards of honour, German interpreters, printing facilities, furniture where needed, barbers, chiropodists – in fact everything necessary for the support of a delegation which, from an original planned size of one hundred and thirty people, ended by being double that number, plus visitors with official business to transact. It was a honey-pot to which the busy bees came. Brigadier Wales's headquarters announced that there were six caravans in the British Delegation Area for unexpected arrivals and that,

> These would be on an area of ground between 14 and 28 Ringstrasse. The Royal Engineers would cause all grass to be cut on this ground, obstructions removed and the main gates opened. Caravans would move in under the directions of a Q (Maint) a.m. 9th July 1945. Other rank driver/batmen would be rationed and accommodated at Camp. The Royal Engineers would construct a deep trench latrine on a suitable piece of ground adjacent to the caravans. Box covers would be provided and shelter.

What the British Army could not provide we sent for from England. For Colonel Crankshaw, food and drink, cooking utensils, cutlery, ashtrays, table linen, glass, china, caterers, cooks and waiters. Chief Petty Officer Pinfield, Royal Navy, who, at Teheran, had supervised the construction of the Persian ice pudding, returned to take charge of the Prime Minister's kitchen. My telegrams to William Armstrong included requests for such things as:

> Bell transformers 230 volt, bells, bell wire, cotton-covered, five hundred yards. Wood screws one by six inches, wood screws one and a half by six inches, staples, insulated, four gross.
>
> Two thousand Conference Passes.
>
> One hundred transfer Union Jacks for cars, size six inches by four. Sixty dustpans, brushes and brooms, pails, scrubbing brushes. Two hundred house flannels. Sixty mops. Twenty-four saucepan brushes. One hundred cups and saucers white. Two gross dusters.
>
> Thirty three-tier bunks with palliasses and pillows. One hundredweight soda and one hundred tins bath and sink cleaner. Two hundred cotton sheets.

> Chiefs of Staff batmen must bring electric irons and shoe-cleaning materials.
>
> Could you ask Winnie to bring with her a precious pocket comb I left in my office?
>
> Could you tell Chiefs of Staff military assistants that no fly-fishing here. Chiefs of Staff can fish from garden edge with bent pins and worms. No boating or we are liable to be shot by the Russians on the other side of the lake.

It was Yalta all over again only this time we were having to do it ourselves.

Because there was no guarantee that the water in the green Babelsberg oasis was pure, a daily supply of sterilised water was delivered to each house.

Just before the Conference opened, two Post Office engineers who had come from London completed their careful search of the delegation houses and reported them clear of bugging apparatus.

The arrivals of the delegation proper were phased over three days and this made a big difference to us in the administrative office. We were able to give them proper attention and not, as in the past, throw them into rooms and offices and hope for the best. By the evening of Sunday 15 July, the Prime Minister, Mr Attlee, the Foreign Secretary and the Chiefs of Staff were tucked into their houses, staffed and cared for. The weather was fine and the lake reflected back the green of trees and clipped lawns.

On one of the previous evenings, Betty Gibbs and I had gone to 'tea' with General Karanadze, Nina Alexandrovna and Gala. By 6 p.m. after the usual vodka marathon, we managed to get out and into an army car. We told the driver to drive anywhere, while we sat by open windows and tried to get the fumes of drink and cigarette smoke out of our system. That same evening there was a 'Three Power' Administrative Staff party at 43 Ringstrasse; Colonel Frank McCarthy, who had been making advance arrangements in the American area, was there and others from the American delegation; the Russians came – about six of them – with General Karanadze, and I noted that one of them who had been at 'tea' that afternoon was not in nearly as good shape as were Betty Gibbs and I.

The Conference settled to its work. The atmosphere was relaxed because, this time, a period of three weeks had been allowed for. The only time limit concerned Mr Churchill and Mr Attlee, who needed to be in England on 25 July for the General Election results. In the event, the American and British Chiefs of Staff also left at this time, their three and a half years of joint consultation as a Combined Chiefs of Staff Committee, though they did not know it yet, at an end. At one of their Potsdam meetings, General Marshall informed them, in closed session, that an atom bomb experiment in New Mexico had been a complete success. It was not their responsibility to decide on its future use, but, in August at Hiroshima and Nagasaki, it decided the future and finished the war against Japan.

With Mary Churchill, who had come with her father, I dined at General Marshall's villa. He fetched me from 43 Ringstrasse. As we drove into the American delegation area, it was sundown and the military detail was preparing to lower the Stars and Stripes. He climbed out of the car, I followed and waited, while he, and others in the vicinity, stood to attention. Through a loud speaker there came with haunting beauty the tune of the 'Star-Spangled Banner'; it was a privilege to share the moment.

General Arnold, whom I had not met before, and Frank McCarthy were at dinner. There was a fine library in the villa; we spent some time looking at the books and wondering what would become of them when Babelsberg reverted to Russian control. The Russians had been suspicious about us all, and had demanded that we give them an inventory of the contents of each of our houses. We did not do so – nor, to my knowledge, did we remove any article from any of them; there was no temptation, anyway, because most of them were furnished in extremely bad taste – except, for me, the pianos.

The general atmosphere at Babelsberg, between the British and American sectors, was that of a community compound, where people lived in self-contained working units, invited each other to their houses, greeted each other in the street. The security cordon around us was absurdly tight. I remarked, in exasperation, to General Karanadze that I thought the whole point of these tripartite meetings was for us to move about freely and meet each other; he and other Russians could walk into our sectors, but we could not go into theirs except by invitation.

As for the world press correspondents, there were about one hundred and eighty of them growling at the gates, frustrated in their efforts to find out what was going on. Mr Churchill did his best to get from Truman and Marshal Stalin agreement to hold a press conference, but he failed.

In the British sector there was one person it gave me infinite pleasure to see, and she was my sister Pamela. This time her presence with us had not been secretly arranged by General Ismay and Mr Burgis. I had asked General Ismay whether he thought we could bring her in as an Army Nurse in charge of our delegation medical centre. He had kindly made the right noises to Brigadier Wales, and she had been transferred from her Casualty Clearing Station in Schleswig-Holstein. Since D-Day + 4, Sister Pamela Bright had followed the British 30th Corps in its battles across Normandy and into north Germany; she had nursed under fire and had been awarded a Royal Red Cross medal for gallantry and service. She wore the dark blue ribbon on her khaki tunic. At the Potsdam Conference she sat in her little surgery and dealt with the minor injuries and ailments which came to her from our delegation and from the No. 4 Lines of Communication unit. When it was over, she returned to her army duties until she was demobilised.

The Cecilienhof Palace, which had been chosen by the Russians for the meetings of the Big Three, was outside Potsdam. I had seen it when I came over in advance, and Arthur Cox was given charge of the British part of it. It had been built in 1914, a comfortable imitation of an English country-house with mock-Tudor beams, and was surrounded by a park. In the park there were rough graves covering the bodies of the men who had died fighting hand to hand and between the trees. Incongruously, in another part of it, there were small headstones commemorating the life and death of pet dogs and cats of the Crown Prince's household. At the pretentious portico entrance flower-beds were responding to Russian treatment by showing bright red and blooming heads of begonias whose roots lay buried in their separate pots below the ground.

Inside, it was elegant and luxurious. The Russians had collected together all they could find of the original furnishings and had made good from German houses anything lacking. The Prime Minister's rooms upstairs had been the Crown Prince's blue and grey suite, President Truman's the Crown Prince's pink and silver one. Marshal Stalin's quarters lay behind the fixed bayonets of sentries standing guard.

Downstairs, in the main conference room, there was a large round table, three armchairs, with unarmed ones set round between them, a red carpet and red curtains at the tall windows. On the table were three flags, round the room three doors of equal size and one double one.

The easiest way for the Prime Minister to reach the conference room from his upstairs suite was to come down the main staircase and go through the double doors. But this door was locked. I asked the Commandant, who was showing me round, whether it could be opened and so save Mr Churchill having to traverse an extra length of corridor. He shook his head.

'Not possible,' said the interpreter, 'they use the three smaller doors, one each.

The intention became obvious to me; they must sit coequally at the round table, their entrances and exits must be through doors of the same size.

The Commandant looked at me and said something.

'He asks if you are pleased,' said the interpreter. 'Yes? No?'

'Yes,' I said. It was a hot day.

We stole two books from the library of the Cecilienhof. Colonel Mark Norman, on General Jacob's staff, who was at Potsdam, was a friend of Prince Frederick of Prussia, a refugee living in England and son of the Crown Princess Cecily after whom the palace had been named. We took one which had an inscription in it from his father, and one which had been given him by his mother. 'I was very touched to see *Faust* again,' he wrote, 'the book which I have read hundreds of times in my schooldays. I am dying to see you and hear from you what my home looks like, if you met any of our old servants and if the house was completely stripped by the Russians, as I was told.'

Berlin was not yet tied into its Allied Control Zones; there was still freedom to go into the Russian-occupied area where Hitler's Chancellery gaped in ruin. For the Prime Minister and others who went on the first day, it was possible to see the bunker in which the Führer and Eva Braun had committed suicide; but, when I went later in the week, the Russians had sealed this part off. We were free to roam at will over the Chancellery building, to look and pick at the files, papers, pieces of broken furniture; in one passage there were hundreds of new Iron Cross medals strewn about the floor, their shining metallic faces a travesty of the reason for which they had been made. It was a horrible and macabre place, its evil spirit hanging over the grim city it had destroyed. The smell of Berlin, as of the military suburb of Potsdam, was quite definitely the smell of decayed death.

Whether it was because the horror was so close it could be felt; whether it was that Germany and 'music' are synonymous; or whether it was just chance, but it did happen that the Potsdam Conference was richly supplied with musicians. When Marshal Stalin entertained the President and Prime Minister there was a concert after dinner given by leading Russian soloists. President Truman, at his Big Three party, produced Eugene List to play the piano; Mr Churchill's hospitality was accompanied by the string section of the Royal Air Force Symphony Orchestra playing a selection of his favourite pieces in a room next to the dining-room. The 'Destiny Waltz' was one of them, another a march recently composed by a Londoner entitled 'The Sons of the Soviet'. As this was new, and there were only two copies of the score, the sixteen musicians had a hard time of it, especially as there were calls of 'beautiful . . . beautiful . . .', 'louder . . . louder' from the apparently entranced listeners next door.

The administrative staffs were not to be outdone; Frank McCarthy had Eugene List go and play at General Marshall's villa; the Royal Air Force string section entertained a party at 43 Ringstrasse from a raft on the Griebnitz See; and Frank McCarthy and I combined with the Russian administrators in a magnificent concert at the Neues Palast, the 'Sans Souci' palace which had escaped serious damage on the outskirts of Potsdam.

We had the Symphony Orchestra billeted in the British area; under its conductor, Wing-Commander Macdonell, it was one of the finest of its kind; we had the audience – our two delegations; we had the evening – 24 July, the last day before the military staffs were due to leave. All we needed was Russian permission to use the orangery in the Neues Palast.

We got it, after having to endure 'breakfast' with the Russian caretakers. Wing-Commander Macdonell, a teetotaller, who had been with us, was less than happy as we walked up the street afterwards. A strong wind was blowing the line of trees to one side. General Hollis, who saw us approaching, said that we were leaning one way and the trees the other; the effect, he said, was strange.

The programme included Tchaikovsky's 6th Symphony, asked for by General Marshall, and Handel's 'Largo', a favourite of Field Marshal Brooke's; King, Portal, Arnold, Cunningham and Ismay had nothing to offer us, so a member of the orchestra, Denis Matthews, the English pianist, played Beethoven's 'Appassionata' Sonata.

Just as the first item, the 'Largo', ended, the electric lights went out. Efforts by Russian Army electricians failed to put them on again. But Arthur Cox and Hugh Lunghi who had come to Potsdam with the Military Mission were prepared; their resourcefulness and their years in Moscow had caused them to bring some packets of candles. These we stuck wherever we could round the pale grey and gold orangery. The concert continued in perfect beauty in the candlelight.

When it ended, we said goodbye to General Marshall, Admiral King, General Arnold and Colonel Frank McCarthy and went back to our houses to bed. For the British Chiefs of Staff the farewells to their American colleagues had been said at a dinner they had had together. Here, toasts were drunk and friendship broke through the reserve.

On 25 July, the next day, there was an exodus from the British delegation area. Field Marshal Sir Alan Brooke, Admiral of the Fleet Sir Andrew Cunningham, Marshal of the Royal Air Force Sir Charles Portal left Babelsberg. Behind them, as they headed for home, lay Germany, the land of one of the enemies they had striven so hard to conquer. Behind them lay five years of constant and honest work carried out to the best of their high ability as a Committee, as Commanders-in-Chief and as heads of their three services. Never again would it be my job to give 'CIGS', 'CAS' or 'First Sea Lord', a compartment on a train, a bed in a villa or a cabin in a boat.

'I'm so sorry to trouble you on such a small matter,' said Sir Alan Brooke one day at Potsdam when asking me for something for their villa.

I am sorry, I thought as I saw them off, that you will no longer have to.

General Ismay left with Mr Churchill, his heart heavy with foreboding that perhaps the British electorate had decided not to send his 'Master' back to Babelsberg.

At his last Plenary meeting at the Cecilienhof, Mr Churchill had made a speech about democracy, had thanked the leaders of the two other nations for allowing the General Election 'break' and had said that it was possible Mr Attlee would be returning to take his, Mr Churchill's chair.

'I don't think,' remarked Marshal Stalin, 'that Mr Attlee looks like a man who would seize power.'

Mr Attlee's return three days later must have confounded the Marshal.

For Mr Churchill the journey home was his last as Prime Minister of Great Britain in time of war. The people he had led from threatened defeat and enemy occupation to a victorious and honourable place at the peace councils had cast their votes and rejected him. They had not rejected Winston Churchill, they had rejected war and its leadership. He would remain for all time one of their great Englishmen; they would always be in his debt.

On the evening of 26 July in London he broadcast his farewell as Prime Minister and expressed his gratitude to the British 'for the many expressions of kindness shown towards their servant'.

At Potsdam he had had to leave two most serious issues unresolved – the Polish–German frontier and the place in history of the atom bomb; but it was certain that the wide and far-seeing perspective of his views would not be forgotten.

For the staffs waiting at Babelsberg the three-day pause ended on Saturday evening, 28 July.

The Prime Minister, Mr Clement Attlee, Head of Britain's Labour Government, and Mr Ernest Bevin, the new Foreign Secretary, returned. It was an occasion without parallel in history, and a tribute to the united Government we had had in Britain throughout the war that our policy at the conference table would remain the same. Mr Attlee had been present at Potsdam from the beginning and knew at first hand all that had passed at the tripartite meetings. He and Mr Bevin would continue to be served by the same men who had served Mr Churchill and Mr Eden: Sir Edward Bridges, with his high standards of integrity and intellect, Mr Norman Brook, his deputy, human, able, just and dedicated, and all the others who, in their dark civilian suits, had worked alongside the blue and khaki uniforms of the Armed Services. They would still be there to sort and sift the debris of war when peace came, by their presence proving that the continuity inherent in the British Civil Service is a phenomenon of the British way of life.

Neither was there a change where the military staffs in the War Cabinet Offices were concerned. General Ismay, General Jacob and

General Hollis were there until after the end of the war. Hollis then took over from Ismay, and Jacob decided to take himself out of military matters and accept an offer from the British Broadcasting Corporation. The Assistant Secretaries of the various Strategic and Intelligence committees continued to work as before, remaining until either a posting elsewhere or a decision to retire took individuals out of the War Cabinet Offices and brought others in. The Secretariat system was as vital a part of the Committee system as the Civil Service was of the British form of government. It was as corporately objective and politically unbiassed and it kept the trust of those it served because it did not try to usurp their functions nor intrigue for position; its own position was secure.

Those of us who were not established Civil Servants, or in the regular Armed Services, would have to decide our own future for ourselves. The protective and privileged clothing we had worn for five years would soon be stripped off us; we would no longer have our 'war work' as an excuse for escaping from our personal obligations towards family or friends; and we would have to compete on equal terms with the thousands of men and women who would be pouring out of the war machine into a civilian world.

But in Babelsberg we still had four days until the finish of the Potsdam Conference, and – after our return to England – two and a half weeks before the surrender of Japan and the end of the Second World War.

General Ismay was not so tied in time with the new Prime Minister as he had been with Mr Churchill, and we saw him often at 43 Ringstrasse. He was, as always, outwardly calm and cheerful, but we knew that, in fact, the loosening of the threads of his intensely concentrated and selfless war service was making room for the fatigue which he had never acknowledged was there, as one long year of duty had followed the other. He performed one military ceremony when he conferred a knighthood on General Kruglov, made General Karanadze a Commander, and Colonel Kuznetzov, the Prime Minister's personal liaison officer, an Officer, all within the Order of the British Empire. I was happy about General Karanadze's especially as he looked so pleased about it. General 'Pug' was not so sure that he enjoyed putting his arms round General Kruglov's neck when he encircled it with the pink and grey ribbon of the Order, but he liked little, bald-headed General Karanadze and was willing to come with me to breakfast with him on the morning of the day when, with all the other VIPs, General Ismay left for London.

For the last Plenary Meeting I had gone with General Ismay to the Cecilienhof, and had watched Truman, Attlee and Stalin go into the conference room, with its round table and three armchairs. But the magic had gone and the term Big Three had lost its meaning. Marshal Stalin did not look well; he had aged in the five months since I had seen him at Yalta; his hair looked almost white – perhaps because he was wearing a white tunic, and not a beige one, though it had the same cut and stand-up collar.

On our last day, Thursday, 2 August, when all but a few of us on the administrative staff had gone, Arthur Cox, Hugh Lunghi and I went to the Cecilienhof where, with Arthur making the little speeches, we gave presents – this time intact and complete – to the Commandant and others who had looked after the British delegation. They were clearly pleased and we received from them, not only glasses of vodka, but sincere expressions of friendship. Then, in the inconsequential way that Russians do things, we found we were expected to be present at a dinner-dance that evening as guests of General Kruglov. It was a sit-down affair in the conference room, and we were 'placed' by cards with our names on them at tables decorated with bright flowers and loaded with wines and food. I was seated between Kruglov and a nice, quiet, grey-haired Russian general called Ivanov, whom I had not met before but who spoke good English. There was music, there were speeches and toasts, it was gay, friendly and relaxed. I felt I was in a dream and knew that, when it ended, reality would return and life resume its normal pattern of work and effort, love and friendship, certainty and doubt.

Next day we packed up and said goodbye – to Nina Alexandrovna and Gala; to our friends of No. 4 Lines of Communication we gave drinks at 43 Ringstrasse before lunch; and at some point General Karanadze came round and presented me with two buttons off his general's coat. In the afternoon, in a cavalcade of friends from the British Army and from our Military Mission in Moscow, we drove to Gatow and climbed into the Chiefs of Staff special 'York' aircraft to fly home to London. How this particular machine happened to be there I do not know, but it added a comfortably rounded full stop to my life as a conference housekeeper.

Index